D0742590

DOWN AND IN

BOOKS BY RONALD SUKENICK

Down and In: Life in the Underground
Blown Away
The Endless Short Story
In Form: Digressions on the Art of Fiction
Long Talking Bad Conditions Blues
98.6
Out
The Death of the Novel and other Stories
Up
Wallace Stevens: Musing the Obscure

DOWN

AND

IN

LIFE IN THE UNDERGROUND

RONALD SUKENICK

BEECH TREE BOOKS
WILLIAM MORROW
New York

Copyright © 1987 by Ronald Sukenick

Brief sections of this book have appeared in *The New York Times Book Review*.

I would like to acknowledge gratefully the University of Colorado, Boulder Council on Research and Creative Work, for its support for research on this book.

All rights reserved. No part of this book may be reproduced or utilized in any form or by any means, electronic or mechanical, including photocopying, recording or by any information storage and retrieval system, without permission in writing from the Publisher. Inquiries should be addressed to Permissions Department, Beech Tree Books, William Morrow and Company, Inc., 105 Madison Ave., New York, N.Y. 10016.

Library of Congress Cataloging-in-Publication Data

Sukenick, Ronald.
  Down and in.
  1. Sukenick, Ronald—Homes and haunts—New York (State)
—Greenwich Village (N.Y.) 2. Greenwich Village (New
York, N.Y.)—Social life and customs. 3. Bohemianism—
New York (State)—Greenwich Village (N.Y.) 4. Bohemianism
—United States. 5. New York (N.Y.)—Social life and
customs. 6. Authors, American—20th century—Biography.
7. Authors, American—New York (State)—Greenwich
Village (N.Y.)—Biography. I. Title.
PS3569.U33Z465   1987   974.7′1043   87-11412
ISBN 0-688-06589-9

Printed in the United States of America

First Edition

1 2 3 4 5 6 7 8 9 10

BOOK DESIGN BY RICHARD ORIOLO

BĪB

The word "book" is said to derive from *boka,* or beech.
The beech tree has been the patron tree of writers since ancient times and
represents the flowering of literature and knowledge.

PREFACE

Souls of poets dead and gone,
What Elysium have ye known,
Happy field or mossy cavern,
Choicer than the Mermaid Tavern?

The tradition of Bohemia has been traced back to France in the 1830's, where it began as a by-product of the Industrial Revolution, bourgeois society, and the Romantic movement. The story that follows begins 120 years later in a different country. Although I have a part in the story, it is mostly a collective narrative about the rise, decline, and future prospects of a phase in that tradition. The bourgeoisie has been replaced by the middle class, the Industrial Revolution by the Cybernetic Revolution, and Romanticism by Postmodernism. The subterraneans, as Jack Kerouac called inhabitants of the underground who started turning up around 1950, are not the same as the older Greenwich Village Bohemians inspired by Freud, Marx, and Modernism. But the tradition endures its changes precisely because it is not the result of a willed strategy, but responds to an unchanging antagonism between the way of life imposed by our pragmatic business society and the humanistic values by which our culture has taught us to experience and judge the quality of our individual and collective lives.

For me, sneaking over to Greenwich Village from high school or living in the East Village in the sixties, the descent into the underground was a matter not of tradition but of an absolute need. The possibility of better worlds was suggested to me as a kid when I came across a small number of other kids who, like myself, were dissatisfied with the upper-middle-class milieu of Brooklyn's Midwood High. I was not alone—there were others whose values were not those of Dun and Bradstreet. Once discovered, the underground became an education in survival—emotional, creative, and intellectual survival—that schools did not offer. And it provided a supporting community of like-minded hold-outs from an imposed way of life that I knew was not mine.

Much of the attraction of the underground derives from the circumstance that it pursues the tiger of pleasure instead of yoking itself to the oxen of duty. Before hurling the usual charge of irresponsible hedonism, it is a good idea to reflect that the sign of free people is that they are able to do things because they like to. Bohemians do what they feel like. Desire becomes a positive force rather than one to struggle with. For all of its negations of the status quo, the underground is finally based on affirmation. A few years ago a mass-media journal not only accused Jack Kerouac of being an anti-Semite, which he was, but also charged Allen Ginsberg with being one, which he isn't. I called Ginsberg and urged him to write a denial, but he said that negation leads only to further negation. Several months later I happened to be sitting in a Polish restaurant in the East Village on Yom Kippur eve when Ginsberg, a dedicated Buddhist, came in wearing a dark suit, tie, and yarmulke, urgently wanting to know where he could find a temple. The meaning I take from this coincidental parable is that the positive force of desire is more compelling than the negativity of denial.

I question the very possibility of moral power without this affirmative emotional dimension. Ought is not a positive number. Ought is neutral, neutered, nothing. No feeling. Ought requires enforcement and generates resentment. Even conceding the rule of law, ultimately a democracy can be based only on people doing what they want to do. That is a fact that lawyers may not like but artists can understand. "Poets are free, and they make free," says Emerson. And they do. In both senses. The poet unlocks the chains of thought, Emerson continues, "whether in an ode, or in an action, or in looks and behavior," and the power to impart this emancipation, "as it must come from greater depth and scope of thought, is a measure of intellect." Unlocking the chains of thought and expressing that liberation draws out the whole of our intelligence, which does not consist merely of the rational and analytic faculties. Subterraneans of the artistic underground, as distinguished from political dissenters, are among other things researchers in the risky discipline of living in contact with the deepest impulses. This constitutes basic research, whose practical applications will have to be left to the political intellectuals and other social engineers. The ongoing explorations of the underground, which involve not only what artists produce but how they live, can best be observed in the bars, cafés, and public places where they hang out. Keats's Mermaid Tavern is a sacred place, where talking, drinking, and carousing unleash the chained gods, obscene and holy, dangerous and creative, that can destroy us or lead us to a greater depth and scope of thought. Or both.

This is a collective work in the sense that it is based largely on interviews, and I would like to express my gratitude to the people I interviewed, both those I quote in the text and those I do not. Talking to so many people about a common subject convinced me that the science of comparative experience, which I have been pursuing for some years as a novelist, listener, and, occasionally, talker, is one of our fundamental sources of knowledge. The fact that it is a soft science rather than a hard one from a quantitative point of view makes it no less useful and perhaps more pleasant. In fact many of the interviews took place in the kind of bars and cafés I was investigating, a circumstance that made my research even less quantitative but probably more informative. The book is collective also in the sense that the manuscript has had many invaluable readers whose sense of the subject and the way it should be imparted has been gratefully incorporated into the text. Finally I would like to salute all my subterranean companions who have prowled the underground of the slums and saloons or that of the psyche, whether they are mentioned herein or not. It is to you the book is dedicated.

CONTENTS

THE
REMO

I'm sitting in a cavernous cabaret off Bleecker Street near Washington Square called the Open Door, talking to a junkie musician named Tony Frusella who's playing here tonight. For a while now in the early fifties the Open Door is the center of the Village scene and the music scene. It books the hippest groups, and jazzmen come down to jam after they finish their gigs on Fifty-second Street. Tony plays a big mellow trumpet and he's good, though some people say he sounds too much like Miles Davis.

"When I got out of the army," Tony says, "I got this hot-shit gig with Charlie Barnet. It was a big band and I was in the trumpet section. But like it was bull shit because all you'd do was get up and blow the same notes with a bunch of other guys. It was just like the army. And besides, it's like too piercing. So one day we're playing and Barnet points at us to get up and blow our notes and I don't get up. He points at me again and I refuse to blow. Everybody else in the line is blowing, see, and like I'm just sitting there. Then he starts making fun of me right on stage. Like he's got a real attitude on him. I just sit it out. Finally he fires me in front of the whole audience. Never do what they tell you just because everybody else does it."

"Shmucks," I murmur.

Who are the shmucks here? Tony? He's the hero. Charlie Barnet? No, he's the heavy. The shmucks are the guys who get up when told and play their notes together. To understand what follows, you need to know what a shmuck is. It's not just a jerk or a wimp, it has to do with a particular time and place. A shmuck is somebody with a certain way of thinking, a combination of caution, conformity, and mercenary values. An idolater of Things, a consumer at the feet of the Golden Calf. If you're Jewish like me and from Brooklyn, "shmuck" is a word without which you could not have made it across the bridge from Flatbush to a dubious salvation in the underground of Greenwich Village. "Shmuck." Or some equivalent. If you don't have a word for it in teen-age James Dean America, then you're lost. At the end of *Huckleberry Finn,* Huck forgoes the confines of the settled town to "light out for the Territory" and freedom. Huck Finns are still lighting out for the Territory. Even though there is no Territory anymore. The underground is the Territory and they keep lighting out from Fargo and L.A. and St. Louis and Brooklyn. Why?

We're all less individual than individualism permits us to imagine. The tension Twain sees in America between stability and freedom is not something peculiar to an individual or an era, but still conditions the moment. At the rough parts of the road the culture offers only a limited number of detours, of possible options. To anyone. In this respect we're interchangeable with anyone else in our generation. You can serve as that anyone as well as I, and what we have in common may be the most crucial part of our stories. Certainly it is of mine. The rest is incidental.

Any moderately well informed kid around 1950 knew about the going romance of Bohemia, with its peculiar mix of both pleasure and salvation so attractive for kids in pre-sixties puritan America, where sex was a commodity you traded for marriage. We knew about its mythic figures. We knew about the artist's life, Toulouse-Lautrec's legendary penis, Pollock's fabled drunks, van Gogh's mythic ear. *La vie de bohème.* They say that Dylan Thomas had a sweet tooth for chocolate and that when he was especially drunk he would sometimes shit in bed, usually somebody else's, so you couldn't tell whether he was wallowing in shit or chocolate or both. On the other hand Robert Creeley tells a story about waking up on the edge of the Pacific after a night of partying, Jack Kerouac looking into his face asking, "Are you pure?" Even thirty years later, if you are anything like me, you will still be moved by Gregory Corso's faith in the tradition when he tells you, "If you believe you're a poet, then you're saved."

It's 1948 and Henry Wallace is running for president on a third-party ticket. All over the United States idealistic liberals are getting behind Wallace and pushing hard. Every bright kid in Midwood High School in the middle of middle-class Brooklyn is campaigning his ass off for Henry Wallace. Henry Wallace wants peace, Henry Wallace wants social progress, Henry Wallace is against Red-baiting, Henry Wallace is a liberal's dream. *Village Voice* libertarian columnist Nat Hentoff, at fifteen heavily influenced by Arthur Koestler's anti-Stalinist *Darkness at Noon,* says, "I was very unpopular on my block in Boston when I refused to support Henry Wallace, and I gave as my reason that the Commies were running his campaign." Wallace is the guilty conscience of the well-to-do liberal establishment turning on itself, although you shouldn't put down guilty conscience. It's better than no conscience.

But if, like me, you don't feel part of that establishment or, like Hentoff, you don't like Stalinism, you don't have that kind of bad conscience. You don't like Red-baiting any more than the liberals but you also don't like pious Communist-front youthniks. Worst of all, you don't like folk-singing, or folk dancing for that matter, with its heavy ideological freight. You never dreamed you saw Joe Hill last night and the hora seems no less out of step with your reality because you're Jewish. But my bit, unlike Hentoff's, is not especially political. For one thing, the alternative to righteous liberals at the time consists largely of reactionary fanatics, capitalist dupes, and cynically manipulative politicians, which makes Wallace boosters appetizing by comparison.

In 1948 I've just joined the middle class, or I'm trying to, having moved three blocks from the Gravesend Avenue neighborhood of the impoverished Malamud Delicatessen under the El, which was the original for the deli in Bernard's *The Assistant,* to the affluent Midwood High district at Ocean Parkway. I always seem to assume the position of an outsider looking in, even when looking in at outsiders. But the radicals are also affluent here, so who are the outsiders? One problem is that, being anti-Wallace, I'm considered deficient in social conscience concerning those less fortunate than ourselves, but coming from Gravesend Avenue, I already feel less fortunate than ourselves. Besides, the ambience of Gravesend Avenue has given me a permanent distaste for the middle-class Jewish facility for bad conscience later so well represented by the movies of Woody Allen, who attended—what else?—Midwood High School.

Down at the Gravesend of things you don't have the luxury of either no-risk liberal idealism or Jewish guilt, you have enough to contend with surviving as a Christ-killer among the local Christians. But the future firemen, postmen, mechanics, cops, and crooks of Gravesend Avenue are my pals, even if they are subject to irrational racist behavior that, however, I know cannot be put down as endemic stupidity. At this point I still feel a lot of loyalty to the guys in the gang. Stupidity is their refuge, their protection from the unreachable middle-class world beyond Gravesend, and they take me into it. If they refer to my Yiddish grandmother as a kike, they also call Blacks niggers, Hispanics spics, Irish micks, and Italians wops, even though a lot of them are Italians themselves and occasionally get sore about "wop." One time I start talking about wops in front of an older Italian kid and he grabs me by the collar and warns me, "Never call a guinea a wop."

What is the attraction of the underground for kids? Why won't Huck stay home? Midwood kids apparently thought that getting straight A's and going to Harvard Med School was all there is in life. Unreal. These were the days when any self-respecting college had strict Jewish quotas. What were they going to do with five hundred Jewish kids a year with 99.8 averages from Midwood High School alone? The resulting crazed rat race was what passed for reality at Midwood. For me, coming from Gravesend Avenue, the effect of this mad struggle was astonishment. First of all it was clear that even playing along with a system like that was participating in a racist insult in which the price of success was self-contempt—try to be better because you're actually worse—and there we are back to the joke of guilt and inferiority enacted by Woody Allen. Very funny, Woody.

My sense of unreality is verified by the great socialized-medicine debate. I already have a reputation for stupidity, the stupidity I've learned from Gravesend. Stupidity is a form of resistance, and provokes not only contempt but hostility. The irate response to me is always "What, *you* got a hundred on your geometry regents?" "*You* won a scholarship?" But with the socialized-medicine debate I know I have it made, because I'm at last on the smart, liberal, righteous side of things. I'm emphatically in favor of socialized medicine in a big, formal high-school forum. I'm in for a shock, because when the day of the debate comes around it turns out that all those future doctors and lawyers think socialized medicine is the worst thing that could happen to a bunch of upwardly mobile dermatologists, gastroenterologists, and malpractice experts. You'd think I'd got up there and told them—ultimate insult—that they were "bujwah." Of course I will come to detect the inevitability of neoconservatism here when, decades later, these people are forced to confront their real interests, but at the time I stagger off the stage in confusion after a barrage of sarcastic and contemptuous questions, thinking, *Shmucks.*

"Shmuck" was a code word for a condition whose alternative in Flatbush was vague. But in Greenwich Village at the time there was a strong sense of alternative identity. In the underground of Greenwich Village you not only knew who They were, you also knew who We were. America was one thing and Greenwich Village another. Village people might go Uptown but it was a kind of slumming in reverse. Yoram Kaniuk, an Israeli who had already fought for Jerusalem in the War of Independence, found the promised land again in a way as a painter in underground New York of the fifties and its center, the San Remo bar. The plunge into the underground, with all its implications of the infernal, is nevertheless an attempt to resurrect the mythic Holy City within the profane polis. It involves a notion of the good life beyond "mercenary" concerns. The spiritual geography of the underground describes a promised land of freedom, illumination, and excitement beyond the provincial ego, the constrictions of social class and ethnic heritage, beyond the conventional altogether. A new Athens, a new Jerusalem—and let's not forget Sodom either.

"Out of the bar were pouring interesting people, the night making a great impression on me," writes Jack Kerouac of his version of the San Remo in *The Subterraneans*—a book supposedly about San Francisco but actually about the Village with names changed, according to Allen Ginsberg—and here you can see not only Kerouac's romantic attraction to subterranean life, but also the kernel of his run-on, innovative, improvisational style incubated in that jazz-influenced underground scene, in his riff on the coinage or typo "birl"—"some kind of Truman-Capote-haired dark Marlon Brando with a beautiful thin birl or girl in boy slacks with stars in her eyes . . . and with them a guy with another beautiful doll, the guy's name Rob and he's some kind of adventurous Israeli soldier with a British accent whom I suppose you might find in some Riviera bar at 5 A.M. drinking everything in sight alphabetically with a bunch of interesting crazy international-set friends on a spree."

Kaniuk, graying, decades later an eminent Israeli writer, will reminisce to me in a café in Tel Aviv almost with a sense of wonder about his Village days. When, back then, he goes to a posh Uptown party for Tennessee Williams with painter Gandy Brodie it's in the spirit of an expedition among the Philistines. Brodie spots Ginger Rogers and tells her, " 'This guy here is a Russian, and he saw you when he was in the underground, and he admired you, and he was in the KGB, and his great dream was to once be like Fred Astaire and dance with you.'

"So she got all excited. And I start speaking in bad English, not that my English was so good but I made it worse, and I said, 'Me dreaming about you. Underground. You. Fred Astaire.'

"And it was a strange thing, she looked glittery, beautiful, and when we danced together I saw that all her age was in her neck, you could see the wrinkles of her age, and she was trying to patch herself up. And I played it all the way."

Kaniuk isn't buying into Uptown, he's putting it on.

Around the time of the socialized-medicine fiasco, selling out became the hot topic among those of us in Midwood who weren't shmucks, what was selling out and what wasn't, who was selling out and who wasn't. Selling out applied to those who assumed the moral superiority of leftish views while maintaining shmuck-materialist values about money, success, and sexuality. It never occurred to any of us that shmuck materialism and dialectical materialism had any relation. The dialectical lefties were stuffy, but the shmucks were not even "subtle." We thought of ourselves as in the spirit of the true left, unaware that we might be something else, something for which there was perhaps no political category, or at least not yet. Not till the sixties, if then. So selling out came to mean not only working for advertising companies and corporations, but almost any of the normal shmuck-materialist ambitions when pursued by leftish classmates. Selling out, finally, meant becoming even a doctor or a lawyer, because such choices denied the promise of a more "valid" kind of life beyond the middle class from which we all came. For some, selling out was simply the synonym for making it—at anything. *Who are the shmucks here?* "Tradition has been broken, yet there is no new standard to affirm," observes writer-intellectual Paul Goodman of "the young." We were growing up absurd, though we didn't know it till Goodman's book of that title articulated our mystique in 1960. The lack of a myth appropriate for us begat a sour negativity.

But the mystique of the Village seemed near irresistible: Money isn't important. Sex is. The value of art is taken for granted.

"I came to the Village because sex was very uptight in the fifties," says Howard Smith, longtime author of the "Scenes" column for *The Village Voice*. As such, he was the man from whom a few decades of undergrounders and would-be undergrounders picked up their cues about what was considered in—and especially, sexy and in. Smith, with his rumpled five-o'clock-shadow look, has even these days a certain puppyish quality that conflicts with his pitch for raunch. "I wanted to fuck. I wanted women who would talk to me. I wanted women who didn't wear padded, wired bras with a slip over it and a sweater. I knew I was going to do something in the area of the arts with my life but I had no idea what. I came for sex. In the Village some girls didn't even wear bras. At all. God, to me that would be like seeing five fashion models walk by nude right now, that's how far out that was. At Pandora's Box, I used to go to that coffee shop all the time and this waitress would lean over and say, 'Anything else I can get you?' and she wore a low-cut peasant blouse and no bra and I would almost fall out of my chair."

"Suddenly, I *was* free, I felt," writes poet-playwright Amiri Baraka—then known as LeRoi Jones—of the first impact of the Village on him. "I could do anything I could conceive of.... The idea that the Village was where Art was being created, where there was a high level of intellectual seriousness, was what I thought. And the strange dress and mores that I perceived ... I thought part of the equipment necessary to have such heavy things go on.... So that I did think that coffeehouse after coffeehouse and the other establishments down around West 4th and MacDougal, Bleecker or 8th Street, were filled with World Class intellectuals."

MacDougal Street in Greenwich Village was not so different in 1948 from what it would be if you fast-forwarded all the way to 1984. In thirty-six years Minetta's would still be there, and the Kettle of Fish too, if soon to close. Minetta's was where you were when you weren't in the San Remo, the bar down the block at the corner of Bleecker Street. The Rienzi, an early hip non-Italian espresso place, started by five or six artists of various kinds, would not be there, though the Figaro would, rebuilt in the same place. But way back in 1948, if you wanted a hip cup of coffee, you went to the Waldorf Cafeteria—thirty-six years later a bank—on Sixth Avenue off Eighth Street, where the artists went to snack and talk, since the Rienzi and the Figaro were not yet built. The Kettle was the bar you went to if you wanted a somewhat rougher scene, which you didn't. You wanted the Remo because the Remo was the place, in 1984 a Chinese restaurant, in 1948 the mecca for refugees from places like Midwood. You were headed for the Remo, where you'd try to look old enough to be in an actual Village-Bohemian-literary-artistic-underground-mafioso-pinko-revolutionary-subversive-intellectual-existentialist-anti-bourgeois café. Real life at last.

I edge into the Remo, which luckily is crowded so I don't look conspicuous. I'm looking for my sister, Gloria, a regular, who has left Yale Art School to become a belle of Bleecker Street. It's the kind of bar that in the 1970's ambience of accelerated nostalgia might be considered "campy," but now in 1948 it's just an aging New York bar with old wood, white-and-black-tiled floors, a pressed-tin ceiling, wooden booths, and a busy backroom restaurant. I find Gloria, wearing jeans, in the proletarian-looking crowd at the bar in the front room. She waves me toward a booth and joins me in a minute carrying a martini. Gloria, an occasional waitress and model, is maybe the first girl to scandalize the gray-flannel generation by wearing what, at the time, are still called dungarees. Jeans in 1948 are considered shocking on men, much less women. Not that I'm much aware of it then, but in retrospect it would be clear that men find Gloria's voluptuousness and curly hair insanely attractive.

"Have an espresso, they serve the strongest espresso this side of Sicily," she urges, thereby neatly avoiding the legal-drinking-age problem. She keeps waving to friends as she talks.

"It was really like the home away from home for thousands of people," she'll explain years later. "Everybody was living in cold-water flats or tiny little apartments so everybody used to gather there. Nobody spent time at home, I mean the Remo was really like the living room hearth, kind of, except there was like also a lot of heavy drinking going on. The martini scene."

"Not beer?"

"Beer was for the weekend crowd. For the hardcore drinkers a martini was the most alcohol you could get for the least amount of money. Cause everybody was always broke."

A tough Italian guy comes by and Gloria asks him to send the waiter over. "He's one of the bartenders," Gloria says. "A real ass pincher." A lot of the guys in the Remo, it seems, are "semi-Mafia-connected," what poet—then painter—Ted Joans's friends refer to as "the Minor Mafia."

The Village was much more a village in 1948 than in the sixties,

when it would get to be a tourist mecca and Bleecker Street on weekends would resemble Coney Island. In 1948 it was all Italian with
some underground people attracted by the Bohemian tradition, cheap
rents, and its insulation from the middle-class world of Uptown, which
began at Fourteenth Street with a few Village beachheads further
north like the Chelsea Hotel on West Twenty-third where Dylan
Thomas died. And the Italians were very insular. Tribal. Hoods loaf-
ing around storefront social clubs directing dead deadly looks at Bohemian interlopers, especially if they seemed to be gay or, in their
view, worse, were like Ted Joans, Black. Pre–civil rights America.
Years later Gregory Corso would remind Allen Ginsberg about an
incident involving LeRoi Jones/Baraka. "Remember how we went to
read in Washington, D.C.? He crawled underneath the backseat. I
never saw a man in my life do that, and I said, 'Hey, LeRoi, what're
you doing there?'

"He says, 'Don't you understand, I'm in Washington, D.C., I'm in
a place where they don't like Blacks.'

"I said, 'What, the capital of the United States?' So he woke me
up to the ball game on that. Right. This class guy."

"He wouldn't get out of the car to go into a drive-in," says Ginsberg. "And he was right at the time, I didn't realize."

"Me neither. I figure, all right, I'm Italian but at least I'm white so
they can't fuck with me too much."

Thirty years later in Boulder, Colorado, I encounter a courtly Baraka, with frosting hair and beard but still formidable gull-wing eye-
brows and the projection of a raging mental intensity, and I try to
put together this anecdote and his history of quick-change ethno-
political ferocity—I remember Ted Joans telling me that being friends
with LeRoi is like riding the back of a shark. The two takes merge
into a new image of the man.

"For a while I lived on Thompson Street," says poet Tuli Kupferberg, leading member of the dirty-talking, rabble-rousing music group
the Fugs, his almost pedantic intonations belied by a mad clown face,
scraggly beard, glittery eye. "That was called the South Village, less
desirable and infinitely more dangerous. Racially mixed couples, if
they wandered in there by mistake, they were taking their lives in

their hands. I finally decided to get out when I came home very late at night and there were two people in front of the bar, badly dressed, one was on the ground, the other one was kicking him in the head. So I decided this was not a nice kind of neighborhood."

"I motioned with my head to one of the two waiters standing around," writes Chandler Brossard of his version of the Remo in his 1952 novel, *Who Walk in Darkness*. "He came to the booth and I ordered a glass of beer. He did not say anything. I liked him less than any waiter I had ever seen. He looked deadpan at us, and went to the bar for my beer. The Italians who worked in the restaurants down there disliked all non-Italians. Some of them disguised it better than others."

The Italian hoods in the Village represent a leitmotif of fear for the classless subterraneans in Brossard's book, alienated as they are from both the Downtown proletariat and the Uptown bourgeoisie. This accurately reproduces the feel of the streets at the time, and in retrospect I see it corresponds to the situation of the cultural underground in the forties and fifties, with its hostility toward the middle class and its ideological divorce from the working class in consequence of the failed socialist movements of the thirties. It was a situation that vitiated the politics of the older Bohemia and largely depoliticized the new underground until the social protest movements of ten years later, in which the always political Living Theater took the vanguard. A deemphasis of politics and, especially, ideology marked the transition from Bohemians to "subterraneans" who, it might be said, initially moved further underground. But for a kid like me, this enclave of hold-outs had the power of myth and the sanction of tragic genius—Poe, Rimbaud, van Gogh. If you had to choose between wordly success and tragic genius, and this scene implied that you did, you would gladly have chosen the latter.

Joe Santini, owner of the Remo, would "stand at the bar and watch all the funnies come in," says Gregory Corso, implying a contained antagonism toward the underground types in the interests of business. Corso should know. He's a native, born across the street from the Remo at 190 Bleecker, did time in an orphanage, already in jail at twelve and in Dannemora at seventeen. Corso as a member of the underground does not have the same problems with the working class as do some still measuring things by middle-class values. Anatole Broyard sees the scene, in his 1950 article "Village Café," as a sardonically romanticized Inferno whose bizarre inhabitants are paralyzed as if in the circle of ice by their own hang-ups, compared to which the bartenders seem normal. But Corso felt right at home. "One bartender, Nick Colossi, became a National League umpire. And he, whenever there was a fight in the bar, would get a baseball bat, dig it? And beat up on the fuckers. Because, you see, people from all over the city would go to that bar."

"All the bartenders were pretty tough?"

"They were Italians, Italians are like that. And I guess they had to be at that time with so many people coming in. You know why people go to bars. Either they got a problem, either they get drunk and act dumb, or they go there to pick somebody up. So these guys, especially if they're Italian—like yegods."

It's true there was a certain hostility in the air, not only in the Village but in the whole forty-eight states. It was the beginning of the cold war. Waves of superpatriotism were emanating from Washington. Pinkos and faggots were in trouble in the provinces. The first list of subversive organizations was just out of the attorney general's office, quickly becoming a job test for members of listed groups. And from another point of view, the left, still going to demonstrations in jackets and ties, seemed hopelessly Victorian and out of touch.

"Early in the fifties I became associated with an anarchist group called Resistance," says Tuli Kupferberg. "They were still living in the Spanish Civil War. All the foreign anarchist groups, the Italians, the Jews, and the Spaniards, were much stronger than the American group. It had a lot of people who went into the War Resisters League, Ralph DiGia, Dave McReynolds, Paul Goodman, Judith Malina, and Julian Beck. But we just felt we were holding on. The Europeans were still living in Europe. I remember one guy got up once and he said—he'd fought in the Civil War—'My friends, there is only one way. *Machine guns! Machine guns!*'"

A lot of the veterans of the old left were hanging around the Village bars, blacklisted and unable to find jobs, unemployable merchant seamen, men with memories of the Spanish Civil War. "It was really a bummer," says Gloria, "because never having had any particular personal life because they were always going to sea, they were now stuck in New York and they had no personal life, so it made for a particularly chaotic kind of scene." Writers and actors who could no longer get work drifted down to the Village. Zero Mostel took up painting.

The tone of the bars was strictly macho. Broyard writes admiringly about a bartender who "can break your nose over the bar." Judith Malina of the Living Theater records in her *Diaries* a fight involving the manager of the Remo, the owner's stepson. "Johnny Santini's face grew more and more brutal with satisfaction as he struck again and again his already unconscious opponent, crumbled on the tiles, inert. Johnny kept striking till they pulled him away." Gays were out, though Corso insists that "Thursday night is faggot night" at the Remo and Broyard says some gay activity was tolerated and that the tension with which it proceeded, "so much deeper and more equivocal than at the regular markets, is like a delicious knotting in the bowels."

Some people dig the edge of violence that shows in these precincts those years. You experience a knotting of the bowels, delicious or not, walking past the hoods at 121 Prince Street, where Broyard lives in a cold-water flat across the hall from Gloria, as does Carl Solomon, to whom Allen Ginsberg's *Howl* is dedicated. The building has a quirky population of Bohemians, one of whom "threw his bed out the window and painted his apartment black to end his marriage," according to Beat historian John Tytell. One of the subterraneans in Brossard's book is nearly beaten to death by hoods at the end, and Ginsberg will try to recollect close to four decades later where it was—in Minetta Lane, outside the Remo, at the West End Bar near Columbia? —that Kerouac was beat up.

"Kerouac did get beaten up at the San Remo, didn't he?" asks Ginsberg.

"No," says Gregory. Corso describes himself these days as simian, but his face has fleshed and softened in mid-age so that if you put a babushka on him he'd look more like a sly old lady. "That motherfucking, what's that place called, across the street?"

"The Kettle of Fish," I say.

"The Kettle of Fish," Corso affirms.

"That was a rougher place anyway," I say.

"Yeah," says Corso. "I knew the guy that did it, and you know what happened? See, Jack when he spoke was like me. Open. First thought, best thought. Okay. We were walking on the street, this guy suddenly grabs Kerouac. Kerouac was much stronger than him, but he wouldn't touch him. So the guy grabs him, and I saw the worst thing in my life. He's bouncing Kerouac's head on the ground, like this"—Corso jumps up and starts acting out the scene—"and I suddenly realized. And I screamed, '*Sto-o-op!*' and he keeps on doing it, and I grabbed this motherfucker back. *Uuuh!* And he looks at me like a drunk man, and walked away. It was the scariest thing I ever saw."

"Just completely spontaneous for no reason?" I ask.

"Yeah. It was fast. All I could do was scream, 'Stop!' "

"What was the reason the guy grabbed Kerouac?" asks Ginsberg.

"Because Jack, like me, we speak the unspeakable. And we feel free. We're Americans, why not? We're not insulting the guy. No, but that day his head was being bounced on the ground, I saw a smile on his face. And I knew that man never hurt anybody in his life. Monsieur Kerouac. I love him. I love him very much."

In another fight, at the Cedar Tavern, painter Franz Kline, repeatedly provoked, blows his stack at his good friend Jackson Pollock and starts punching him hard in the gut. Pollock, the biggest and toughest of all the painters on the scene, does nothing but double over in pain, laugh happily, and, according to the account by writer Fielding Dawson, whisper to Kline, "Not so hard."

Despite all the aggression floating around in the warm gas of tobacco and beer filling the San Remo, there was also a certain careless freedom in the atmosphere. Carlos Castaneda would preach to a later generation of youth about the existence of alternate realities. In the fifties there was only one, challenged occasionally by, say, an old book that escaped current categories, like *Leaves of Grass* or *Tristram Shandy,* or a way of moving and talking, such as James Dean's, or the tone of a bar like the Remo. What a relief for teen-age rebels fleeing across the bridges and tunnels from the rat race for success that made Sammy run from World War II and the Bomb and the Holocaust through the fifties, so frightened, his hysteria fed by McCarthyism, that he didn't stop till he got to the sixties. Reality was middle class. If you stumbled in the race and fell out, you faced the frightening prospect not so much of starvation or even of "failure," as simply of nothing. The "working class" had not been real since the decline of the working-class movements in the late thirties; the "masses" were being absorbed in the mass market. "Negroes" certainly were not real—they weren't even visible. The upper class was a myth presumably neutralized by FDR along with the monopolies, monopoly having been reduced to the status of a game. Doctors, lawyers, and especially businessmen were real, maybe even, at the limit, professors. Politicans and celebrities had a tantalizing meta-reality. Beyond that, you ceased to exist.

What's fascinating to me about the Remo is that the habitués are doing nothing, they're wasting time. "Hovering halfway between the pleasure principle and the death instinct"—a phrase Broyard means as a putdown—they are at least in contact with the pleasure principle and the death instinct, something that middle-class existence at the time does not dare permit. America, innocent victim of Russian aggression, persecuted by the Rosenbergs and Alger Hiss, and sneaky subversives who hide behind the Fifth Amendment, is itself too aggressive to allow the dream, the revery, the passive attention required to recognize its deepest impulses. The smile on the faces of Kerouac, of Pollock, as they are beaten is a smile of perverse beatitude, emblem of breakthrough to the primal pleasure of giving in, giving up, of failure, loss, defeat, the other side of the fifties drive for success.

In the underground you learn to violate the taboos that support middle-class reality. You learn not only to waste yourself, you learn to waste time, disrupting the countdown toward death implicit in the chronology of production, with the timelessness of pleasure. You have to know how to hang out. Some people have a talent for it, others learn. It requires a certain amount of stupidity, which, for those brought up to pursue middle-class ambitions, is often hard to muster. For many people, and especially those like intellectuals whose goals are internalized, hanging around doing nothing can be a trial of patience. Drinking helps, so do drugs, but at its most refined hanging out is a form of meditation. You let your mouth gape, you stare dully into space and let your mind go blank. It's not easy, but it's worth the effort. Sitting in the bars and espresso places, browsing bocce courts, the 8th Street Bookshop, Fred Leighton's Mexican boutique, Fred Braun's sandal store, or the offbeat jewelry store run by Sam Kramer with the earring in one ear on Eighth, the various pottery shops and importers of cheap exotica—hanging out in such places digging the merchandise and members of the opposite sex becomes an end in itself.

But the hanging-out place par excellence is, I quickly discover, Washington Square. Maybe its relaxed, dead-end ambience has to do with its position as cul-de-sac at the bottom of Fifth Avenue, or with the fact that it served as a paupers' graveyard around the beginning of the nineteenth century. You can almost always find anyone you want to see there if you hang out long enough. Meanwhile you can enjoy sitting on a bench watching the mix of bohoes and middle-class ladies, Italian hoods, hip sex mothers playing with their babies and hip dogs, knowing adolescent boys and newly nubile sexpots from Little Red School House down the block or private schools Uptown, preening Blacks cocksure and superior from their place in the Bohemian pecking order, intellectuals in proletarian clothing, young folk singers gazing into infinity as they let their fingers trip across their guitar strings, emaciated Bowery types, NYU college kids, and a miscellany of loafers sitting around the circular fountain in the center with a certain casual inner-than-thou look.

This was the crowd on a sunny weekday afternoon. Starting with the sixties, the Square increasingly became a place where small-time drug dealers would congregate, but those were already the days when the Hippies were lounging on the lawns, with rarely a blue uniform in view. In the old days you got tickets for sitting on the grass. Howard Smith remembers "getting tickets for my kids being nude on the grass when they were crawling, they didn't even walk yet, and the cops gave them tickets for indecent exposure."

At this time the Square is run for the gentry coming down through the Arch from Fifth Avenue and the hoods coming up from the Village past the fenced playground where NYU's Loeb Student Center will later stand. Neither group wants drugs, noise, vagrants, musicians, queers, hoboes, bohoes, or Negroes. Decadent loafers. Hanging out. Wasting time. Corrupting morals. But this is just what they start to get, plus attendant tourists in large crowds on weekends, despite the cops. In fact, the real enforcers are the Italian hoods. Anything they don't like they beat up. If it doesn't vacate the premises fast. Two swarthy types approach a wispy-looking youth who is neither with a girl nor looking like he wants one, which can mean only one thing to them.

"Hello, Mary," says the hood on the right.

"Waiting for your boyfriend?" says the hood on the left.

"Ain't he pretty?" says the hood on the right.

"*Mah-rone!*" says the hood on the left, shaking his wrist.

At this point the wispy youth remembers an urgent errand and leaves.

My first take on the underground is that it's a class of outsiders experimenting with an idea of the good life beyond stable middle-class constraints. Since I believe that to be my inclination, I'm willing to give subterraneans the benefit of every doubt. Those rebels inclined to waste their lives and get on with it, to embrace failure at the start and opt for excitement over security, are then confronted with the promised land of previously repressed impulses, a risky new underground landscape to explore consisting of everything deemed unreal by the dominant culture, which amounts to almost everything. The risk is becoming a victim, a risk that is totally taboo since the Holocaust. But those who go all the way in defeat and become victims are, like Dylan Thomas, at least victims of themselves, achieving sometimes an inverted saintliness symptomatic of the culture—the last is first and the best is worst. This underground saintliness of the beaten is a phenomenon that has been noticed by many, among them Norman Mailer and Broyard, negatively, as well as by Malamud, and above all by the Beats. As in the perverse purity of Maxwell Bodenheim, for example.

Bodenheim drifts into the Remo, poet and novelist, relic of an older

Village Bohemia that thrived between Wars I and II. Gloria points him out, bummy looking, a local fixture, selling his old books. Bodenheim becomes for me, even in his seedy decline, a symbol of the dark glamour of the underground. "How dumb I was at that time," says Ted Joans, an avid collector. "Bodenheim would wander around with maybe five or six copies, hardcover copies, of his book *Naked on Roller Skates*. 'Give me thirty-five cents, son, I'll sign it, thirty-five cents.' Isn't that something, you can't even buy a copy for three hundred and fifty dollars in cash. And I, like a dummy—and I had the money—didn't buy it. Cause I looked at it wrong."

Judith Malina—who told me only half joking in Paris that the ground-breaking Living Theater, so influential in the sixties, was born in the Remo—writes in her *Diaries* in 1952 of "Bodenheim's queer remembrance of poems past, and his terrible face. There was a mocking item about him in *Time* magazine, a story of his arrest some nights ago for sleeping in the subway. With it was a picture of him much as he looks now, though sober. He passed it around and confided to me that he will sue for libel. A recent benefit for him given by some Villagers put him in possession of some money, so he bought me beer, and gin for himself, and became quickly incomprehensible."

Flash forward: We're sitting in Allen Ginsberg's slum apartment on East Twelfth Street near Avenue A, his neighborhood since the fifties, Peter Orlovsky just in from Boulder and Gregory Corso from Paris, talking about Bodenheim. "Gregory's still sleeping on my floor," says Ginsberg, thinking back thirty years. Allen now at sixty, with *terribilità*-lined Moby Dick brow in contrast with a sensual fish mouth, which possibly provokes Corso's characterization of him as guppy, has a face slightly skewed by Bell's palsy from right eye droop to mouth twist above his beard, as if distorted by a perceptive Impressionist painter to capture the interaction of poet-crazy and rabbinic moralist.

"Before us was the Bohemians," says Corso, in many ways Bodenheim's successor. "Now you know what the Bohemians did. Mr. Bodenheim would go around and sell a redundancy of a poem for fifty cents to buy a drink. He didn't join Ben Hecht or any of those assholes to whatyacall go to Hollywood and play the game," says Corso.

28

"No, you know why?"

"Why?" asks Corso.

"He was drinking and he took a pee in the National Academy of Arts and Letters meeting, and they kicked him out of the National Academy. My father told me because my father and mother were there. He pissed on the floor of the National Academy. Just like you," says Ginsberg laughing.

"Fuck them, man," says Corso.

"And so they drummed him out. We nominated a whole bunch of people and you know what happened? We nominated Robert Duncan, Robert Creeley, Gary Snyder, and Kenneth Koch and maybe somebody else, I forget. Not one of them made it, instead Russell Baker, E. L. Doctorow, William Gaddis—all right—Donald Justice, Charles Rosen, Paul Theroux, Lewis Thomas. Isn't that incredible?"

"I'm just happy Koch didn't make it," says Corso. "I'm happy he didn't make it because he wanted to make it. I'm happy the motherfucker didn't make it. I'm happy about Koch. I'm not a bad man, y'know, an evil man and all that shit, but I always thought he was a little ambitious. If you believe you're a poet, you don't fuck about anything, you got it made."

"Do you think that kind of ambition is always bad?" I ask.

"I think so, because you gotta know who y'are. If you believe you're a poet, then you're saved."

In a diary entry on art in relation to suffering and hedonism, Judith Malina writes, "Do we idolize its victims and priests? Do we not idolize Maxwell Bodenheim although we are sometimes loath to talk to him and always ashamed of our condescension to him? The bartenders of the Remo have put a photograph of him over the bar.

"What we admire is Bodenheim's refusal to resist," continues Malina. "We fight all the time, resisting temptation. We admire those who don't even if it's suicidal."

In the Remo, Bodenheim is this very minute reciting one of his poems over at the bar, which he does for drinks, when he's abruptly interrupted by the cry of a sea gull piercing the bar noise.

Joe Gould, Harvard 1911, small, bald, toothless, gray-bearded, frail, is standing in the middle of the room, strung over his shoulders his cardboard sandwich sign that advertises poems for sale from his "Oral

History of the World," carrying a huge bundle of papers, presumably the "History" itself. Gould puts down his papers and starts flapping his arms while making sea gull noises—he can imitate sea gulls. He stops when someone buys him a beer. He stops to drink the beer. Gould says he understands the language of sea gulls and claims to have translated Longfellow into Sea Gull. For this talent he has earned the name Dr. Sea Gull.

"Gould had something called 'The Oral History of the World,'" says social historian of the hip Seymour Krim, whose writings were instrumental in demystifying the old Bohemian mystique that Gould represents. "He took down what people said, it was very interesting, this was the theory of it. He would write down common speech, or uncommon speech, and he was supposed to have had thousands of pages, I think selectively but I don't know what his criteria were. He used to carry around these tattered red folders."

Actually, years later, Izzy Young, impressario of the influential Folklore Center, found Gould's handwritten notebooks. "And you know what?" says Howard Smith. "They stink. You know the theory was he listened to everybody's conversation, especially at Minetta's. There was also a great portrait of him in the Kettle of Fish, a kind of caricature. Izzy found tons of notebooks. This is what they said: 'Overheard woman in next booth ordering shrimp marinara. Her boyfriend said, "Want another cigarette?" She said, "No." People in booth in front of me ordered another bottle of wine. Can't make out what they're talking about.' Izzy said you had to read about six notebooks till maybe there'd be one line anyone would have been interested in. He was obviously over the hill into heavy alcoholism by then, or older age or whatever, and these notebooks were a great myth created by the guy who wrote them up in *The New Yorker*." Though as John Tytell says, Gould's method could be considered "the original tape recorder," incorporating an important principle employed later by people like Kerouac and John Cage: "No discrimination, which is a Beat as well as a Buddhist tenet, but hard to realize because of academic conditioning."

As a neophyte, I watch Gould and Bodenheim with utter fascination. After a while, I also become familiar with the strange figure of

Moondog in medieval-looking leather, blanket, and Viking horns, usually stationed in the middle of the sidewalk on Broadway or Sixth Avenue, selling sheet music. Moondog, crackpot composer and inventor of bizarre instruments such as the "oo" and the "trimbas," like the clownish Puerto Rican street poet Jorge Brandon, whom I later encounter with his talking coconut in the East Village, turns out to be a fairly interesting artist, or so say those who attend his occasional rooftop concerts. Philip Glass once let Moondog live at his place when he had nowhere to go. It's not the oddball quality of these figures that attracts me, but rather the way they throw themselves on the mercy of others, their willed destruction of pride, self-respect, and even ego itself. If you are seeking distinctions from the aggressive egoism of the fifties success cult, Gould and Bodenheim are especially instructive examples.

Both Bodenheim and Gould "were clowns in a certain way," says Krim. "I mean bitter clowns, to make a dollar."

Maybe court jester would be a more appropriate category, one that Ginsberg and Corso in their poet-crazy mode have found effective, but if Gould and Bodenheim are clowns, they are so in a lineage of underground clowns descending from Dostoyevsky's *Notes from Underground*. Decades later, talking to Ginsberg, I'll suddenly realize how important Dostoyevsky is to the Beats in their formative years, and to the underground mystique. Dostoyevsky's original subterranean, spiteful and belligerent, is also an exhibitionist who knows how to keep you amused. You tolerate his hostility while being entertained by the spectacle of his self-humiliation. The bitter clown of *Notes* pays for his contempt with total lack of respect for himself.

I would come to understand that the flagrant self-destructiveness of the underground of Bleecker Street is an expression of its total contempt for the cautious pragmatism of the middle class. Dostoyevsky's antihero reserves for us the right to destroy ourselves in spite of all rational arguments. His psychological self-dissection may make *Notes*, after *Tristram Shandy*, one of the first self-conscious works, as defined in Postmodern fiction to denote consciousness by the narrative voice of itself. In *Notes* the insistent nonconsciousness of the normal bourgeois world would make any kind of introspection, or even self-awareness, seem self-conscious if not downright sick. In fact "sick" was used as a strategy by the rebellious "black humor" comedians of the fifties, like Lenny Bruce and Mort Sahl—not to mention cartoonist Jules Feiffer and his "Sick, sick, sick"—who in turn influenced a number of novelists in a modest attempt to break away from established styles. Self-awareness is against the interests of a dominant class that wants to maintain power without thinking too much about motives or consequences.

However, at the end of the forties we began to see the intellectual chic of Auden's "age of anxiety." It attempted to domesticate the underground mystique with the housebroken fifties version of "alienation." Alienation dignified the situation of underground man with the idea that the anguish of a heroic disaffection with the culture was necessary to produce the awareness that would ultimately validate the culture. It was a doctrine that led you to reject the mainstream only in expectation of eventually being redeemed by it as a hero.

So it would become hip to be self-consciously neurotic in the fifties in opposition to the healthy, normal louts in the gray flannel suits. The fifties was the age of breakdowns. The insanity bit had a heroic hue. There were times when you felt like an outsider by the mere fact of not being in psychoanalysis. That I avoided the shrink was not because of any virtue of my own, but rather because of not having enough money. Whatever its therapeutic benefits, psychoanalysis kept you on the straight and narrow of social conformity just so you could earn enough bread to pay for it. But in the sixties even madness would get to be transvalued by R. D. Laing via Freud heretic Wilhelm Reich, by redefining madness as a form of sanity.

Reich's orgone psychology, which insists on the integrity of the human organism no matter how maladjusted to society, was throughout the fifties influential on a long list of creative people interested in resisting that society, from Bellow to Mailer to Kerouac to performance artists and dancers like Carolee Schneemann and Ann Halprin. William Burroughs, who is dubious about Reich's therapy, defends his orgonomic cancer research quite vigorously. "The function of the orgone box, as I see it, is to raise the electrical tension at the surface of the cell and that's exactly what it seems to do. You get a tingling sensation in the surface of the skin, and I think that would be definitely anticancerous. The discovery of the electrical cell theory of cancer has been enunciated by others with no acknowledgment to Reich, although it's his discovery."

Most Reichians place credence in both the healing power of the orgone box and the effectiveness of the therapy. There was a time in the Village when practically every hip apartment or loft you walked into had a restored brick fireplace and an orgone box or "accumulator," as they're called, a metal-lined wooden closet you sit in to charge up on healing orgone energy, the basic energy of the universe. But hardcore subterraneans will never, like R. D. Laing, rationalize madness as an impulse toward a higher form of normality. Gould and Bodenheim had to know that self-destruction is self-destruction, desirable only because the burn-out it leads to is preceded by incandescence.

This attitude is sardonically illustrated by a story repeated in one of Bill Manville's "Saloon Society" columns, which appeared in the early *Village Voice*. "Say, you know that hotel I'm cooling it in? The rat manager comes in this morning, he says to me: 'Sam, that blonde on the second floor, they found her this morning. She must have been on something powerful, she was dead. She was all blue from the junk, all shriveled up.' Man, you know what I said to him? I said: 'Oh, lead me to that connection!' Imagine, Bill, how strong that junk must have been. Imagine, not *only* to die—*but to turn* BLUE *and to die!*"

Though I don't realize it at the time, Reich's theories are appealing to me during the McCarthy era because they provide a rationale for underground values in the absence of radical politics, and encourage the Bohemian yen for Dionysian freedom. As a recent article in *Partisan Review* puts it, "Sex, for Reich, *was* politics, and the contentious language of his manifestoes ... made his system [sound like] a regrouping for a war of liberation against the residual Puritanism and production-oriented austerities of American life." Unsparing in its critique of the authoritarianism of revolutionary society as well as the constraints of capitalism, Reich's attack on sexual repression finally links for me the apparently opposed oppressions of dialectical materialism and shmuck materialism, between which it formerly seemed necessary to make a choice. Though the middle class, deenergized by its self-imposed suppression of biological instinct, is not really free, revolution is not necessarily liberation. Despite McCarthyism, it's possible to fight the system without being a Marxist. As a friend says, "Now you can be a rebel, if not without a cause, then without a Cause." From then on for me, and I think many others, sex becomes a weapon and dissipation a form of dissent, instead of merely a way of having fun in defiance of the work ethic. I know a guy who convinces himself that seduction is a duty, though one he manages to enjoy, neatly combining the righteousness of the work ethic with the pleasure-prone underground mystique.

In the underground, hostility toward middle-class values tends to be ambivalent. In the Village bars, this envious hostility toward the middle class—even the cultivated middle class—could be seen any weekend in its attitude toward the Uptown tourists willing to buy drinks to watch the clowns perform. People remember, for example, Terry Southern coming Downtown with a bankroll, looking. And eventually finding "the funny man," as Corso calls him, Mason Hoffenberg, co-author with Southern of *Candy*. In Brossard's novel an ad-agency account exec named Russell Goodwin turns up in the bar. He lives Uptown and has a charge account at Abercrombie and Fitch. He reads *The New Yorker* regularly and thinks it's "really terrific." He listens to WQXR, the classical music station, goes to the Museum of Modern Art, and prefers French films to American movies.

" 'Don't *bring us down*,' " one of the underground regulars says.

" 'Oh. I get it,' Goodwin said. 'I get that one. It's a jive expression. Right?'

" 'You're in,' Porter said.

" 'He's a very solid citizen,' Harry said. 'He makes four hundred a week.' "

Behind the self-righteousness of the subterraneans is an assumption of superior virtue, even of a certain purity. In fact, at this time in the early fifties, I am credulous enough to credit a kind of grungy purity to the Village scene in its deliberate isolation from the world of Uptown. Before Mary McCarthy's article about the Remo in the *New York Post*, which simultaneously popularizes it and puts it down

—a strategy also dear to Time-Life, which used it on Jackson Pollock to ridicule and vulgarize him at the same time—Broyard says the bar "hadn't even an obscene scrawl in the men's toilet." It's the tourists who come to check it out who "decorated it with the images of their disappointment." There is a kind of communality down here after all, the good side of tribalism. You don't foul your own nest, you take care of your own shit. Ginsberg has the impression that the neighborhood was familial toward Corso as a native son, but even the tough bartenders at the Remo extend credit to regulars, and the bartoughs are tender toward exotic characters like Bodenheim after they've been around long enough.

A hood comes over to sit in our booth a while talking to Gloria. This guy is a real gorilla. He communicates in gutturals and grunts, punctuated with jabs and animated gestures. After he leaves, Gloria says he's more or less a hitter for the Mafia and she didn't understand a word either. She just keeps smiling and nodding. She says he speaks a language known to only a few intimates who live on his block in Little Italy. Later, after this guy learns to talk by associating with the subterraneans, he gives up hittering and becomes a rather well known actor.

"Let's make it over to Minetta's," says Gloria. "Maybe we can eat something if Manny's there." The MacDougal Street regulars are on a shuttle between the Remo and Minetta's a block away, seeing who's where when, and what parties are happening later in the evening.

"Why do we eat only if Manny's there?" I ask out on the street.

"He lets us charge food."

Minetta's has the same kind of clientele as the Remo, sawdust on the floor, the walls covered with caricatures, many done by Franz Kline. Joe Gould is usually stationed at the door. Manny is there. He looks a lot like a grasshopper. We order eggplant Parmesan and slather it with lots of grated cheese to make a whole meal out of it. Costs around seventy-five cents and we don't leave a tip. "Every now and then somebody comes into some money, then we tip him. He's nice."

We check out the Remo again. Gloria points out jazzman Miles Davis nodding in a corner. The going drugs are pot and heroin. Gloria says hello to a woman who comes on as if Black. "Junkie to

35

the musicians," says Gloria. "Supplies a lot of people with junk. And bisexual," which is not too usual at that point because it's a very macho scene going on down there. "But she's the only one who holds her own with everybody." Judith Malina of the Remo crowd says that Paul Goodman, her guru and analyst, and whose plays she is directing, is "of the opinion a woman couldn't be an artist." Malina also has to struggle with the problem that he wants all her boyfriends. Stanley Gould of the junk-blue eyes is around as he always is, making drug deals. " 'Listen, man, this is really great charge,' " says Cap Fields quaintly in Brossard's book. " 'The best.'

" 'How much?'

" 'An ace for two sticks.' " Cap himself is already high on the weed, talking "thick and strange" as he sits down in the bar.

In her article, which I will remember because it gets a lot of attention in the Village, Mary McCarthy puts down the Remo because, she says, its habitués Do Nothing. McCarthy's generation of Bohemians, the political intellectuals around *Partisan Review*—which in any case is Upper Bohemia—is tuned in, she says, to "the battle of ideas and standards." The "ideas and standards" her group is involved with, however, are those of Modernism, which American art is about to leave on the beach. One of the tragedies of American culture is that the political intellectuals usually haven't a clue about what cutting-edge contemporaries in the arts are up to, and care less unless it fits into their doctrines. In his well-known study of the avant-garde, Renato Poggioli asserts that the political intelligentsia typically focuses on subject matter rather than aesthetic considerations. In painting, this period is an exception. Clement Greenberg and Harold Rosenberg, polemicists of Abstract Expressionism, demonstrate the power, for better and for worse, that intellectuals can generate when they make contact with formal developments in the arts.

The San Remo underground, succeeding the older Bohemians, besides being a new generation, which is always difficult for the preceding wave to make out, just may have been too low for a high intellopol like McCarthy to see clearly. If she could she might have spotted, for example, Paul Goodman in the Remo, musicians John Cage, George Kleinsinger, and Miles Davis, dancer Merce Cunningham, artists William Steig and Jackson Pollock, Julian Beck and Judith Malina of the Living Theater, social activist Dorothy Day, and writers as diverse as James Agee, Brossard, Broyard, Ginsberg, Corso, Kerouac, and many others who, it might be argued, were doing something, even if it was something Miss McCarthy wasn't aware of.

It helps me to make sense of my experience with Bohemians, and it may help you with yours, to understand that when you talk about the difference between Upper and Lower Bohemia you're talking mostly about life style. Upper Bohemians happen to have radical, or at least heterodox, ideas, but they live middle class. Or even upper middle class. Or even rich. The distinction between Upper and Lower Bohemia should not be confused with the distinction between the hardcore and softcore underground. The latter is well described in Malcolm Cowley's 1934 book about the Bohemia of the 1920's, *Exile's Return*. " 'They' [the hard core] had been rebels: they wanted to change the world, be leaders in the fight for justice and art, help to create a society in which individuals could express themselves. 'We' [the soft core] were convinced at the time that society could never be changed by an effort of the will. . . . But it was fun all the same. . . . We lived in top floor tenements along the Sixth Avenue Elevated because we couldn't afford to live elsewhere. Either we thought of our real home as existing in the insubstantial world of art, or else we were simply young men on the make, the humble citizens not of Bohemia but of Grub Street."

I have often been puzzled, along with many others, by the spectacle of a former subterranean known for an unconventional or even radical way of life suddenly turning up in an ad agency, say, coming on straighter than straight. Bohemia, Upper or Lower, is for softcore subterraneans only a matter of life style. They are along for the ride. When it's no fun, or a better ride is available, having no necessary stake in the underground or anything but career, they melt into the middle-class mainstream. "We took our little portion of the easy money that seemed to be everywhere," writes Cowley, "and we thereby engaged or committed ourselves without meaning to do so. We became part of the system we were trying to evade, and it defeated us from within. . . . We laughed too much, sang too much . . . and after a few years we were, in Zelda Fitzgerald's phrase, 'lost and driven now like the rest.'" Never confuse a life style with a commitment, son, or you'll end up committed to nothing but your stock portfolio. For example, Abbie Hoffman tells me that Jerry Rubin, notorious for his switch from Yippie to Yuppie and who himself seems lost and driven now like the rest, "used to always talk about his career—this is good for his career, this is bad for his career."

"Even in the old days?" I ask.

"Yeah, he used the word 'career.' And I always used to go"— Hoffman assumes a helplessly astonished expression—" *'Career?!'* "

Cowley himself, after zigging to support the Moscow trials and turning away from the avant-garde to endorse a Party-line cultural nationalism in the mid-thirties, zagged to recuperate the reputation of America's greatest "experimental" writer, Faulkner, in the forties, then sold Kerouac to the publishing industry in the fifties, but only after *On the Road* had been subjected to a certain amount of censorship in the name of revision. Ginsberg says the revisions were negligible, though others disagree, but he adds that Kerouac wrote *Dharma Bums* in response to Cowley's request for something the public could understand more easily.

However, Kerouac ambiguously craved the public acclaim that Cowley made possible and that helped to destroy him. He once said that fame was "like old newspapers blowing down Bleecker Street." But in a 1957 article in *The Village Voice,* Howard Smith observes Kerouac after reading from his work at the Village Vanguard: "The applause is like a thunderstorm on a July night. He smiles and goes to sit among the wheels and the agents. . . . He is prince of the hips, being accepted in the court of the rich kings. . . . He must have hated himself in the morning—not for the drinks he had, but because he ate it all up the way he really never wanted to." Many subterraneans want to violate the taboos of the middle class, while simultaneously needing its indulgence, as if you could bite the hand of oppression and then expect it to feed you. With those contradictory needs, success may be as unsatisfying as failure. But there are subterraneans who see the underground as providing a permanent moral perspective on the dominant culture, as well as subterraneans who are ambivalent, or even what you might call honestly opportunistic.

Cowley's career is exemplary. Cowlies are indispensable to the underground. When Ginsberg berated Cowley for not publishing *On the Road,* Cowley reminded him he was the only editor around at least trying to do so. It is the cowlies who always sooner or later discover the commercial value of the underground and figure out how to vend it to the middle class, either diluted by time, or in denatured imitations, or filtered through a de facto censorship. So Cowley is able to rediscover Faulkner for us, whose greatest work was done twenty years earlier, and manages to "discover" Kerouac, if in a revised version. So the underground becomes "offbeat," weird but fun, or rather, weird and fun. "There must be a new ethic that encouraged people to buy, a *consumption* ethic. . . . Many of the Greenwich Village ideas proved useful in the altered situation," says Cowley of the Bohemian rebellion of the twenties in a passage that previews the commercialization of the sixties "counterculture." "Thus, *self-expression* and *paganism* encouraged a demand for all sorts of products."

It's not for me, voyeur of bars, vagabond of coffeehouses, itinerant outsider, to put down the cowlies. When your orientation is looking in, you have to accept that your position will be outside. But when you do want in, these middlemen to the middle class are among the few connections available. And why shouldn't you want in? There's a difference between selling and selling out. So what if cowlies are sometimes only joyriders—at least they know joy when they see it. In fact, that will be part of the appeal of subterranean life in the sixties—we're having more fun than you. Why shouldn't everybody have the chance of buying into a good thing once it's discovered? But something new will soon start happening to this familiar American dynamic of cultural opportunism. To an unprecedented degree it will become the artists themselves, in a strategy that can be traced back to the French Surrealists, who sell themselves to the middle class. Norman Mailer's *Advertisements for Myself* is an obvious case in point. And when you start selling yourself, you may stop selling your art and wind up selling your life style.

On any night in the Remo you might hear about a certain ongoing party over in Sheridan Square in the West Village. There's a kind of open-house potluck dinner in progress there, supervised by this huge Black guy, an unemployed merchant-seaman Spanish Civil War vet who watches over a gigantic communal pot of something that's been on the stove continuously for weeks. Anybody who's hungry dips in; anyone with food to contribute adds it and stirs, fish, a piece of chicken, a can of baked beans, as long as it's edible. There's also one gigantic ashtray to emphasize the collective tone, from each according to his ability, etc. The Iron Curtain has closed, Tail Gunner Joe McCarthy is gearing up, and a lot of these old lefties can't get any work other than driving cabs, moving furniture, occasional carpentry.

"This isn't the time to sell out and take a steady job anyway," says a guy in a black turtleneck, munching something nameless he's fished out of the pot. "This is the time to wait and organize while the inherent contrafuckingdictions of the system start to tear it apart." He's got me trapped in a corner. People in this kind of scene like to give me advice, maybe because I'm a kid. "You got to use your head"—he taps his and gets a surprising castanet sound. "Like I used mine in the Lincoln Brigade. That's a steel plate, kid. You think things are bad but the worse they are the closer we get to the revolution. Bad is good, kid. Use your head."

I don't say anything. What can you say to a guy like that? Stay away from magnets. These guys, stuck in a stagnant ideology, are programmed for wipeout. In a few years the big Black will be living in a rathole apartment next door to a crazed alcoholic pal on the Lower East Side where they will break down the wall between the two apartments in a drunken fit and end up with a duplex rathole. "They were like so crazy," says Gloria, "the two of them. The roommate would come around to my loft pounding on my door, screaming in the street. You know, the kind of drunk where you roar and you scream and you pick up rocks, I mean it was crazy. And I never saw him in any other condition. Ever. He was like a killer type, it was horrible."

Soon, for me, the party melts into pleasant confusion, through which I stray dazed by beer, cheap wine, and generally overloaded circuits. At some point I notice a blond girl sitting, knees crossed, on a couch across the room. I say "girl" though she must be at least five years older than me and way ahead. She's wearing her blond hair short and straight and is the first woman I've seen dressing in what I later come to think of as existentialist style—black stockings, black sweater, pallid makeup. Marilyn Duport, whom I will come to know on and off through the years of her short life, is starlet-pretty and Bohemian-sexy, and one of the nicest people I'll meet in the underground scene. Poised, if not a little detached, as if skating maybe on thin ice, on this occasion she looks like she could have walked out of Saint-Germain-des-Prés.

In fact, a lot of American painters used to drink their *demis* in exile at the Select and the Coupole through the fifties, Sam Francis and Ed Clarke among them, and some Black writers, including Richard Wright, used to hang out in a café near the Luxembourg Gardens called the Tournon. There was a kind of easygoing traffic between Montparnasse and the Village.

I see that Marilyn is rolling a cigarette and I will later remember thinking, *Shit, that must be a reefer.* The existential pallor tends to make girls look blank-faced, as if, I always think, they're in shock. But when Marilyn looks up and notices me staring, her face breaks into this warm, wide smile, so I go over and get my first taste of marijuana. Marilyn assumes an easy camaraderie with me, despite my age, in the spirit of the giant cooking pot on the stove. It's us against the world of gray flannel and attaché cases, I feel, the crumbling solidarity of the underground against the triumphant middle class, the doomed fellowship of resistance, the poverty and isolation of losers. The romance of it, the bitter pathos of it. In fact, no more than fifteen years later, after the last of several acid-induced institutionalizations, Marilyn would be out of friends, money, and places to live. One vagrant night she asked an acquaintance in Brooklyn if she could crash in her apartment. When she was turned down Marilyn walked up to the roof and jumped. You would have to realize then that the inverse of her openness and generosity was an underlying acceptance of a darker fate, and that her archetype was Marilyn Monroe, the tragic mess of de Kooning's *Marilyn* implied under the glossy image of Warhol's.

When the only energetic collective effort around is the united front of shmuck materialism, it's easy to see that Tony Frusella is right not to stand up and blow for Charlie Barnet. It's easy to see, coming from Midwood, where everything is overstuffed—the furniture, the people, the heads of the high school kids trying to make it into Columbia, Harvard, Yale—that Bohemian self-denial is virtuous. It's easy to see, coming from the conspicuous consumption of the middle class, why romantic poverty should be worn like a badge. It's easy, too easy, to see, in face of the concerted success drive of Luce's American Century, how a career of solitary self-destruction could be a heroic course. To discover these truths in a going scene, with its own sense of prestige and its own kind of tradition, is an irresistible revelation. So what if Seymour Krim starts his underground career by sweeping out a book store, when the book store is owned by Joe Klinger, who had published one of the classic literary magazines, *Pagany,* and supposedly discovered doomed, self-victimizing, visionary *poète maudit* Hart Crane? You do not question too much the bitterness of veterans of Bohemia, like the one-eyed Klinger, while fighting off the wide-eyed optimism of post–V Day booster America. You expect to be bitter, you prefer it.

Years later, over lunch in a small café in Paris, Ted Joans and I get to talking about the habit of tough independence, the adversary stance, retained by the Abstract Expressionists even after their sudden success in the early fifties.

"That strikes me as the last generation of painters that had been really completely separated from the establishment."

"That's right, that's it," says Joans.

In fact, Abstract Expressionist Adolph Gottlieb has said that "during the forties, some artists were painting with a sense of absolute despair. . . . Things were going so badly . . . I felt free to do whatever I wanted, no matter how absurd it might seem; what was there to lose?"

"Like with the writers hitting a brick wall in the fifties," I say to Joans. "You know in 1957 when *On the Road* came out, Kerouac had already written most of his novels and none of them had been published, except his first one in 1950, which wasn't real Kerouac. There was hardly any chance to become establishment."

"All of them were like that then," says Joans, almost as if he's acting everything out with his loose body and mobile face, creating in the process a persona with the name of Ted Joans, to whom he often refers in third person. "See, Pollock remained a Bohemian, the true maverick, even with money. It bothered him that he became a celebrity. In 1951, two weeks in New York, I walked into the San Remo, which is right on the corner of Bleecker, so if you came in one door you could go out the other right onto MacDougal, so I was doing one of those things instead of just going around the corner, and I saw him and I said, 'Excuse me, are you . . .?' And he said, 'Yeah, yeah, I'm Jackson Pollock. Who are you?' You know, like that. Sort of like a surly John Wayne." Joans goes into a sort of shit-kicking cowboy act. Ted's a great mimic, so that for example when he does his hilarious imitation of Gregory Corso, it's so precise that I sometimes think I'm actually looking at Corso despite the difference in complexion. Now he slips into a version of himself as naïve young painter.

" 'Oh, oh, my name is Ted Joans, I, I just graduated from Indiana University, I studied painting there, and this is my first time in New York and I'm going to Europe.'

" 'What are you going to Europe for?'

" 'Well, I'm going there to advance my painting.'

" 'I thought you graduated.'

" 'Yeah, I . . .'

" 'Well, what in shit you going to Europe for? Unless you want to learn to paint the hair in somebody's nose or asshole. What's happening is happening right here. What's happening is happening right here in this goddamn United States, especially in this city. What are you drinking?'

" 'Well, I don't know, I'll have the same,' I said, which was a mistake because he was drinking little glasses of gin, and then washing them down slowly with beer, let me tell you."

"Looks like all those guys were doing their best to drink one another to death. How'd you know who he was?"

"From *Life* magazine! But see, he didn't want that kind of celebrity. Those guys, see, like de Kooning still refuses it."

"That's interesting, because now, at least, everybody wants to be a celebrity."

"Well, they had that tough American maverick thing, like cowboy stars. Once you become a star like that, it's like in the Wild West, somebody's gonna come up and try to outdraw you."

"Or outpaint you."

Around the Village, after the myth of collectivism had shattered and the cult of heroic individualism had grown, of necessity, out of the social rejection of the great Black bop jazzmen, the isolation of the early Abstract Expressionists, and a disillusion with grand social movements, I sometimes thought of the big pot. In an ambience so fragmented that the so-called Abstract Expressionists vehemently rejected any common label and people had a hard time agreeing on common interests, much less the common good, the Spanish Civil War vet's big, communal pot seemed a lot more appetizing than it once had.

2

BOHEMIA
IS A
COUNTRY
IN EUROPE

What are you going to Europe for? Americans discover America periodically and it was in process of being discovered again shortly after World War II but word was not quick to get about. Berets were still to be found around the Village, partly in deference to *la vie de bohème* and partly as a result of the heavy traffic between Bleecker Street and Boulevard Saint-Germain. Existentialism was at the peak of its influence, and the beret—especially favored by Bop-oriented hipsters— was more a response to the middle class than to the weather. In the Remo you could hear many a tale of recent European adventures, and a little later in the White Horse over in the West Village, starting in 1950 or '51, you might have found Dylan Thomas, or gossip about Dylan Thomas, dominating the conversation. Why was Thomas such an influence on the American underground at the beginning of the fifties? One reason, certainly, was that he wasn't American, and that his voice, its singing Welsh accent, carried with it the full, resurgent glory of the British lyric tradition. Another was that he came as an emissary and exemplar of the European tradition of Bohemia, with all its inverted, rebellious prestige.

One evening I drop by the Remo and it's dead. So I wander west to Sheridan Square and look in at Louis' on the way. Louis', just off Sheridan Square, has its own clientele of locals, writers, students, and actors from Circle in the Square next door. At one point or another you could see William Styron there, or Jason Robards, and Steve McQueen used to go over on his motorcycle when he was an unknown. Tonight it's also filled with the Bleecker Street crowd. Soon it would get so crowded some weekends you'd have to wait on line to get in.

"One day," says co-founder of *The Village Voice* Ed Fancher, "I don't know what happened." Fancher, now a psychotherapist, fits the part with his distinguished-looking white beard and deliberate manner. "What I was told happened is that one of the bartenders at the Remo bounced one of the regulars in a very brutal way. One of the Italian guys behind the bar beat up one of the regulars. And everybody just said, 'That's it, that's enough, we're not gonna take it anymore.' And they all moved to Louis'. Like, Louis' was empty one night, and somebody says, 'Well, I know a bar which has a lot of space and they won't treat us this way, the hell with the Remo,' and they simply went. I remember going over to the Remo and seeing it empty, and somebody says, 'Hey, the place is Louis',' and Louis' was jumping. And then from Louis', the spillover I believe went to the White Horse, which may already have had a small group. The White Horse was already well established before Dylan Thomas went there. I mean he was like a tourist. I mean people took him there because that was the place to go. I saw him there, I guess, a few days or a week before he died."

The White Horse was still in when Howard Smith arrived on the scene in 1957. "Of course all anybody could talk about when you went in there, which bored the shit out of me, was Dylan Thomas.

'Oh yeah, right where you stand now, I used to buy him drinks.'
Everybody in there claimed that without him, Dylan Thomas wouldn't
have been able to drink in America."

The White Horse has since become passé, the days long past when
Dylan Thomas used to pass out there, but his benders are remem-
bered by the elbow benders at the bar. The stories they tell about
Thomas are mythic, impossible to disengage the man from the legend
and maybe even to say which finally is more important. According
to one story told by a guy who says he's a poet and looks like he's
been drinking a long time tonight, Thomas was once assigned to the
house of a young untenured professor in a university town where he
was giving a poetry reading. Thomas's spectacular readings in the
early fifties were the beginning of the poetry-reading boom that later
became the economic staple of the poetry business. It seems his host
didn't provide an appropriate playmate for Thomas—how was he to
know assignation was part of the assignment?

"I mean in those days Thomas was like the fucking first rock star
already—that's when the whole celebrity bit began for artists. I mean
I have nothing at all against poets being rock stars, right, as long as
it doesn't confuse anybody. But it does. People get to think rock stars
are poets. God knows what they think poets are. Anyway, there was
Dylan Thomas doing his Dionysus number and it seems that the
professor's daughter was there, thirteen years old but ripe, and Thomas
kept demanding the girl be allowed to go upstairs with him. Not very
nice, but it wasn't easy to say fuck you to the decade's supposedly
greatest poet, and besides the professor thought of himself as very
with it."

It's Friday night at the White Horse, though the place is not so
jammed as it once was when you had to fight your way to the bar
and you might glimpse writers like Norman Mailer, William Styron,
Vance Bourjaily, or Frederic Morton moving through the crowd. They
were part of a group of novelists that actually held literary meetings
there. But the old wood and glass of the bar is the same, and you
can still practically hear the singing of the Clancy Brothers off to the
left, coming from the back room where they used to hang out.

"Maybe the professor got off on having his daughter deflowered by

Dionysus. And if Thomas was torn to pieces by the throng, destroyed by his public, then why shouldn't his daughter get her piece? The tight-ass Eisenhower age needed a Dionysus real bad and Thomas was elected it. Right. Thomas was the man who relived that myth for us, in the flesh, the poet as provocateur of joy, frenzy, drugs, drink, and sex. Think of old T. S. Eliot writing poems about gods he wouldn't have dared sit down to tea with. Thomas was an *enfant terrible* or, maybe, just a terrible infant with his baby face and total self-indulgence. In those days sex had a subversive force, now it's a consumer item and Dionysus is getting rich on the record charts. Thomas fucking blew it apart, he made art spread its legs and the word became flesh, it wasn't always pretty but it was fun. Poetry is a voice that comes out of a body and goes into other bodies. Forget the page, it's what's on stage that counts. So now the reading circuit is heading back to vaudeville—I hear some poets are actually taking up tap dancing. Hi, honey, buy you a drink?"

The guy gets distracted talking to a woman next to him and I never hear whether Thomas goes upstairs with the girl, so your guess is as good as mine, which is that he did. It suits the myth.

It's initially surprising that Thomas's version of high poetry, as influence, will ultimately lead—in one direction—to an idea of art as entertainment, as a way of tapping the marketplace. Our populist notion of art for everybody is confused all too easily with the necessities of the mass market. Ideas, or even attitudes, often do not travel well across the Atlantic. The Bohemian vices, like Thomas's flagrant alcoholism, that are sometimes attendant on dedication to one's artistic evolution become in America a form of public spectacle. Readings are more interesting than reading, and artists more interesting than art. The occasionally suicidal avant-garde assault on mercenary values, symbolized in the public mind by van Gogh's severed ear, itself becomes salable in this country. Even the largest talents are not immune from the contending pressures of a precious Bohemian alienation and a debased public acceptance. Though the title of Ginsberg's poem "Death to van Gogh's Ear" signals a rebellion against a doomed marginality in the tradition of *La Bohème,* if not against happier styles of self-destruction, once upon a time the Bohemian mystique at least served to insulate artists, even despite themselves, from the pressures of the marketplace. But Bohemia is a country in Europe.

"When I hit the scene," says Ed Fancher, "it was immediately after World War II. My generation was part of that group of soldiers returning from the war and who went to the New School," that Village institution off Fifth Avenue that might be described as the first free school, and that had been one of the main refuges for scholars fleeing Hitler. "There was a very heavy European influence, particularly in the graduate faculty. But there were writing seminars there that were more in the American tradition. It was a leading place for writers, Bill Styron was a student there, and they were the ones that hung around the Remo. Hiram Hayden was one of the teachers, Don [not Dan] Wolf. Bill Welbourn, who wrote a novel that was never published, was an important part of the literary set. He became an alcoholic, he died many years ago in total poverty. The Remo was kind of international, people were always coming back from Majorca or Italy or Rome or someplace. The literary *Zeitgeist*, I guess you'd call it, or weltanschauung, around the Remo and the New School was the intellectual heritage of the *Voice*."

The misunderstood genius starving in the garret was the role model for artists of all kinds at the time. I myself could hardly wait to start going hungry. Luckily garrets, or at least cold-water flats, were cheap. "A lot of guys were on the GI Bill, which paid for the New School," Fancher says. "The only thing is in those days you could get a three-room apartment for eighteen dollars a month. That's really what *The Village Voice* was built on. A writer could live on so little he could afford to work for us for little or nothing. When I moved to Christopher Street for twenty-two dollars a month I really had to think whether I could afford those extra four dollars. I lived for one hundred fifty dollars a month. I mean, most of the people around the *Voice* were poor."

"You almost reveled in your poverty," says Seymour Krim. "It was romantic. You took certain interior vows to write as best you could."

At the time the underground was living in cold-water flats in the Italian Village, near Bleecker, or in grungy lofts slightly uptown around

East Tenth Street. Ted Joans has written that he "gave big costume balls to raise money for rent." At one such party, Charlie Parker attended. "It was dedicated to Surrealism, Dada, and the Mau Mau. Bird arrived late but he hastily improvised his own Mau Mau image, plus aided other hipsters. He insisted that we play no recordings of his, or Dizzy Gillespie, 'his worthy constituent.' So we played other hip things, even popular stuff of Slim Gaillard, Harry The Hipster Gibson and Louis Jordan. *Life* magazine cover girl Vicki Dugan was the Queen of the affair. Montgomery Clift took invitations at the door for awhile. It was held in a photographer's studio and we earned enough money to pay rent for a year."

The area around Bleecker and MacDougal was still central, including the San Remo, even after Louis' and the White Horse way over on Hudson became hip, and the Cedar had hardly begun to be a scene.

"Jackson Pollock turned me on to the Club," says Joans, "the place down there run by artists where most of the Abstract Expressionists met. Another thing, a lot of the Abstract Expressionists, including Franz Kline, used to show in the Village outdoor show in the spring. See, the outdoor show hasn't always been a crappy place. People like Rothko used to walk around and talk to people, there were a lot of good painters in there. It was just a place to expose and you could sell some of your smaller things. Hans Hofmann had a school up above the Eighth Street Playhouse, which was one of the first movie houses that would show avant-garde type of things. Hofmann was very nice. At that time America was still on a European kind of influence, and with that accent he had, you know, that carried weight. But there was a little schism there between the Hofmann and the de Kooning school. You could see it in the Cedar bar, because they would come in and start talking about Hofmann's push and pull and this and that, and de Kooning would go, 'Bull *shit*.' De Kooning was a tough, outspoken guy, man, and for a long time he didn't have American citizenship, so they used to call him the Dutchman, you know, like he was a foreigner, but that foreignism was really great, because, see, de Kooning could outdraw the average man there."

While I and my friends, and probably some of yours, were still dreaming of ways to escape to Paris and live in exile like the Lost Generation, the whole picture had changed. Europe had come to the States. There could hardly be a better illustration than Hofmann and de Kooning of the effects of the European talent infused into American painting beginning before the war and massively accelerating with the arrival of the refugees from the Nazis. Hofmann's work retains a certain meditative and composed quality in comparison with de Kooning's. Hofmann's canvases still make sense in the same room as certain European paintings like, say, a Mathieu, a Hartung, or a de Staël. De Kooning's paintings, like Pollock's, are records of performance rather than premeditated fabrications of consciousness.

If, as Joans says, de Kooning is like a cowboy, Hofmann's authority is more like that of a professor. They say that in class, Hofmann rarely says anything about anybody's paintings. He just goes around, looks at a painting here and there, nods, and mutters, *"Nicht wahr?"* which, as someone remarks, is like German for "Ain' it?" Sometimes he doesn't even say *"Nicht wahr?"* He just mutters something like *"Nekke?"* which is short for "Ain' it?"

One time, recalls sculptor Zahara Schatz, Hofmann was criticizing the work of his advanced students, "and there was somebody who had a large canvas with nothing but squares of primary colors or brilliant colors all over it. And Hofmann looked at it and looked embarrassed about it and didn't know how to say or what to say. In the end he got the right expression: 'You're missing color in your painting.' The student was using so much color there turned out to be no color. But he said this very simple thing and everybody got quiet looking at it. It was the best way of expressing for the whole group that you could use hardly any colors and get the color you need and use an awful lot and have none."

The difference between *"Nicht wahr?"* and "Bull *shit*" was the difference between influencing and assimilating. At the time, I would have believed anything anybody told me if it was followed by a knowing *"Nicht wahr?"* "Bull shit" was just street language to me. Actually, as everybody now knows but I didn't then, a new situation had started at the end of the forties that would cut American art loose from Europe and lead to its domination in the international scene for the next thirty-five years. It took the emergence of Jackson Pollock to make people realize what was happening. Pollock was pretty close to being a real cowboy, having been born in Wyoming and grown up on farms in Arizona and California. There's a striking photo of Pollock at fifteen, working as a forest ranger at Grand Canyon, looking like the real thing compared to a John Wayne or Gary Cooper.

Once the subterranean scene hit the White Horse over near the Hudson River, the tide reversed and moved back east for the next two decades, heading for the farthest East Side. By the time things moved from the White Horse and the Remo to the Cedar Tavern a little uptown from Washington Square in the early fifties, Pollock had already pulled the rug out from everything. Pollock had this trick he did at the Cedar. On weekends the tourists came to see the painters hanging out and the management put tablecloths on the tables. Pollock knew how to jerk the tablecloth off a table leaving everything in place, glasses, plates, silverware, saltshaker. After Pollock did his trick everything looked pretty much the same but everything was completely different. That's why de Kooning said Pollock broke the ice.

"I thought of him in the beginning," says publisher Barney Rosset of Pollock, "as a very incipiently violent person. He sort of scared me." Rosset, whose demeanor is crisp old gent, vintage World War I, knew the Abstract Expressionists through his wife at the time, painter Joan Mitchell. "But he actually wasn't. His violence really was self-violence. I was in the Cedar bar one night with Pollock and de Kooning and Kline. They got into a big fight. Pollock went and knocked down the door to the men's room, just smashed it, and he broke two chairs, the place was in shambles. So we all went out on the street finally, thrown out, Pollock and Kline kissed each other and said good night. Then they wouldn't let Pollock back in for a month. And he would come and look in the window at night. You'd see this face in the window—'No, Jackson, can't come back, two more weeks.' But he wasn't that unusual. De Kooning was also, I think, more violent. Potentially. But they were really poor, let me tell you. But it didn't seem to affect them whatsoever." Rosset says that Mitchell and de Kooning were in the habit of making fun of Kline's paintings to one another, like de Kooning pointing to the tape on windows of a newly built house and saying, "Oh, look, that's a Franz Kline."

As soon as you walk into the Cedar in those years you have the sense of something new going on. Though still barely old enough to buy a drink, and lacking connection with the real actors on the scene, when I go to the Cedar for a beer it has for me the power of a ritual that puts me in communion with the gods. I stand and watch the blur of activity, people talk to me casually, and though I have no idea who they are, I'm aware that, as in the Homeric epics, any disreputable-looking half-drunk bullshit artist might turn out to be an Abstract Expressionist Apollo, Dionysus, or even, hopefully, Aphrodite. You have the feeling that everything has become an open question that everybody is trying to answer at once from the bar up front to the wooden booths in back. There's a kind of dank austerity to the place, no jukebox, no TV, nothing on the walls but Hogarth prints. It's a distinctly macho bar, where gays are hard put to make any headway. At a certain point there's a graffito in the john that reads, "I'm ten inches long and all man," under which somebody has written, "Great! How big's your dick?"

"The Cedar Tavern," says Robert Creeley, always an impressive dark presence, peering at you out of his one eye, "had not in some sentimental sense, but almost in a practical sense, a mythic dimension." The artists who hung out there, "at least for my particular cluster of people, are heroes. They also were great readers," and had "the most forward and freshest way of thinking, in my generation, certainly." He feels they were extraordinarily articulate, and avoided the limited thought patterns of others in their generation.

The intellectual openness of the Cedar may be clarified by a story I'm told at the bar by a young artist, paint-smeared work clothes and the whole bit. "Once I'm in here and I have to go back to take a piss, and Kline and de Kooning happen to be in the men's room talking about where to put this line, where to put that line. So I'm fascinated and I stand there at the urinal as long as I can without being considered a pervert. They're talking up a storm behind me. 'You got to put it up here,' one of them is saying. 'No, no,' says the other, 'up here. Like this, then it goes down here and across and goes off that way.' I zip up my pants, trying to think of some innocent way of loitering in the john listening to maybe America's two greatest painters, Pollock already dead, telling one another how to make a painting, when I suddenly realize, because of something one of them says, that they're trying to figure out how to install the plumbing in a loft. Shit, I think, disgusted, but then later on I figure, Wait a minute, you wouldn't catch Braque and Picasso talking about plumbing the way they talk about painting." "Kline had no attitudes," painter Ed Clarke says. "You could talk to him about anything. He was completely open."

This openness is soon to be reflected stylistically in the diminishing importance of the frame of the canvas. Several years later, a guy just back to the Cedar from France around 1958 tells me the only thing happening in Paris is a painter and karate expert named Yves Klein, who did a series of monochromatic canvases painted with nothing but a certain uniform violent shade of blue, which this fellow refers to as "clean slates," followed by a series produced by pigment-smeared nudes squirming on empty canvases, which he says are like "imprints of reality," the visual equivalent of tape recording. He says they are the precursors of a radical realism moving beyond the canvas into the world itself.

"Bull *shit*," says another artist at the bar wearing a house painter's cap. "I'm already doing that. I paint apartments for a living. Of course, if you're an Action painter it probably doesn't make any difference to you where the action is."

It looks like the guy on the other side of him, a second-generation Action painter, is about to slug him, but the first painter continues in a hypnotic monotone without a pause.

"One day I found myself in Paris with a Pollock and a Mathieu in the same room, and looking at the dates of the pictures, it seemed that the Frenchman, Mathieu, had been doing the same kind of drip and slash paintings in Paris at the same time, or even before, Pollock was doing them in the States. Then I realized the paintings had nothing to do with one another. The Mathieu was elegant, lush color, very composed, and still used an illusion of depth. Truth and beauty lurked in the background, that tradition, you know, Europe, with the required profundity, transcendent to a tee. The Pollock went right off the edge of the canvas, used industrial paint that was plain, downright ugly, and was done flat on the surface. Everybody knows Americans are more superficial, right? After a while the absolute presence of the Pollock made the Mathieu look like a postcard."

This is a little over my head at the time, maybe because I've never been to Europe.

"That was the day I decided to leave Europe," he continues. "I realized then that what they called a painting in Europe was a strictly European phenomenon. Or to put it another way, as Rothko told a friend of mine after he finally had the money to go to Europe, there paintings haven't been invented yet, not at the level of abstraction of a Bach or a Stravinsky. Not in the sense of independent objects that do more than reflect the human ego. Pollock was producing something more like objects, but magic objects that could change your life. They changed my life. I suddenly realized that my ego was nothing but the interaction of genes and circumstance. Before Pollock I was always searching for who I was, like a character in a novel. After Pollock, forget it, I understood I wasn't anybody. Just as I'd always suspected. Ever since, Europeans have seemed like characters in a novel, heavy with their fates. Americans are more like accidents, reacting to the random. Ciphers in a situation."

"Yeah, right," says the house painter. "The bottom line is Americans don't have to think about anything."

"Pollock's paintings could have extended indefinitely over the edge of the canvas and sold like wallpaper, rather than like the unique and sacrosanct icons of European painting. The action is on the wall, along with the handwriting. Part of life, not about it."

"Sure. The next step is graffiti," says the house painter. "Or billboards."

In fact, one of evolutions in the opening out of the art scene, soon to become manifest, was the phenomenon of commercial artists—billboard painters like Rosenquist and illustrators from the advertising world like Warhol and Jasper Johns—moving successfully into serious painting, a development that helped fuzz the distinction between the art underground and the commercial mainstream.

The old Cedar, by the time it closed in 1963 and then reopened slightly uptown on University Place, had served as the intersection of two underground generations. When the Beats came back to New York from the west coast toward the end of the fifties after *On the Road* was published, they helped break the Cedar open to a whole younger set. The older subterraneans, coming up from the Bleecker Street scene, especially the Abstract Expressionists who were responsible for the Cedar's renown, and the New York School poetry people around Frank O'Hara, were joined by newcomers in the second wave of Abstract Expressionists, writers and painters associated with avant-garde Black Mountain College where Franz Kline had taught, and, to a lesser extent, the Beats.

"All of us hung out at the old Cedar Tavern," writes Amiri Baraka. "Jackson Pollock died before I got there, but he was one centerpiece. Franz Kline, Bill de Kooning, Philip Guston, Ray Parker, Norman Bluhm, Mike Goldberg, Al Leslie, John Chamberlain, David Smith, Dan Rice, and even Larry Rivers were regulars. They were the big names, people we respected. Franz Kline's style, not only his paintings but his personal idiosyncrasies, we set out to emulate. Kline seemed always a little smashed, drink in hand, cigarette dangling, talking in drunken parody as abstractly as he painted. Basil King, Dan Rice, Joel Oppenheimer, and Fee Dawson used to do takes on this style, personalized but legitimately drunk. To talk in a fragmented, drunken but hopefully profound ellipsis was the goal. The torture of genius, genius unappreciated, genius assaulted by philistines, this is what was implied. Genius was not easy to understand or put up with."

Sometimes genius is hard to put up with even for the Cedar. Not only is Pollock himself eighty-sixed at times, but Ted Joans remembers a sign that's up for a while that misspells NO BEATNIKES ALLOWED, stemming, he says, from an incident in which Jack Kerouac pissed in a stand-up ashtray and Helen Frankenthaler snitched. The artistic license of unappreciated genius is one of the bonuses of cultural alienation, which was still the going pose, but it also helps to infantilize and, therefore, neutralize that genius as well.

"The Cedar was so male," choreographer and performance artist

Carolee Schneemann told me recently. She resembles an earth goddess and her work—often nude performance pieces—has always insisted on her female physicality. "It was so sacrosanct in that way, even with the implicit kind of male violence, or male importance. Everything was charged with the dominance of the male lair—it was like going into their cave, their hang-out where they were what you focused on, and if you were pretty enough and sexy enough they might bestow a little bit of their regal eye, or a beer." Going to the Cedar was like going to a certain kind of church, she says, compared to the mix, flow, and constant redefinition of Max's Kansas City, the art bar that became the center of the scene in the late sixties. The style during the Cedar's preeminence was black stockings, black eye makeup, and very long hair. One night at the Cedar, Schneemann "saw light flaming out from one of those booths. I saw a feathery illuminated light, and I wasn't taking dope in those days, I was about eighteen, so it was just alcohol. And I was captivated by this mysterious figment and I went to see what it was, and under it I saw this man with an almond-shaped face, a very pure oval face, and the light was radiating out of him. And I was feeling transfixed and I said to somebody, 'Do you know who that man is over there?' So he says, 'Yeah, that's Bill, that's de Kooning.'"

The White Horse was where Schneemann "used to pick up older men. And went home with them. Writers and film people and wickedness. It was incredible, when I think about it, what was I doing. Two drinks and anyone who looked interesting, he was mine for the night. I had it all reversed. I thought that men were created for my pleasure, and I was in the nice position of being able to pick one anytime I needed one. And that was the adventure. Although they were often odd, and sometimes disappointing. Especially, I never understood why they were being mean to their wives, that disturbed me a lot. I wanted them to be just pure gazes across the room, that would then be embodied with wonderful passion and sexual delight, and not that I would find somebody else's dresses beside the bed. The White Horse was a lot more fun. It was a little younger, and yeah, maybe it was less defined in its self-seriousness. At the Cedar it was either the very grand important men and the women that, sort of, I don't remember them being there very often."

If the painting scene seemed more consciously American after 1950, the uniquely native American art form, jazz, became, through the fifties, more central than ever for underground artists of all kinds. It came together at the Five Spot, a bar on Cooper Square where the brothers Iggie and Joe Termini hosted a basically flophouse clientele until the artists started coming in during the mid-fifties. Painters like Grace Hartigan, Al Leslie, David Smith, de Kooning became habitués. Larry Rivers, the painter, played jazz there, poets read poetry to jazz, and avant-garde film makers even showed their films to jazz. Writers like Kerouac, Frank O'Hara, and Kenneth Koch moved in, and finally the great jazzmen themselves came down to play—Charlie Mingus, Sonny Rollins, Cecil Taylor, Thelonious Monk, Ornette Coleman. Before the old Five Spot was demolished around 1963 to reopen down the block, it had become one of the main jazz places in the city. But part of the importance of the Five Spot was that finally it belonged to a new era of the underground, one that happened more and more outside of the old Village scene. "I still went to the Cedar and bellied up to the bar, but now I was much more into the Jazz clubs that were opening," writes Baraka. "The Five Spot was the center for us. . . . In one sense our showing up on Cooper Square was right in tune with the whole movement of people East, away from the west Village with its high rents and older bohemians. Cooper Square was sort of the border line; when you crossed it, you were really on the Lower East Side, no shit."

But even back toward 1950, if you are a kid living in New York like me and have any pretension to hipness at all, you are heavily interested in jazz and you start going to Birdland and Bop City in Midtown Manhattan. One day I run into Marilyn, who says she has some freebies for Bop City, if I want to use one of them. It seems that she's been hanging around with some musicians and one of them, a guy who does arrangements for Miles Davis, got the tickets. Bop City, on Fifty-second Street, is the big jazz scene at the time.

When I meet Marilyn in Midtown, she's with an emaciated-looking woman and a white horn player who seem very zonked out. I clumsily try engaging the guy in conversation by mentioning a few people we might know in common, and at every name he jerks his head up, thinks a while, and says, "I don't know man, like, what's his instrument?" At one point the skeletal woman goes to the ladies' room to fix her makeup, she says, and a while later the musician looks up and asks, "Where's Carole?"

"She's fixing herself in the john," I answer.

The other two at the table look at one another and laugh. "Out of the mouths of babes," says Marilyn, then apologizes with her beautiful smile.

The musician knows Symphony Sid, the MC at Bop City, so he comes to sit with us during breaks. The immortal Sid is the only DJ playing Bebop on the radio, doing his late-night show out of Bop City. Sid's hemp-coarse nasal voice is itself an affront to the middle class, knowingly assuming bourgeois hypocrisies the good burgher refuses to be aware of. The antimellifluous drive of his delivery mirrors the music he plays—Charlie Parker, Dizzy Gillespie, Max Roach. The harshness of his sound, like Parker's, eliminates bullshit, and the hard swing of his rhythms often works against the sense of what he's saying so that like Parker it's as if he's saying two things at once. This is especially true of his commercials, which always sound tongue-in-cheek and sometimes like ads for something subversive, violent, and unspeakable. A commercial for mail-order cutlery ends up with the cryptic and sinister appeal: "Send knives." The thing that impresses me most about Sid is his green skin, due undoubtedly to total lack of exposure to sunlight and fresh air. I've never seen anyone with green skin before. It makes me think twice about the virtue of sunlight and fresh air, health and normality. Sid comes on cool, like he takes your bullshit for granted, but every once in a while his attitude irritates the powers and he's banished from the airwaves. During one period of exile he cleans up his act in Catholic Boston by doing a gospel music show, coming on as "Brother Sid," and still playing great stuff. Later on he gets into hot Latino music, Willie Bobo, Eddie Palmieri, Mongo Santamaria, a couple of decades before it's called salsa.

Marilyn is making it with a string of guys, that's how she likes to live. She doesn't want to be tied down, she just wants to do what she feels like. Some of the guys would get pissed. This is a time when even hip women are laying down everything for their men, right? Marilyn has the utmost disdain for the "chicks" who hang around the writers and painters on the scene, catering to their egos. Besides, she finds ego trips tedious. You might find Marilyn in any one of the hip Village bars. She always goes alone. She often leaves in company. You might meet Marilyn, for example, at the bar of the Open Door, a cabaret known in Kerouac's *The Subterraneans* as the "Red Drum," according to Ginsberg, where you're waiting to hear Charlie Parker play. Around then you could see Bird handing out posters at Louis' for his weekend gigs there.

"So there we were at the Red Drum," writes Kerouac, "a tableful of beers a few that is and all the gangs cutting in and out, paying a dollar quarter at the door, the little hip-pretending weasel there taking tickets ... a wild generation party all smoky and mad ... all sitting together, interesting groups at various tables ... and up on the stand Bird Parker with solemn eyes who'd been busted fairly recently and had now returned ... the great new general gang wailing and gathering there, so here he was on the stand, examining them with his eyes as he blew his now-settled-down-into-regulated-design 'crazy' notes—the booming drums, the high ceiling ... to hear Bird, whom I saw distinctly digging Mardou several times and also myself directly into my eye looking to search if really I was that great writer I thought myself to be."

After the set, sitting there, exhilarated, I see Marilyn drifting over from a table. Noticing me, she flashes her big smile and stops next to me at the bar.

"Have a seat?" I ask, offering her my barstool. She sits down. She's wearing black turtleneck and jeans, cheeks peachy beneath chic pallor, very blond, very stacked. If you're a neophyte, like me, you too would probably be wowed and a little awed by Marilyn because she's so hip, so carelessly in. Looking at her you know she's the kind of woman who can have anything she wants. Except that the way she comes on is like she doesn't want anything. Sometimes her problem is fending off things she doesn't want, like some drunken writer at her table who is "like coming on and being a real drag."

And here he comes, maneuvering heavily among chairs and tables, waving here, smiling there, as he zigzags to the bar, a good-looking very well built guy in a plaid shirt stationing himself on the other side of Marilyn's stool. I don't get a chance to chat, because after a few exchanges between them that I can't hear over the noise of the bar, she says, looking at me, "And besides, I'm just about to cut out with him."

The guy looks at me with dark eyes, reaches across the bar in front of Marilyn, grabs my glass of beer, and finishes it in one long chug.

"Crazy," he says.

"Don't mention it," I mutter. He zags back into the crowd and I head for the door with Marilyn.

"What's his name?" I ask.

"I forget," she says. "There's a whole bunch of guys like that on the scene all of a sudden, very aggressive. They're kind of boring—they don't talk to me, they talk to one another about how they're going to be great writers. Then when they're done jiving one another about how great they are, they expect to get laid, who needs that? Besides, I think they're basically queer."

This is the kind of remark you hear from certain hip ladies around Bleecker street. These new guys on the scene are not laid back like the jazz musicians you meet or self-contained like the writers around of a slightly earlier vintage, some of whom it would be difficult to distinguish from editors and academics, and some of whom are. Maybe the new guys are just running into the kind of reception with which the musicians greet any outsider, no matter how good: "Like, he doesn't know his instrument." Or maybe, before the myth cultivated by the media is pinned on the incipient Beat style letting everybody know how exciting it is to be a Beatnik, the way they live is boring. At least to someone not tuned in to the literary evolution involved that, ten years later, will have irreversibly shaken the uptight writing establishment coming out of the fifties. Maybe the question of how boring the artist is, contrary to the myth of the Artist's Life, is completely irrelevant to his art.

I walk with Marilyn up to Eighth Street, stopping briefly on Sixth Avenue to look into the Waldorf Cafeteria, sometimes known as the

Waxworks because of the eerie pallor its lighting casts on the customers, then across Sixth Avenue to the Jefferson Market Diner, then
over to Sheridan Square, where Marilyn wants to check out Jim Atkins. "Friday nights Saturdaynights all out late seemed to windup
there oneway or another," writes Bill Amidon of Atkins in his novel
Charge . . !, which is mostly about the underground Lower East Side,
"fags hookers trade pimps JDs junkies ... whitepeople and all
differentcolored ones motor-cycle people and mortgage-people actors
painters and every writer in the city made it there when he needed
that extra goose of color. It was a hip Horn & Hardart." Whatever
Marilyn is looking for it isn't there, and she heads back to Sixth
Avenue looking in at a bar named Fugazzi's, then at a little hash
house on Cornelia around West Fourth, but that isn't it either.

"See that guy in there?" she says. "That's Stanley Gould. I wouldn't
be surprised if he's looking to sell."

"Sell what?"

"Stanley's always selling something. He's always around."

Stanley Gould was an occasional drug connection for William Burroughs, who says, however, that he wasn't much of a connection.
Later Burroughs would slip him ten bucks now and then when he
was broke and living in the Hotel Chelsea. Gould was one of the
early admirers of Charlie Parker, according to Ted Joans. "He knew
Bird personally before any of us." Corso admired Gould's intelligence
and dedicated a book to him on grounds of his endurance as an
underground figure "who remains and keeps on going." Norman Mailer,
it is said, once bought him a set of teeth. Gloria in later years always
referred to him as "America's oldest living junkie."

But Marilyn isn't looking for Stanley either, so we drift east to
Stewart's Cafeteria on Cooper Square for a cup of coffee. Stewart's,
an all-nighter, is the grimmest joint of all, inhabited by types who
look like they don't have any place to sleep, or who look like they
don't sleep, skeletal specimens nodding over dirty Formica tables,
scabby men and women even I recognize as junkies, standing in strange
impossible postures against the walls, complexions ghoulish in the
green light. Anyone with a practiced eye would know Marilyn isn't
a hardcore junkie. What is she doing here? The place gives me the

total creeps. One look at the steam table with the week-old vegetables and other items that appear to have been cooked in mucus is enough to turn your stomach for the evening. I don't dare set lip to coffee cup for fear of catching something awful.

Marilyn says she expects to meet some guy here but he's not showing up. After a while she might look at you with a resigned smile, but in a different way. "Oh well," she might say if you get lucky, "let's make it over to my place," and you go with her, still further east and up broken stairs through cat piss corridors to her cold-water flat, scrofulous kitchen linoleum with tub in center, living room–bedroom jungled with green plants—"One thing about living on the fifth floor, you get plenty of light"—knowing it's not you she's looking for that night and wondering what connection she hopes to find.

Marilyn was completely in the tradition of adventurous Bohemian women, going all the way back to Murger's nineteenth-century classic treatment, *Scènes de la Vie de Bohème.* But while Mimi and Musette were free spirits moving out of the lower social ranks to seek their fortunes, Marilyn, in typical American style, was moving out of middle-class security to seek her freedom. The problem was that she needed not only to seek it but to define it as well, requiring an open and experimental attitude toward experience as demanding as that which an artist, working at the cutting edge, must maintain toward his or her art. It is no doubt partly because of the pressure of this demand, endemic to Bohemian life, that Murger wrote that Bohemia "is the preface to the Academy, the Madhouse, or the Morgue." Certainly many Village subterraneans passed through the second, including Ginsberg and Carl Solomon, who met there, and Marilyn in later years was no stranger to Bellevue. The myth of Bohemia, as Murger notes, can be devastating for hangers-on who have no strong artistic vocation providing a purpose for that kind of life.

No matter what the commitment, the scene was especially hard on women. A few made it: There's Louise Nevelson, who had a loft at the time on West Third, and Joan Mitchell and Helen Frankenthaler, but they're said to be rich. And there's a tradition, tinctured with tragedy, for creative women in the Village going back to Isadora Duncan, Emma Goldman, and Edna St. Vincent Millay, and before that to Ada Clare and Pfaff's beer cellar where Whitman was a habitué.

"A lot of your women friends kicked off," I remark to Gloria, looking back many years after the fact.

"Yeah, that's probably very significant. Iris Brody jumped off the roof, Sonya OD'd, Marilyn also jumped off the roof." Gloria had spent time with Iris in the fifties, living with her in the Bahamas *chez* Eugene O'Neill's son, Shane, in his mansion. Burroughs remembers Iris as being the secretary of Maurice Girodias, who published *Naked Lunch,* and there's an Allen Ginsberg photo of Burroughs that has one of her paintings in it. "Iris," says Gloria, "after she had a baby with this musician, she'd been in the Women's House of Detention innumerable times. She was with this guy who was also a junkie. Her thing was to be very thin all the time because she had been a model. She was really very beautiful. A very interesting if somewhat effete painter, her paintings were really quite lovely. She was on junk and she would get busted and she would go to prison and come out and she'd be fat as she could be. And then she'd get back to junk and get very thin and interesting looking again. I would see her in the Four Seasons Book Store, which was run by Etta Rice and her husband who was a poet, it was the first kind of interesting MacDougal Street book store, before the 8th Street book store, and it was a little place, like with a lot of writers coming in and the kind of books you couldn't find in the other places, in the late forties. And I would see Iris Brody there selling everything she owned, books, prints, paintings, and barely coherent, desperate to sell whatever she could sell. Really, like totally incoherent. But thin. What happened to Iris, she married a Black musician, had his baby, had a mother ran a beauty parlor somewhere in the Bronx or Uptown, she dumped the baby at her mother's, the guy abandoned her as they say, she was living with her mother and she just went up to the roof and jumped."

Each time an acquaintance jumps off a roof or OD's, I'm reminded that the Bohemian life has always been risky. But looking back I realize that between the old Bohemians and the newer subterraneans starting with the Beats, there's a difference. Things have become less sentimental, even in matters of life and death. It would be hard to imagine Gregory Corso declaiming in a Village bar, as Bodenheim was wont, "I have a malady of the soul." Even if he happened to have one. For these newer subterraneans, the underground is a way of getting something they want and there is no need to mystify the situation with high-flown ideas about art, purity, and self-sacrifice on the altar of a higher ideal. It may be that your motives are noble, but if you're into self-denial for noble motives then that's what you want, so don't bug me about how noble you are.

When I discover the underground, I see it solely as an enclave providing the chance for a principled resistance to an unacceptable status quo. It will take some years for me to desentimentalize the underground, differentiate the interesting from the merely seedy, and begin to acknowledge its darker, unredeemed, infernal aspects. It might be argued that tapping the infernal is necessary to release the darker powers of consciousness that energize art, but not everyone is an artist and not everyone can handle it.

There are many different tendencies in subterranean life, some considerably less kosher than others, and representatives of all of them could be found any night in an ample hip cabaret like Max's Kansas City, which, after 1966, would bring them all together in new combinations and recombinations. The avant-garde is that part of the underground concerned with the thrust of innovation. But for the most part the clientele of any of the public houses and meeting places of subterranean society would consist of people who drift into the scene without any particularly considered cultural, intellectual, or political "position." Many of these, writers and artists of various métiers who cling to no special group or persuasion, are the outsiders of the underground, involved in subterranean life mainly because it allows them to do their creative work. Ballasting the famous, the flashy characters, and the socially adroit at the center of the scene, they are usually anonymous though occasionally one will hit the limelight, whereupon some barroom genius is sure to remark, "Oh, *that* guy? *He's* a painter?" Others might simply be considered marginals, subterraneans as a matter of taste, as in Talking Heads' line about the suburbs, "I wouldn't live there if you paid me." "Marginal" also indicates the indefinite borders between the underground on one side, and the demimonde, the underworld, and simple vagrancy on the other.

The Beat movement picked up on the itinerant mode in American culture, the idea of the hobo, as had Vachel Lindsay, who had also rediscovered the vitality of poetry as oral performance almost half a century previous to the Beats. A hobo is not a bum, nor a simple vagrant. Vagabondage is a self-sustaining way of life, a refuge for outsiders and underdogs like Chaplin's tramp. The "demimonde" in France originally indicated a milieu of semiprostitution, a phenomenon hardly unknown stateside in life on the margins. In the American underground the term is applied to the hip relaxation of social and financial distinctions that allows financiers, whores, film stars, painters, criminals, politicians, and street people to mingle in the same milieu, as would happen most spectacularly in Max's. In addition there are always any number of unaffiliated and peculiarly American types around, outlaws, urban cowboys, lone strangers, too much self-styled outsiders to be part of anything.

It's a population not so much of drifters as of what you might call floaters, people who have no particular schedule or nothing special to do, a large portion of whom are always on the make for something —sex, money, drugs—and who are always on the lookout for tourists, people from Uptown, the Bronx, or Jersey, types often all too eager to be taken thrillingly advantage of. One barroom story related to me by a moderately talented bull shit artist illustrates a fairly normal level of sexual con practiced mercilessly on willing outsiders to more or less mutual satisfaction. "Pete and me are sitting on the rim of the fountain," volunteers this guy while drinking at the ancient bar of McSorley's on East Seventh just off Cooper Square, centerpiece of a book of stories by *New Yorker* writer John Mitchell and later hang-out for a segment of the culture underground and especially poet Paul Blackburn. The fountain referred to is of course that in Washington Square, its rim being the preferred perch of the innest of the subterranean floaters. Washington Square has always been a well-known pickup area, to the point where Jane Kramer, in a piece on the Square, once described the best route for a girl who wants to be picked up—"once around the fountain, and back up the path again.

Should a girl fail there, she ends up conveniently near the coffee houses, where she then goes to try her luck again."

"Anyway," the guy continues over his ale, "these two chicks stop in front of us and proceed to look lost.

" 'Whatcha lookin' for?' Pete asks.

" 'You know where to find Bleecker Road?' says one of them, a redhead.

" 'Where you from?' asks Pete, without a blink at Bleecker *Road*.

" 'Bahstin,' says the redhead.

" 'What part of the country's that?' asks Pete.

" 'Y'know. Mayass,' says the chick.

" 'Whose ass?' asks Pete.

" 'She must mean *Baw*ston,' I tell Pete.

" '*Baw*ston,' he says. 'What're you doing in New York?'

" 'We want to meet some ottists,' she says. That's what she says. She wants to meet some ottists, 'Do you know where they hang out?'

" 'Ottists, oh sure,' says Pete. 'Lots.'

" 'Really?' says the other one. 'Is it on Bleecker Road?'

" 'Yeah, some,' Pete says sort of casually. Meantime I can see he's trying to figure out what the hell an ottist is. So am I. Otter experts?

" 'Why do you want to meet ottists?' asks Pete finally.

" 'We go to Bahstin Univursity,' says the redhead. 'We're taking a course on ott.'

"So Pete looks at her like she's crazy and he says, 'They have courses on Mel Ott? What are you majoring in, baseball?' And the chick says"—the guy snorts and bangs the bar—" 'They don't cover Mel Ott, it's only van Eyck to Van Dyck.' "

After they get that straightened out, they take the girls over to the Rikers on Eighth Street because it's the cheapest place around, while letting them know it's the hippest in-scene in the Village, where all the ottists and writers go. In fact a lot of them do hang there at a certain epoch, especially after the bars close, but when they get the girls to Rikers, which specializes if anything in lack of ambience, they clearly don't believe it's hip, proving that unlike Rikers, an in place has got to look funky, or chic, or funky-chic, because from the outside it's not what's going on that's in, it's what it's going on in.

"By the time we get out of Rikers it's dark, see, but it's warm. So Pete has an idea. He tells them, 'What a lot of really in people in the Village do, see, is go swimming in the Carmine Street pool at night. There's a fence you can climb.'

" 'But we don't have bathing suits,' they say.

" 'That's all right,' says Pete. 'At night you don't use bathing suits.'

" 'Oh, in that case,' they say, 'fine.' So we know we have it made right there."

Pete wasn't completely bullshitting. The Carmine Street public pool was a hip Village scene in the fifties, and on warm afternoons there you could see many glamorous faces from the decadent Bleecker Street night looking oddly healthy in the everyday sun. And subterranean Villagers did go over at night to swim nude, a practice that went on for years till the Village hoods got wind of it. Naturally they figured any girl swimming nude on their turf must of course be asking to get gang-banged, and they closed down the scene with some really hairy rape incidents.

Six months before Howard Smith actually moves into the Village, still living in Jersey, he decides he'll con himself into the Washington Square Outdoor Art Show. "I'll just knock out some things, hang 'em up, and it'll be a way to meet people, especially to meet girls. I'll tell 'em I live in the Village. I entered the outdoor art show—all you had to do to pass, it didn't matter what your stuff looked like as long as it had no nudes and no antireligious content. They told me where to hang my stuff, I hung it, I sat there and got picked up by a lot of tourist girls. I had nowhere to take them. I lied and said I lived in the Village. And they were just dying to jump into bed with some Bohemian freak, they were from Iowa or whereever. They took me to dinner every night and I made up a story of being a starving artist. I started picking up the *Voice* and I noticed they had a few articles putting down the art show, and I certainly agreed because I was actually selling this crap I had knocked out. I took poster board, took watercolors, stood there moving the board around as the paint moved around in big fields of color and sat them down to dry and every night I did a few more of them back at my house in New Jersey. Then I'd drive in and stick 'em up and say, 'Award-winning painting.'

And I actually sold 'em. I didn't do so badly—I was shocked. I didn't go into it to sell anything. I didn't think anybody would buy this, it was on poster board. And so I wanted to tell my story, I thought it would be funny," and so Smith calls up John Wilcock at the *Voice,* starting an association with that journal that lasted through most of its changes till very recently.

The con quotient in the underground shades easily into petty and not so petty criminal activity and, especially through drugs, into the underworld itself. The wave of shoplifting that came in with the Hippies exemplifies the vague antiestablishment license involved in marginal crime. There is a current of feeling that crime is just the flip side of a commercial culture, and that, as Max's Kansas City proprietor Mickey Ruskin observed, "No great fortune is ever made without a criminal act." There's always a criminal edge in the underground scene.

The Beats turned the rock over and hipped themselves to the flip side of American culture in Times Square, hanging around with junkie Herbert Huncke and the floating, hiptalking, hustling, petty criminal lumpenpopulation on the scene. Their sex habits at the time, melding into those of Forty-second Street, even became subjects for study by Kinsey and count among the statistics in *The Kinsey Report.* This was a world, according to John Clellon Holmes's roman à clef *Go,* about the Ginsberg-Kerouac group just after they left Columbia in the late forties, "of dingy backstairs 'pads,' Times Square cafeterias, bebop joints, night-long wanderings, meetings on street corners ..." Grant's, on Forty-second Street, called Lee's by Holmes, is described as "the huge, teeming cafeteria on the corner of Broadway, where even steam tables fouled the air with a wild conflict of smells, and servers, presiding over them like unshaven wizards, imprecated the shuffling crowds indifferently, while greasy, beardless busboys, like somnambulists, moved among the littered tables mechanically." It's here, in this infernal atmosphere, that Holmes chooses to have his Kerouac character describe the Dostoyevsky-like revelation that "life is holy in itself. . . . Just loving all things, all ways!" This suspiciously resembles a programmatic reenactment of the romantic idea that immersion in the infernal is good for attaining enlightenment and, along with the rebel's need to violate the laws and taboos of an unjust society, helps explain subterranean sympathies for the criminal.

Kerouac got involved in a homosexual killing that a friend of his served time for. Burroughs, who likes guns, killed his wife in Mexico playing William Tell, shooting her through the head. Ray Bremser had a habit of knocking over gas stations and getting sent up. Ted Joans tells a hair-raising story of Bremser walking into a gas station unarmed with his hand in his coat pocket as if he has a gun. He tells the guy behind the register to hand over the cash, and suddenly notices the guy's hand moving toward a gun in a drawer. Whereupon Bremser says "I see what you're doing and don't try it" convincingly enough that the guy doesn't, allowing Bremser to take the money and walk out. I suppose it's not even worth mentioning more friendly stuff like Gregory Corso ripping off his pal Ferlinghetti's City Lights Book Store. Or talking about tricking and drug traffic. Especially since junkies are always ripping off their friends. If you have any junkie friends it's not even worth buying furniture. Just put in a camp bed and a few crates on end, otherwise goodbye. If your junkie friends don't clean you out, you can almost consider it an unfriendly act.

The violence was not confined to the Beats. Reading Norman Mailer's essay "The White Negro," with its promotion of pathological behavior, you might conclude he was a natural mark for Jack Abbott, the writer he sprang from prison who killed someone first chance. Philip Rahv was outraged because Mailer wrote a novel where the hero murders his wife and gets away with it, but Mailer managed to stab his wife in real life and get away with it. Given, Mailer was seriously disturbed at the time; his mystique nevertheless encourages violence and the rip-off mentality of the later "youth culture." As Herb Gold observes in an early attack on the underground mystique, "One Rimbaud may be a genius; a crowd of them is a fad."

At the end of the forties, Burroughs tells me in Boulder, Colorado, where he has lived on and off, the cafeterias were the gathering places for petty criminals. "All over the city the Automats, not only did they have very good food, excellent food and very cheap, but also they were all meeting places, drug meeting places, you had to be careful that the manager didn't spot it. But all the cafeterias were meets. The

Forty-second Street Bickford's was a notorious hang-out for thieves and pimps and whores and fags and dope pushers and buyers and everything." His flat, nasal Midwestern accent and his impatient factuality give him the air of an entomologist talking about intergalactic insects, while his face, going through a series of complicated tics and twitches, projects the impression of someone himself fighting off alien possession. Among the people he knew through drug contacts "there were a lot of cheap thieves, knocking down drunks, and that sort of thing. Yeah, they were involved in that kind of cheesy violence."

When I first walked into the Remo at the end of the forties, the sinister side of underground life was beside the point. For me the discovery of the underground released an aggressive optimism. It was a question of morale. One subterranean friend used to make fun of me, calling me the Dale Carnegie of the counterculture. While I found in my discovery of the underground an avenue to alleviate my anxiety about cultural amelioration, his take was that the underground leads nowhere. That's why he liked it. He said the middle class is always trying to improve things, that's why they keep getting worse. Because they keep getting more middle class.

But the fact is at the beginning of the fifties things are beginning to warm up under the ice of the cold war. Kids are getting restless with the Silent Generation. You're nineteen years old, away from home the first time, and as long as you can remember the dead weight of cultural conservatism has inhibited you from pursuing sexual satisfaction, self-expression, adventure, risk—what would you do? I drop out of college and join a small experimental school on the west coast filled with refugees from shmuck materialism who educate one another in cultural resistance. Then I blunder into Cornell through a scholarship. Cornell at the time is a school dominated by fraternity bull shit, but I resolve to turn things to account by trying to change the situation as much as possible without succumbing to it. I figure the ivy scene is so corny it must be ripe for change. *Bad is good, kid. Use your head.* My strategy is to fit in, working on the inside to change things, just the way they taught us democracy was supposed to work in Midwood's civics course. I even buy a tweed jacket.

Then one day down from Ithaca I walk into the Remo and run

into an old high-school buddy with whom I used to go to the Village, sitting at the bar. He doesn't even say hello. He just looks at me and says, "What have you got on your feet?" Novelist Steve Katz says in a published interview that he knew me when I was wearing white bucks. But they weren't white. They were tan. Light tan, it's true, maybe very light tan. But white bucks, no. You can ask anybody. Yes, I am making an effort, I'm even wearing button-down shirts. I don't yet realize how hopeless, at this point, things still are. My friend is wearing a leather jacket that looks like it crashed in a World War II Flying Fortress.

It isn't till I meet him in the Remo that I realize how much we've changed. He's sitting there at the end of the bar, pale and tight, bitching about life in the city. I'm feeling real positive when I meet him. I've recently driven in from California across those wide empty spaces of the West, a completely different trip from any I've had before and one that only reinforces my sophomoric optimism. He doesn't even drive, while I'm full of the freedom, partly phony, that you feel from rolling nonstop along the endless American highway. Me and a friend have been driving a '37 Ford, the kind of car used to crisscross the continent in *On the Road*, I discover when the book appears. We bought it from a painter in 1952 who said he bought it from "some of those Beatnik poets in San Francisco." That was the first time I heard the word "Beatnik." I've always wondered if it was the same car. How many could have been on the road by '52?

I've been spending a lot of time outdoors, I'm tanned, I'm in good shape. My friend looks gray-green, like a negative. I've dropped my wise-ass cooled-out Brooklyn street smarts, he's developed his into a fine art. He's still working out of the kind of cool that got us both through the hypocrite bull shit of Midwood High, hipster cool, the cool that came in with Bebop, which, according to Baraka, "meant to be *other* than that which was everywhere perceived deadly in day-to-day American reality." Cool is to comprehend the world going by you as an entomologist might comprehend a bug, while refusing to have anything to do with it. My friend's weapon is negation and I recognize it all too well. Tense, cold, and ironic, he makes me feel naïve, overenthusiastic, finally a little foolish.

Years later I meet him in Max's Kansas City dressed in a wide-brimmed black hat and flowing scarf, looking a lot like a pimp, or painter-on-the-scene Aristodimos Kaldis, or a Toulouse-Lautrec poster of the late-nineteenth-century Bohemian cabaret personality Aristide Bruant. I've just arrived downtown from City College, where I'm teaching an exhausting, slave-labor composition course, and I'm wearing my archaic, threadbare, undergraduate tweed jacket. It turns out he's made a lot of money in the ad business. Broke at the time and trying unsuccessfully to write my first novel, I remember thinking, *Shit, I could have made a lot of money in the ad business. Then I could afford to dress like a real Bohemian.*

"You remember that time at the Remo?" I ask him.

"Sure, I remember. You were coming on practically like a flower child, and that was before Hippies were even invented. Very obnoxious."

"Remember I had the copy of *Partisan Review* with me?"

"Sure, with the symposium. 'Our Country, Our Culture.' You were using it to prove we were moving into a new era. That it was time for the underground to surface. That it was possible to rejoin the mainstream. Right?"

"Yeah, Norman Mailer objected, but he was still objecting on grounds he himself later helped destroy."

"Like what grounds?"

"That the writer doesn't need to be integrated into his society, and often works best in opposition to it. Strictly out of the old leftist avant-garde idea of alienation. Thing is, I still think Mailer had a point," I say. "But so did the symposium."

"Maybe, but you were full of shit then. In 1952. Whose country and whose culture? Maybe Joe McCarthy's."

"I think what I sensed was the end of the old-guard fantasy of holding out for the revolution."

"Well, those guys were tired."

And maybe they thought they had it made. Or maybe their claim to the culture was premature, and merely proposed as an excuse for assimilating into it. Suddenly the Abstract Expressionists were riding high, and the movement had heavy *Partisan Review* connections. Jackson Pollock had already been anointed, if left-handedly, by *Life,* in 1949. But it was an ambiguous success. When Mark Rothko was congratulated by sculptor Zahara Schatz for the recognition implied by his first exhibit at the Museum of Modern Art, his response was "What do you mean, recognition? Some of my best friends don't recognize me anymore." They say that one Abstract Expressionist, invited to an affair at a Rockefeller mansion, was appalled to spot a painter friend as he walked up the grand staircase. "What are *you* doing here?" he's said to have said. Pollock was taken up by *Life* and Rothko by *Vogue,* but for what? Pollock was promoted as a scandalous crazy who mixed sand, broken glass, and an occasional dead bee in his pigment and poured the mess onto his canvas, while Rothko was pushed as the latest chic in decoration for the modern home. They might as well have been imitating sea gulls like Joe Gould. Their notoriety resembled that of Henry Miller at the time, who was famous despite, or maybe because of, the fact that his best books were unavailable due to censorship.

The differences that developed between me and my high-school friend were a reflection of the cultural situation. If intellectual energies were exhausted at the moment of an uncertain kind of success, subterranean currents were renewing the underground, though in two competing streams, both of which would surface in what is now known as "The Sixties." Ideological polemicists like Norman Mailer were more in sympathy with attitudes laid out by the Hipsters than the Beats. The Beats at the beginning seemed to think of themselves as anti-ideological dropouts although, clearly, a doctrinaire anti-ideology can be considered an ideology. However, what Ginsberg calls his "angelic and lamby politics," based on a revolution of the human heart, did not go down well with either old intellectual leftists imbued with *Realpolitik* or Hipsters intent on numbing out of a hopeless scene.

Toward the middle of the fifties, in other words, if you couldn't live with the status quo you had a choice, but it was between two different kinds of withdrawal. Hip or Beat? What would you do? My third course was that of hopeful participation. It was the wrong choice. At the time it simply wasn't a realistic option.

In 1953 and thereabouts, when Kerouac, Burroughs, Corso, Ginsberg, and Co. were goofing around East Seventh Street, the Moloch of Allen's *Howl* was king, Eisenhower was president, the Korean War was going full blast, the Rosenberg case was coming to its grim climax, the cold war was at its most intense, and the Bomb was on everyone's mind. A-bomb shelters were designated in buildings and, somewhat later, protesters including Judith Malina and Dorothy Day would be thrown in jail for demonstrating against civil defense drills. "Do-gooders" stuck their necks out, for others the underground provided a place where they could survive. Marginal types were not appreciated, were harassed. "Hands Off Lenny Bruce!" Cool was, among other things, a way of fending off hysteria on the margins. It helped keep the lid on for fear of what might happen if it blew off. But the quadrangles of the Ivy League were presumably a sanctuary, if nothing else, from the draft, despite the occasional railroading of your odd pinko prof.

The Cornell quad was one of the better specimens of the period. The campus was a refuge for literati, real and would be. Goldwin Smith Hall was especially fertile in fiction writers. Richard Fariña, William Gass, Steve Katz, Joanna Russ were around at various times from the end of the forties through the mid-fifties. Tom Pynchon, according to creative-writing head Baxter Hathaway, was cribbing turn-of-the-century Baedekers as material for *V*. Arthur Mizener, resident representative of the New Critics, dominant literary school of the time, came into class in white bucks, tweeds, and gray crew cut, boyishly twirling his Phi Beta Kappa key, to lecture in praise of "maturity" in literature. Near as I could figure, this meant don't rock any boats. Now and then he found it necessary to allude to "Tom" Eliot. Vladimir Nabokov's *Pnin* is a fiction partly à clef of that era of the campus. Nabokov was teaching literature there and publishing in *The New Yorker*. Unlike him, we didn't know yet that he was a great writer, though that he was a great eccentric was clear. We had no way of knowing that some of his best work couldn't be published in the United States because of censorship. What happened with the campus literary magazine was only symptomatic of what was happening in the rest of the country.

The campus literary magazine. There isn't one when I arrive and we feel there should be. Otherwise what are we going to publish in? Me, David Behrens, later a Pulitzer Prize journalist, Martin Washburn, a painter and during the Off-Off-Broadway explosion drama reviewer for *The Village Voice,* and others, some now writers and editors.

Susan Brownmiller, author of the renowned book on rape *Against Our Will,* and a leading feminist proponent of pornography censorship and supporter of Richard Kuh, who, as DA, hounded Lenny Bruce, will remember the scene fifteen years after the fact in an article in *Esquire.* Brownmiller, a member of a tiny, isolated campus radical group called Students for Peace, is an aspiring actress at Cornell, but is already showing signs of the cultural obtuseness common to many varieties of political leftists. She can never understand why her literary friends would never participate in her political activities. "As I remember the Students for Peace crowd singing worn-out folk songs from the Thirties," she writes in *Esquire,* "I remember *The Writer* crowd huddled at a table ... almost as though they were muttering with Prufrock, the current favorite, 'Do I dare?' ... They clung to each other as if to ward off a chill. You couldn't get them to do anything political." It takes guts at that time and place to sit out on the quad, as Brownmiller does, and solicit signatures for radical petitions. Not long before, the head of another radical campus organization has almost been thrown off a bridge by some fraternity boys. But if the political alternative to the silence of the fifties is yet another version of the uptight peasant-blouse and folk-song crowd, a repeat of the Midwood High left—a school that Brownmiller, incidentally, also attended—revving up with yet another rendition of the Spanish Civil War golden oldie "Viva la Quinta Brigada," we aren't up for it.

The Cornell Writer, it says on the first page of the first issue in November, 1953, should be interesting to readers "beyond what virtues of good literature they find in it," because it reflects "the attitudes of our own generation." An interesting statement, bound to cause difficulties. I am the fiction editor, and the first story in the first issue is by me. "Indian Love Call" makes fun of uptight co-eds and campus pseudointellectuals. The best thing about it is its immaturity. It is not only sophomoric, it is aggressively sophomoric. The characters have absurd names that prevent you from taking them seriously as characters so as not to distract you from the real issue at hand, which is suppression of teen-age lust in the deenergized fifties. And the story is bad. But there are some interesting things in it, mainly a kind of antiliterary energy threatening to explode out of the well-made literary frame of the story, which is badly made.

Well, anything related to lust is taboo at the time, and some people, including Hathaway, who is faculty adviser, try to talk us into toning it down, but we figure that would be selling out. This is a chance to test our principles. The atmosphere at the time is so oppressive that Richard Schechner, later avant-garde director, advocate of guerrilla street theater, and leader of a "piss-in" at the famous Pentagon demonstration of the sixties, will later admit to Brownmiller in *Esquire* that what he learned at Cornell was that "you don't get involved in a political organization. I didn't want it on my record." In the same *Esquire* article I am quoted by Brownmiller to the effect that I was made to feel "un-American" in the Cornell ambience. "I grew up under the assumption that you had to live underground— lie, present a facade, never say what you really thought. . . . *Nothing seemed possible*. We were scared and threatened and defiant." Rather than censor ourselves, here is a chance to break the silence. Something in the issue must hit a nerve, because the magazine sells out in about half a day on campus.

These days nobody will believe what happened next, so I'll quote from an article in the *Cornell Daily Sun*, December 11, 1953: OBSCENITY CHARGES PREFERRED AGAINST EDITORS OF WRITER, by Stuart H. Loory —later managing editor of the *Chicago Sun-Times* and CNN Moscow Bureau chief. "Two editors of *The Cornell Writer* and that magazine's faculty adviser have been asked to appear at the next meeting of the Faculty Committee on Student Conduct to answer charges that an article in the first issue contained 'obscene' phraseology." That's me and Washburn. And Hathaway. The committee had received complaints about the magazine. One of the complainants was Deane W. Malott, president of the university. Another was apparently the Ithaca post office, which had turned issues back to the university as unsuitable for mailing. One complaint, according to the *Ithaca Journal,* "called the terminology and implications of the story 'fairly disgusting.'"

The issue of the magazine, what's left of it, is impounded. Several university organs are convened. Many meetings of various faculty and administrative committees are held, at least one of which lasts four hours through midnight before it even begins deliberations on its decision. Washburn, Behrens, and myself undergo repeated cross-examination and interviews with deans in the presence of the university lawyer. A fight between the liberal arts and the nonarts colleges of the university erupts. Another explodes between the English department and the administration. The story goes out over the wire services. Headlines in the *Brooklyn Eagle.* Frantic calls from home. A letter from Hathaway to my father: "Ronald has absolutely nothing to be ashamed of." An avalanche of editorials and letters to the editor: "I was very happy to buy the first issue, but with my reading of the first article, my disgust overcame my joy.... a bit of trash liberally dashed with the language of the gutter ... vulgarity and plain bad taste ... detracts from literature as a form of art." "I believe Sukenick's story, 'Indian Love Call,' to be a superb example of prose art, akin to the beautiful work of Joyce or Proust." "Clamp down, says a student, or we'll be investigated."

When we come before the committees it turns out the crux of the charges has to do with offensive language, and in particular my use of the word—are you ready?—"birdshit." It sounds funny but it's no joke at the time. It seems the president of the university has tried to expel us on the spot and would have done so except for the nearly unanimous resistance of the English department. When the lid is on as tight as it is in the fifties, it doesn't take much to start the pot boiling. Birdshit. Distinctions are made during committee deliberations like "dam" would have been okay but "damn" is blasphemy, "shit" would have been obscenity but "birdshit" is okay because it's only animal dookie.

The liberals must have won out with their arguments about animal dookie, because after weeks of this they let our asses off the hook, though with a solemn warning. "A Cornell University faculty committee on student conduct decided today to take no action against

two students for an article, described as obscene and objectionable,"
says the United Press story of December 17, though the committee
urged us " 'to be more conscious of their limits in literary fields.' "
The Cornell public relations office, UP continues, said that in " 'the
opinion of a majority of the committee the story contained material
objectionable to a sufficiently large segment of society to make it
unsuitable for publication. . . . There are limits, set not only by law,
but also by standards of good taste and' "—dig it—" 'freedom enjoyed by creative writing.' . . . One part of the story told how Hen-
rietta 'scratched her ear with her big toe, while Bish yelled, "Woof,
Woof." ' Washburn and Sukenick spent an hour and a half with the
committee." Be more careful next time, kids. Woof, Woof.

It seems that birdshit in any form was definitely a no-no these
years. Underground radio figure Bob Fass reports a similar incident
at Syracuse University involving the word "guano."

Five years later, Kirk Sale, then a Cornell undergraduate, helped
organize a student protest against curfew rules that brought out three
thousand students who, among other things, burned Malott in effigy
and broke the windows in his house. This was an unheard-of mani-
festation at the time. Brownmiller relates the apocryphal story that
the wife of a university benefactor dining *chez* Malott called her husband's attention to the students with the remark "Look, dear, they're
coming to thank you for the boathouse."

A decade after the birdshit incident, the students at Berkeley picked
up on direct-action tactics over similar issues in the "Free Speech
Movement." Just to refresh your memory, "There was one guy they
were arresting because he was using profanity and resisting closing
up his table," says Aaron Shatten, owner of Berkeley's Shakespeare
and Company bookstore. "They arrested him, I think it was a Berkeley police car, or maybe it was a campus police car. What happened
was they just sort of crowded around and wouldn't let the car move.
And first it was just a few people and then it went to hundreds and
then to thousands. And the governor called up the state police, and
they formed along Telegraph Avenue, and you could see all these
guys on motorcycles, huge motorcycles, several hundreds, whole flocks
of policemen waiting to come in," and "The Sixties" began.

Next time there was an attempt to confiscate an issue of the literary magazine for pornography at Cornell, it was several years later and a new generation of kids had hit the quad. When the police car drove onto campus to impound the magazine it was mobbed by a thousand students who almost turned it over and the administration let the matter drop, confirming everyone's faith in direct action.

So much for "birdshit," but what I'm really doing in "Indian Love Call" is actually something way beyond my conscious range at the time. The parody of the literary Modernism in favor at the time is unmistakable now. While I'm still worshiping in the church of the Modern Movement, presided over by Archbishop Eliot, Pope Pound, and Demigod Joyce, which sustains me with cultural manna against the hot dogs of my actual milieu, some corner of my consciousness knows we face a clean slate, an empty canvas. Somehow I realize that Modernism is already literary, and while it may be *Partisan Review*'s culture, and its country, the rest of us are living in McCarthyland.

This is confirmed for me, in retrospect, by an odd meeting I have with Nabokov the following year. By now I've published several stories in the magazine, which has survived, and I've heard by grapevine that he likes them. At that point Nabokov must be trying to get his great *Lolita* published, but no dice in the United States. He would have to publish it with Maurice Girodias's Olympia Press in Paris, which specialized in pornography and great books that couldn't be published here because of pornography laws. I remember buying the Olympia *Lolita* a few years later with a brown wrapper on it. I feel I have something in common with this butterfly collector and professor of Russian Literature but I don't know what, so I grope around trying to find out what he thinks of my writing, trying to talk to him about my Modernist gods. Years later when I meet Girodias in Paris the first thing he says to me, before saying hello, is "You look like one of my authors."

Nabokov is not giving me any easy answers. In fact he's not giving me any answers. In response to my questions all he'll talk to me about, in his elegant Oxbridgian accent, is cricket, about which I know nothing and want to know nothing. In my memory he's dressed in white flannels, though that may be just something my memory is doing to harmonize with his conversation. It's clear he's being very friendly in some monumentally oblique way that I can't understand. It's clear to me now that what he was doing was giving me a lesson in disengagement, in the things you care about because they're of no importance, sports, the abstract realm of chess strategies, the formal play of art. My head is urgently filled with ideas about things deriving from the Moderns. Nabokov, like all the best writers, Beckett, Henry James, Rabelais—you can see it in his books—works beyond ideas. This is already erotic, to play with language instead of saying something meaningful with it, something ideational, ideological, idealistic, that's what drives the censors mad with deep fears. It's not a mere word like "birdshit" or even "fuck" they want deleted. It's not punctuation they want conventionalized. It's not the few or many things his editors insist Kerouac change in *On the Road*, it doesn't even matter what they are since, according to Ginsberg, once Kerouac agreed to change them the editors didn't even care whether they were actually changed. It's an impulse to castration, the need for a token of submission, a sign that the writer's agreed to stop jerking off and get down to business.

Herb Gold tells the following story about his first novel, *The Man Who Was Not With It*. "It was indicated to me that if I would change the title—the title they wanted to use was *The Cup of Kindness*—and change a list of about sixty words, and make a few little cuts, that it probably would be the Atlantic Prize novel. First, that would have given me ten thousand dollars, which I could have used, and it could have had a lot of attention—in those days they reviewed those books, the Atlantic Prize novel or the Harper Prize novel. I sent Sam Lawrence [the publisher] a telegram saying, 'The cup of kindness is a many-splendored crock,' and then got a very nice letter from him saying, 'Okay, we'll do it your way.' The book sold, I think, under two thousand copies. They didn't push it. The words were not dirty words, they were my poetic use of carnival slang, and they said it simply wouldn't be understood. They said the title meant nothing. Nobody in the office understood what 'the man who was not with it' meant. That was 1955, two years before *On the Road* was published."

Are you pure? Ginsberg says Kerouac "was mad at me for working in relation to the political scene," because he thought that "was a betrayal or a diversion or a complete divagation from what he had in mind and what I had in mind," which was "the attempt to open up the heart." But Ginsberg told him he thought he could handle it. Ginsberg says the less selfish course is to risk corruption by the world, sell out, and "transform shit to gold." Some of Ginsberg's friends say that in some ways he always wanted to be a rock star—and for a while he was singing with the Clash. Once he told me with a sense of awe that he'd recently read a poem to twenty—or was it forty?—thousand people. Anne Waldman says it was with the Rolling Thunder Revue, and Bob Dylan let him read to the outdoor crowd because it was raining. Judith Malina tells me, "I'm the unicorn's horn, when I go into the poisoned water it's pure. . . . That's the difference between believing that you can change the situation you're in, and believing that you're a victim of the situation you're in." Hemingway says you have to have a shit detector. Dylan Thomas doesn't always know the difference between shit and chocolate. Warhol's gang is less innocent. It seems that no matter where the proto-punk-rock Velvet Underground went, for example, the toilets would stop up, writes Andy Warhol. "So they started scooping handfuls of shit from the toilets and slinging it out the windows. . . . You don't believe stories like that till you see people running by you with handfuls of dripping shit, laughing."

If underground artists are pure, it is not as priests or puritans. I remember Lenny Bruce's last big performance. Just after one of the Kennedy assassinations, in a big theater on Second Avenue. He comes out onstage and doesn't say anything for five minutes. Just stands there cringing against the curtain, which happens to be huge, glittering, gold, looking around at the audience. Then finally he goes, "Don't shoot." He was taking on all that paranoid shit, forcing us to smell it. But to do that he had to play the victim. Always. In the underground you take the creative risk of playing with shit, but it costs.

Like Maxwell Bodenheim, murdered with his woman by the mad point man of a love triangle in a dingy Bowery room in 1954. Or Stanley Gould, "America's oldest living junkie," finally dead of AIDS in 1985, contracted no doubt from shooting shit into his veins.

If you play with shit you get your hands dirty. You want to hold out for the revolution that's your business, it's a dead end. But if you have dirty hands you're not supposed to talk about it. Not in the Silent Generation. Lenny Bruce was hounded to death for saying "fuck," not for fucking. Wilhelm Reich was brought to trial not because of his psychiatric practice pushing liberated sex, but because of the psychiatric journal he published. He died in jail. Birdshit or not, they weren't kidding around in those days. You can still smell the Rosenbergs frying. This was the mid-fifties, remember? Darkest Eisenhower. It was all birdshit then, that's why it's the one thing you ain't supposed to say.

Jack, like me, we speak the unspeakable.

"Paul Krassner introduced me to Lenny Bruce when Lenny first came to New York," says John Wilcock, speaking earnestly with a distinctly non-upper-class English accent in his Hell's Kitchen apartment. Wilcock has the putty-faced pallor of a night person, and in fact he haunts the New York night scene through a complex network of party informants. "Lenny said he was going to open at the Village Vanguard, and I said, 'Oh, I'm right on the corner, I'll give you some keys and you can use my place between sets, and stuff like that. He wasn't known at all, he was just opening for the first time in New York. The very first night he opened in the Vanguard, the very first thing he said, he came in and he looked around this little tiny room with about four hundred people crammed in, and he said, 'I don't know how Max Gordon can afford to pay me a grand a week to work a place this size. I've been thinking about it, I've come to the conclusion he must be a crook.' That was the first thing Lenny said in New York. And almost the second thing he said was to look around and say, 'Well, any kikes here tonight? Oh yeah, there's one sitting there next to a nigger at the bar, and oh, I see a spic down there,' and he went into all this bit. So within about five minutes he'd alienated the entire place including the owner. And, you know, he went on from there. He did for, like, the stage and everything exactly what Henry Miller had done in writing—he'd pushed the limits and gone beyond them, and been slapped back, and in the meantime he'd opened up all the limits again for everybody in that whole area."

"Was Lenny a junkie?" I ask.

"I don't know, what is the definition of a junkie?"

"I guess when you have to organize your life around it."

"I don't think he did that," says Wilcock. "He always turned on to do a show, but he didn't turn on with anything we would know about, he turned on with some prescription stuff. But I remember going into the bathroom one day in the Perry Street apartment and seeing his jacket with all these fucking hypodermic needles sticking out of the pocket, and I was really paranoid. I'd only just gotten onto dope, and it was like, you know, someone with needles in my apartment and stuff, who knows what was going to happen. I was very frightened of that, you know. But he had prescriptions and stuff, nothing happened, I didn't say anything about it, but you know, I had a moment of perturbation when I saw this. He was an amazing guy, actually.

"He was tender," insists Wilcock. "He was very tender. One day I remember my place was being painted, and it was a real mess, you know, and I left a note saying I'm sorry for the mess and stuff, and when the place was finished the next day I came back home, and there were candies, there was candy all over the bed, about ten different kinds of candy laid out in a row, and at the far end of it there was a note saying, 'Happy house painting, wouldn't this be a great gift for a diabetic?' And then another time he came and he brought flowers, right? I mean I'd never heard of guys giving each other flowers, there was nothing gay about him that I ever determined, you know, but he was just really a sweet guy. In contrast to the end when he had nothing on his mind whatsoever except this endless confusion in his head about legal stuff."

Where are you in the mid-fifties? Are you fighting your way up the heart-burning ladder of career, or have you finally decided there's no place to go but down? Burned out into a dead-end underground. Into the shadow world emblemized above all by Bebop. Digging Bop is one of the main ways subterraneans can express their cultural radicalism—if you want to hear Dixieland go to Eddie Condon's on Eighth Street with the fraternity boys. By the end of the forties the scene had moved from Harlem down to Midtown at Birdland and

Bop City. Then it started coming Downtown to the Village, but now things are already moving into a new phase. Parker is off junk, fighting the habit with Manischewitz and huge quantities of aspirin. He says he doesn't want to be a slave anymore. But he also knows he's going to die as a result, according to his pal Yoram Kaniuk, because his body is so fucked up and used to running on shit.

"There was a jam session somewhere around Waverly Place in a sort of warehouse," remembers Kaniuk. "We used to have this kind of jam session that lasted two or three days. Ben Webster came, and Miles Davis was very young, and Charlie Parker. And there were others of course, Charlie Mingus, many played, but as it developed something happened. A contest started between Ben Webster, Charlie Parker, and Miles Davis. It was three generations fighting for something. And it was at a time when Charlie Parker was changing his music, he was putting some classical music in it, he was influenced by, I think, Bartók. And Miles was then also trying to break out of Bop. Ben was still playing the old thing. It was a moment in time when things were changing and we didn't understand it. And it happened without our knowing it. And they were playing, they were angry and loving one another, because Miles admired Parker, while *he* admired Ben Webster, who was always hocking his saxophone at Minton's Playhouse to get some money and then we would collect money and give him back his saxophone. And there were the three great horn players, fighting, and it was beautiful because they loved one another, and they fought with such vigor and venom and hate and love all mixed up together and they were lost in it in father and son relationships. I mean Ben was Bird's father and Bird was Miles' father and the father was against the son and son against father. I remember that some gangsters came in and said something about blowing a torch under somebody's balls, they had a blowtorch, some girls screaming, people were completely, I mean I was drinking but people were taking a lot of hash and a lot of dope and we were really gone, time didn't seem real. There was a rich lady who kept coming from Uptown bringing all kinds of chicken fricassees from some fancy restaurants and some drivers with chauffeurs' uniforms walking into this inferno bringing all kinds of very fancy food and people would take these chickens from silver plates. I don't know, it was very weird, the whole scene. You have to understand I'm talking about thirty years ago."

Dylan Thomas died in 1954 in a room at the Chelsea, hotel to Bohemia, after years of suicidal drinking. Parker went in '55 and Jackson Pollock drove his car into a tree in the Hamptons in '56 after he'd fallen off the wagon for the last time. Three lives without second acts. Charlie Parker, the saint of Bop Kerouac so admired, died on Kerouac's thirty-third birthday, as Kerouac himself would go, also to an early grave, on Dizzy Gillespie's birthday. When they hear Bird had died, Ted Joans and three friends in the Village set off in four different directions by subway and on foot with chalk and charcoal to resurrect his spirit in the underground that revered him. Soon the graffiti began appearing chalked all through the New York subways and then in the johns of underground bars and then in hip places all across the country: BIRD LIVES. The Kilroy sign of another generation. KILROY WAS HERE, the killer king projection of U.S. GI's blasting their way across Europe. BIRD LIVES, the flight of imagination toward freedom and incandescent life.

BLEECKER
STREET

It *was beautiful because they loved one another.* There was no money involved yet, or not much, and the only kind of success in view was limited to clique, cult, and coterie. In-groups huddling in enclaves as here, now, in the dead point of the fifties the youthful patrons of Tulla's coffeehouse in Cambridge, Massachusetts, huddle against the draft, the cold war, and the windiness of academe. One day you are surprised to find this daring bridgehead of Bohemia opening its door to tweedy Harvard Square, at a time when a cappuccino is a symbol of subversive sophistication. Of the couple who run the place, the guy looks wasted by sin, and the woman, vaguely Viennese, ready to waste you with it.

In the mid-fifties the New York Jewish Intellectual Establishment is moving to Brandeis University at a rapid rate, but Waltham, where Brandeis is located, thirty minutes away from Cambridge, is far too blue collar for intellectual tastes, even socialist intellectual tastes. Brandeis is the Ellis Island of academe, funneling the first large influx of Jewish intellectuals, with and without academic degrees, into the American university system. But nobody wants to live on Ellis Island. Despite a certain condescension toward the new school and even hints of a genteel anti-Semitism emanating from the Harvard establishment, noted by Irving Howe, then a Brandeis professor, in *A Margin of Hope*, the faculty shuttles from Brandeis to the academic mainland of Cambridge, or at least to the Belmont, Newton, or Back Bay suburbs of Harvard, Radcliffe, and MIT.

Drawn to Brandeis by the prospect of laying claim to what I consider my intellectual patrimony from proponents of it like Howe, Herbert Marcuse, and Philip Rahv, co-editor of *Partisan Review*, I assume the identity of a grad student. I see Brandeis as a short cut to the underground of intellectual resistance that seems the best alternative to an oppressive middle-class culture. One day in January, 1958, I stroll over to violinist Arnold Fournier's furniture rental shop at 47 Mount Auburn Street not far from Harvard Square to pay an installment on my furniture, and I find that Fournier is no longer the proprietor of the shop. Fournier is no longer there at all, instead the premises are occupied by another coffee shop started by two recent Brandeis graduates that will feature jazz, opening with a trio including still another Brandeis product, Chuck Israels, on bass. I keep the furniture.

Shortly, after being closed by the cops, the coffee shop reopened as a club, Club Mount Auburn 47, featuring folk music. If Tweedsville was proving attractive to the intellectuals after their years of sneering at academe—by a strange coincidence at the very moment that academe is opening its arms to them—the intellectuals and their style were also making an impact on Harvard Square. Tulla's was definitely not derived from the prep school mentality, and Club 47—with its tweedy-rebel and leather-jacket crowd and its barefoot madonna and major discovery, Joan Baez, giving a new voice to folky pieties—was distinctly not "shoe," as they used to say. Baez's first public appearance in Cambridge was an impromptu at Tulla's. Someone was strumming a guitar and Joan, sitting there with her family, started "one of those 'whoo-haa' things in the background, and it just went all over Cambridge. The place froze," according to the guy managing it. "Everybody was staring. What is this singing?"

The influence of Club 47 on the subsequent New Left can be seen in a 1979 statement by folk singer Bobby Neuwirth, habitué of the club, later an intimate of Bob Dylan and, still later, one of the inner circle at Max's Kansas City and companion of Warhol "Superstar" Edie Sedgwick: "Cambridge was one of the navels of the cultural period, and a lot of influence came out of it. It put a lot of intelligence into the guitar movement, and the guitar movement was the forerunner of the peace movement. It made people aware enough to allow the peace movement to enter people's consciousness. Between Elvis Presley and the folk singers, the guitar movement enabled kids to believe in youth and the correctness of their own thinking. So when the peace movement started, they didn't buckle under at the first signs of parental authority—the people who said, 'You're Communists. Shut up and crawl under a rock.'"

By the mid-fifties, middle-class kids were already listening to white rock 'n' roll—"blue-eyed soul." Elvis Presley was getting on national television by 1955–56. "Suddenly white people are feeling things that they didn't feel before. Rock 'n' roll takes off as a rebellious sound," says rock 'n' roll archivist Mitch Blank. "You have people who are rebelling against the normal, everyday concept of what's right and what's wrong, how I should feel."

"Did that have trouble getting air time?" I ask.

"Absolutely. It was race music. White people shouldn't be singing that. Certainly white people shouldn't be listening to that."

Allen Freed's rock 'n' roll revues were traveling all around the country and you started getting interracial audiences. Buddy Holly was the first white act ever to play Harlem's Apollo Theater. But by 1959 Elvis had been drafted, Buddy Holly was killed in an airplane crash and Chuck Berry was in jail on the Mann Act.

"This really knocks the guts out of rock 'n' roll," says Blank. "So instead of these creative people you have synthetic rock 'n' roll—Frankie Avalon, Fabian. They cleaned up rock 'n' roll." So you got Pat Boone and Chubby Checker, both "cover" artists for more authentic musicians, even Chubby Checker's name a rip-off of Fats Domino. At the end of the fifties there was a void, and while the middle class was dancing the twist to Chubby Checker, a lot of youthful, rebellious energy was starting to be expressed through folk music.

Other things were cooking in Cambridge besides folk music and movements emanating from Brandeis. A little earlier Harvard had produced a group of poets destined to be a major influence on literary developments through the fifties and sixties that came to be known as the New York School, oddly, since its first generation was from Harvard and its second from the Midwest. Frank O'Hara, John Ashbery, and Kenneth Koch, plus fiction writer and Parisian exile Harry Mathews, were the main figures who, with James Schuyler, made up one of the most important of the literary elements that would come together and ignite in 1960's New York. The Cambridge Poets' Theater was producing adventurous plays. Gregory Corso, whose book of poems *The Vestal Lady of Brattle Street* was the first significant volume of Beat poetry to be published, was hanging out in the Harvard dorms, cadging money, and sitting in on classes. A more notorious Cambridge development was the experiments of Harvard professors Leary and Alpert, a little later, with LSD. William Burroughs, who visited them at a late stage of the Harvard episode, expresses disappointment with their level of scientific seriousness.

"I stayed with Leary in Newton, Massachusetts," recalls Burroughs, "and I went to his classes, and they were going great guns in seersucker suits just like regular professors. And very shortly afterwards they were discredited and the whole thing collapsed. They thought they had the fix in at the time and they didn't at all. It turned out they weren't into experimentation in a long time—they were, I suppose, fooling around. The man who turned on the world!" snorts Burroughs, his W. C. Fields accents almost breaking into a whinny of nasality.

In 1955 when future activist Abbie Hoffman got to Brandeis as an undergrad, he was living in a dorm, playing poker, a jock. "I come

out of that culture from Wooster, the street culture, the bowling al-
leys, the pool halls, the sports, anti-intellectual. I was smart but I was
a troublemaker." In fact, Hoffman looks a lot like a diabolical Dead
End Kid, though the devilish quality turns out to be an irrepressible
energy and good humor that's evident as he talks. Among Brandeis
students, Hoffman was famous for starting a sub sandwich service in
the dorms.

But by the second half of the fifties America was about ready for
revival. Conversion. Salvation. It has happened before in our history
and it will happen again. Henry Adams has written that his ancestors
"viewed the world chiefly as a thing to be reformed, filled with evil
forces to be abolished, and they saw no reason to suppose that they
had wholly succeeded in the abolition." This is a strain in American
culture that is not confined to Adams's New England. In addition, the
culture will soon be engulfed by the tidal wave of flesh and hormones
known as the baby boom, which will ineluctably generate its own
needs, ask its own questions. The experience providing the answers
could be triggered by opening a book, by hearing a song, by turning
on to acid. It could even be triggered inadvertently by a professor
taken too much at his word. There will be, no doubt, more than a
few professors at Brandeis appalled by the fruition of their abstrac-
tions in figures like Abbie Hoffman and Communist Angela Davis.
Most students cannot be expected to have the history of often painful
struggle with social attitudes and one's own sanity that lends ballast
to those who have evolved a creative style or an intellectual position.
The situation had become volatile, and the touch on the trigger did
not need to be very heavy.

James Dean, whose role as the rebel without a cause carried over
to his public image, in the movie can no longer live with the disastrous
mendacity and compromise of his parents. There is a scene in the
film in which he comes close to patricide. "Kill your parents," Jerry
Rubin would say in the sixties. In California, Kansas, Boston, New
York, kids were disaffected with the dad in the gray flannel suit. New
role models miraculously appeared to answer the need, not that they
hadn't been around before, but it was as if there were an imperceptible
click and the culture suddenly moved into a new gear. The culture

heroes of previous generations had been most influential on a relatively small community of creative people and their hangers-on. All that was about to change. Culture was about to be democratized, and was about to inherit the problems of democracy. There was an older, more self-contained underground that had been quietly accumulating cultural capital for years. Writers like Kenneth Patchen, forerunner and probably superior of Kerouac in the rebellious freedom of his style in poetry and fiction, and poet Kenneth Rexroth, after Langston Hughes and with Patchen largely responsible for the beginnings of the jazz/poetry-reading movement picked up by the Beats, were either bypassed or felt bypassed and turned angrily on the youth wave. So also did the leftist intellectuals who were used to being regarded as the vanguard of the antiestablishment band.

Maybe if you were an older artist and famous, or dead, you were safe—Pollock, Parker, Dylan Thomas—but Kerouac, after years of not even being able to get his books published, was suddenly notorious for reasons so irrelevant to his talent they were impossible for him to deal with. And even among the older and famous there was a high rate of suicide and self-destruction. The times required new role models and, so much the worse for them, this did not necessarily require a very substantial understanding of what made those models important. A flash of recognition would do, at least for a start.

"And then I started to get turned on by some of these teachers," says Hoffman about Brandeis, "and listening to Pete Seeger come and sing songs. And Martin Luther King, I remember, he came that first year, right after the Birmingham boycott. Our cultural life was in Harvard Square. We were influenced by the Beat Generation and their life style and their political outlook and their literature. Of course I went to readings there, and Joan Baez, I remember her riding around on the back of a motorcycle in a leather jacket then around 47 Mount Auburn Street, singing free concerts, Phil Ochs going through. There was a Brandeis connection, that's why we went over there."

"Was your father right to blame everything you got into on Brandeis?"

"I was programmed, trained, encouraged by some of the best minds of the time," says Hoffman of the intellectuals and activists he encountered at Brandeis. "Maslow one, Marcuse second."

"Howe?" I ask.

"No, Howe was the kind of guy that said don't go read the Beats because they're dirty, they're vile. So of course I ran out and read them. Most of these people, by the way, except for Marcuse, would turn against what we were doing in the sixties. Then there were the people that would pass through. Dorothy Day, Martin Luther King, Saul Alinsky, those were three people who had a tremendous effect on me even though I heard them speak only once."

Around college campuses from Cambridge to Kansas students were finding their uncertain, sometimes difficult paths to Bleecker Street. If you were already there and connected with the underground that was continuous with the old Village Bohemia and had risen to prominence with Abstract Expressionism and the cult success of Bebop, life in the second half of the fifties could be a gas. "New York, in 1956, was the wildest, greatest city anywhere," writes Fielding Dawson in his short story "Pirate One." "American painting had just been taken seriously for a first in history, and the city was the art center of the world. Europe was as jealous as all hell, and it was wonderful. You could walk along 10th Street and stop and say a few words with Philip Guston, go into the Colony on the corner there, at 4th Avenue, have a beer with de Kooning, walk over to the Cedar and have a few with Creeley, Dan Rice, or Kline, and that night fall by the Riviera or Romero's and then cross up to the Vanguard on 7th Avenue, dig Getz and Brookmeyer, and then walk down to the Cafe Bohemia, and get your head torn off by Miles, and around one, fall by the Cedar, and pick up some friends and go over to the 5 Spot and completely flip over Cecil Taylor, then afterwards go to Riker's for breakfast, and around dawn head home, maybe with a chick. It was really great. You could feel the exuberance, you could see and hear the dedication."

If you were a little younger, though, if you didn't have connections to the established Village underground and you were living in a tenement on the Lower East Side or in one of the slummier areas up around Hell's Kitchen, things looked a little different. "The affluent post–Korean war society was settling down to a grimmer, more long-term ugliness. At that moment, there really seemed to be no way out," writes Diane di Prima in *Memoirs of a Beatnik*.

"As far as we knew, there was only a small handful of us—perhaps forty or fifty in the city—who knew what we knew; who raced about in Levis and work shirts, smoked dope, dug the new jazz, and spoke a bastardization of the black argot. We surmised that there might be another fifty living in San Francisco, and perhaps a hundred more scattered throughout the country: Chicago, New Orleans, etc., but our isolation was total and impenetrable.... Our chief concern was to keep our integrity (much time and energy went into defining the concept of the 'sellout') and to keep our cool: a hard, clean edge and definition in the midst of the terrifying indifference and sentimentality around us—'media mush.'" The ongoing underground concern about "selling out," however negative and merely reactive to the dominant culture, nevertheless indicates a sustained commitment to alternative values despite the fact that there seemed to be "no way out."

Then, one evening, someone arrives to "thrust a small black and white book into my hand.... I took it and flipped it open idly, still intent on dishing out beef stew, and found myself in the middle of *Howl* by Allen Ginsberg.... I was too turned on to concern myself with the stew. I handed it over to Beatrice and, without even thanking Bradley, I walked out the front door with his new book. Walked the few blocks to the pier on Sixtieth Street, and sat down by the Hudson River to read, and to come to terms with what was happening. The phrase "breaking ground" kept coming into my head. I knew that this Allen Ginsberg, whoever he was, had been breaking ground for all of us, though I had no idea yet what that meant, how far it would take us.... I sensed that Allen was only, could only be, the vanguard of a much larger thing. All the people who, like me, had hidden and skulked, writing down what they knew for a small handful of friends ... all these would now step forward and say their piece. Not many would hear them, but they would, finally, hear each other. I was about to meet my brothers and sisters.... I was high and delighted. I made my way back to the house and to supper, and we all read the poem, I read it aloud to everyone. A new era had begun."

Blond, blue-eyed Ed Sanders looks like a Hollywood model of the all-American boy instead of the scatological rebel, underground bard, and anti-nuke-sub protest jailbait that he turned out to be. "I was born in Kansas City," says Sanders. "I was just a regular American kid, you know, I mean I was a Boy Scout, I was in my high-school choir, I went to Sunday school, it was the whole American panoply. I mean I was an all-American guy. And then, I was browsing at the University of Missouri book store in the fall of 1957, and there was the first edition of *Howl*, which I still have, and *Evergreen Review* number one and number two. There was a whole panoply of writers that I got exposed to in one five-dollar purchase, the fifty cents for *Howl*, two-fifty for the two issues of the *Evergreen Review*, and I was ready to go. I absorbed all that information and, you know, that was it. My life changed overnight.

"This street here we're sittin' on," he says as we sit talking in the Café Figaro on Bleecker and MacDougal, "was where I first experienced the concept of poetry readings. There was a place called the Scene where the Café Borgia is now in 1958 that had poetry readings, and there was the Gaslight where all the Beats read in early '58, there were other places along here, but mainly the Gaslight and the Scene where there were readings all the time."

"Did you start reading at them right away?"

"Oh, no. I was so shy, I would have never approached. . . . I remember once my future wife and I were sitting in the Figaro almost at this table and it was around 1959, and Ferlinghetti walked by and pressed his nose against the glass. Little did I know that a few years later Ferlinghetti would be my publisher and we'd be friends, but I mean this deity pressed his nose against the pane of glass, oh wow. I used to go to these readings and I'd see Kerouac and Edward Dahlberg, and I was too shy to think I had anything. . . . I mean I used to hang out, I would never have made myself known to these people, my God."

But whether as participant or voyeur, Sanders found the Figaro in those days a great place to take in the scene. "I spent many an hour staring in this place," he says. "This was stare headquarters for me. My wife used to come in here and she had this leather vest and Alan Block sandals laced up to her knees, oh man, in a black turtleneck sweater. This was the woman I was later to marry, she was nineteen years old, from Queens, determined to look like a Village woman, you know, not a girl from Queens, with the black kohl around her eyes and straight blond hair and a tight skirt, oh man. We'd sit in here, that table there, trying to figure out where we could go to fuck."

"I thought *Howl* was the cat's pajamas," says Tuli Kupferberg, who was later to be Sanders's partner in the Fugs. "I guess because of its range, you know. It was political and it was personal and it seemed to free the forms up. It was certainly what was needed at the time. It really came like a great cleansing shower, something that opened up everything again."

And not only in America. In Europe, *Howl* had a similar impact, and Yevtushenko, now Russia's most visible poet, told me recently that in the early sixties Ginsberg and other Beat writers hit Russian poets with much the same effect.

America in the fifties had large numbers of people in what today would be called internal exile, a condition creating a kind of subversive sensibility maybe best described by the title Herb Gold refused to relinquish, *The Man Who Was Not With It.* In this mode, even screwing up became a form of resistance. It was the heyday of the antihero and the *schlemiel.* Given the fifties, the emergence of a Woody Allen was unavoidable. If you happened to be one of these inadvertent subverts, your career inevitably turned out to be a painful comedy, psychological slapstick pitting your real self against your official cover identity. I was at Brandeis in disguise, presumably to earn a doctorate I had no intention of getting. Actually I was there because my teaching fellowship both supported me and spared me for two years from the military efforts of an inimical regime, and, more important, because this academy was dominated not by academics, but precisely by the intellectuals I assumed were the vanguard of the underground, and whom I took to be in tune with my real self.

Unfortunately, the Brandeis intellectuals don't recognize my real self. Or if they do, they don't like it. Much to my surprise it develops that what they would like is for me to become a good academic. Yes, they know that my ambition is to become a writer, but they've come across young men with this ambition before. And besides, as I am advised by Irving Howe and poet-scholar J. V. Cunningham on one occasion when I announce my intention to drop out, why give up the chance for a successful career in the university system? A writer's life is precarious. Why not choose security and do both? And besides, what are you going to do in New York? Write ad copy? Become an editor? Write reviews for *Time*? Howe shakes his head. He's tried this stuff, there's no future in it. He argues at me like a shrewd East European Talmud scholar brought up on the spinach of American secular life. The option of withdrawing to the underground and living cheap doesn't even exist. When I finally do this a few years later, Cunningham gets the impression I must be rich since I have no visible means of support.

At stake here was that vague homunculus I chose to call my real self, independent of middle-class definitions of success and failure. This was the phenomenon vulgarized at the time as "identity crisis," but it was a real issue and it will remain a real issue. Is the American personality simply the sum of success-driven responses to the network of cultural pressures? Or is it the stubborn assertion of a virtuous independence, however unexamined? Horatio Alger or the Lone Ranger? Is there such a thing as a real self, and if there isn't, what makes life worth living? Consumption of products? Liberty and justice for clones? Social welfare for pods?

One day in the faculty dining room, Philip Rahv grumbles to me that a young writer, Philip Roth, is pestering him to publish his stories. He claims that Roth's work is at odds with itself. "I told him you can't be Scott Fitzgerald and Franz Kafka at the same time," he grumbles. Everything Rahv says in his rumbling East European mumble sounds grumbling, when you can understand it at all. His speech is as heavy as his bearish figure. The only thing agile about him is his mind.

The difference between Fitzgerald and Kafka is the same difference as that between Horatio Alger and the Lone Ranger at another level.

If Kafka, who had a mind so fine that anything could violate it, had an allergy to entering his mantic projections in the public discourse by publishing them, for Fitzgerald success in that discourse was everything. In the schizoid dialogue of the American psyche, the real self is Emersonian, passive, innocent, and spontaneous, while the public self needs to be aggressive, power oriented, and politic. Part of the implicit strategy of the Beats was to reintroduce the real self into the public arena while the intellectuals, with their consciousness of *Realpolitik*, were still expressing themselves in terms of the power play of polemic. Pre-Vietnam America was still learning about the limits of power, and the idea that it's sometimes better to be negatively capable than positively impotent was still news unless you happened to be a certain kind of artist.

The pervasive intellectual tone at Brandeis was European, and the fact that the original building and center of campus life was an imitation castle seemed a symbolic coincidence. Many of the academics, rather than being narrow specialists, were intellectuals of broad range in the European tradition and there were many professors who were in fact émigrés from a wide variety of European countries. The lingua franca of the Brandeis old guard seemed to be Yiddish. Howe tells of being interviewed for his job there in Yiddish. Any lingua franca helped. At times it was hard to understand the polyglot accents of English spoken by some of the faculty. This communication problem was symptomatic of Brandeis's privileged isolation at the time. It was an exceptional Europhile enclave within American culture. That's why I liked it. That's also why I didn't like it.

The "Permanent Crisis" crisis, which effectively ends my efforts to make a satisfactory connection at Brandeis, involves a public reading of that story—which was later to become the initial story in my first book of stories—to the Brandeis literati. The story, my first real story, is written in one long sentence, a device that can be traced to the circumstance of my studying Faulkner intensively with Howe. Its take is to express a political situation at the level of personal experience, a strategem certainly on the wavelength of Howe's *Politics and the Novel*, which I admire. I realize that the faculty is dominated by professors whose taste for innovation ends with the great Moderns of yesteryear, at best, but I figure Faulkner, politics—Irving will really like this one. When I'm done reading Irving doesn't even say anything to me. Instead he goes and yells at the grad student organizing the readings for allowing this kind of thing to go on at a college gathering. Howe does not intend to be an adversary, and this is undoubtedly a fit of temper, i.e., he means it. If I ever have any illusions that the intellectual's turf is the territory I should be lighting out for, I know right there that I'm making a big mistake.

I did not know yet that in America artists and intellectuals are necessarily different sorts of critters, committed to the schizy split that pits the real self against the public self, even when the two selves are part of the same psyche. Art is impelled by the anarchic force of eros, and pleasure can be experienced spontaneously only by a real self. A public self, insofar as it is divorced from the emotional life, which it puts to one side in the interests of calculation, policy, and power, can register feeling of any kind only in a limited way. In such a situation, the creative arts will always have a potentially subversive force, the more so the more they are innovative and unassimilated at the public level. The effect of such art can be disruptive and without regard to received ideas of what is right and good, as conservative critics and authoritarian regimes are well aware. American intellectuals have tended to be sociopolitical in orientation, and do their best to redirect the erotic force of art toward their concerns with good and bad, right and wrong. Furthermore, from the perspective of form, which is necessarily that of the artist, art does not operate on the ethical plane in so direct a way.

One day Alfred Kazin, another intellectual big shot with whom I expect to connect, comes to give a lecture, yet when I ask some innocent question at the end of his speech he takes off on this five-minute tirade about academics, beginning with "You graduate students," leaving me in a state of confusion and Howe furious. But sometimes it's good to get kicked in the face, because that bit of nastiness exposes to me once and for all my terminally false position. When I get an offer to begin my academic career teaching at a good Midwestern school, despite the urging of my advisers—"So what if you don't like the Midwest," says Irving, "you get a student claque, you publish your book, you stay for three years and find another job"—I turn it down without a second thought, and leave for New York.

When I finally come back to Brandeis a few years later to take my doctoral exams, it's probably more than chance that the night before the exams I fall in with a sexy lady in a black dress who keeps me up all night dancing, drinking, and screwing. The next morning I find myself confronting a day of exams on no sleep and a terrible hangover. Somehow I manage to bumble through and pass, wondering why I do this kind of thing to myself. I did them as assertions of identity, however foolish, against an encroaching and alien mentality. No regrets.

New York quickly confirmed my sense that Bleecker Street and environs was where it was at. A lot of things were opening up in New York toward the end of the fifties, and not only because of poetry. Izzy Young of the Folklore Center on MacDougal Street and Howard Moody, pastor of the Judson Church, an underground culture center on Washington Square, organized and ran the Sunday folk music protests in the Square. There was a city ordinance out that prohibited music in Washington Square Park, which had been a center for folk singers from all over New York. It was an early attempt at gentrification. The protests were "one of the first battles in America where the outs beat city hall," says Howard Smith. "The thing got bigger every week. Each week it drew more and more people. It was huge, it was really heavy."

"Did people get beaten up by the cops?"

"Very badly. Real, heavy riots. And all over should musicians be allowed to play in the park."

"The cops had wanted us to leave," recalls Tuli Kupferberg. "We had sat down in the circle. Izzy had said, 'Let's leave,' and just as he says, 'Let's leave,' the cops come charging in and beating people up. Because they had gotten the command five minutes before.... The guys who were beating us had heard Izzy say that too, they could have disobeyed orders, but no. I think, you know, some of them might have gotten a thrill. Anyway, that was the classical example of police stupidity. They had got what they wanted, and then they beat everyone up anyway."

"Was that the final big demonstration?"

"Yeah, I think permission was given to sing in the park. Somehow the singers won most of what they wanted."

"That was one of the first highly-publicized-all-over-America battles against city hall where city hall backed down," continues Smith. "The next one was when Robert Moses tried to put the highway right through Washington Square Park. And we won that one. Women laying down with their babies in front of the bulldozers. The *Voice* was very instrumental in beating that one, and the Village Independent Democrats. The Village was changing, and a lot of people who were willing to stand up, really stand up for what they believed were moving in. The next big demonstration years later was the Julian Beck–Judith Malina over not taking shelter [in A-bomb drills]. And the first few of those were held in Washington Square Park. . . . There were only maybe fifteen or twenty of them, that's all you could see other than police anywhere. And they did arrest them. But by the sixth or seventh demonstration they filled Times Square. Each one got bigger. And I would say that those were three very important stepping-stones toward later militancy and around the country that gave people the idea that you could fight city hall. That was literally how it was always written about, as an example that if citizens got together in a community feeling, you could win."

The fact that the Village was swinging by the time Sanders, myself, and others like us got there was partly because of the receptivity of a handful of promoters and club owners to what was happening in the new scene. These included Izzy Young, who booked folk singers into Mike Porco's club—which, after being taken over by Porco himself, became well known as Gerde's Folk City, where many famous folksters got their start—as well as Art D'Lugoff, who owned the Village Gate. But most important were Tom Ziegler and especially John Mitchell. Mitchell was the original owner of the Figaro, and Ziegler, who was his manager, took it over from him. Mitchell owned the Gaslight on MacDougal and later the Fat Black Pussycat.

Mitchell ran the Gaslight "with a shotgun," according to Ted Joans. "He literally had a shotgun, he had a single-shot shotgun, and he used to have a sign above the door, 'No, your goddamn friends are not in here.' Because you walk to the door, instead of paying the dollar, you said, 'Well, I'm looking for a friend,' you know. A lot of people used to do that shit. And then they'd come in and wouldn't come out. And then he had a shotgun to back it, and he was training his dog to be mean, but his dog, if you had some food the dog would no longer be mean." When Mitchell left the Village he went to Torremolinos, outpost of Bohemia in southern Spain, where, according to Howard Smith, he opened a Fat Black Pussycat that became the center of the expatriate community there.

One day around 1980, an old friend of Smith, Kristina Gorby, an avant-garde dress designer from the sixties married to painter Jules Olitski, calls Smith and says, "You wouldn't believe who's sitting here in my house. John Mitchell." Mitchell had actually built the original Figaro, before it moved to the corner of Bleecker and MacDougal, and then, in the seventies, to Beverly Hills, then later reopened in the Village at the same corner location. But the original Figaro "was a few doors down from the San Remo on Bleecker," says Smith. "He built it and then Tom Ziegler stole Royce, his girlfriend, that's what I always heard." Then she had an auto accident in Spain. "She came back paralyzed and mentally retarded from the accident and Tom took care of her for the rest of her life. She was not quite a vegetable but wasn't pleasant. She was very well liked by everybody and was beautiful, and they had long since split up. As soon as that happened he went right over, got her, and took care of her, as weird as he was, with all of his girlfriends, right to the end he took care of her.

"Tom and Mitchell were always bitter, vicious, nasty enemies from the day they saw each other. Both are macho, aren't afraid of fist fights with people. So anyway, so I went over to Kristina's house and there was John Mitchell, he was always a small little wiry guy but the type that you wouldn't want to fight with because he looked like he'd kill you. Over anything—if you had an argument over this napkin he'd kill you. And there he was, half his teeth gone, very drunk, a chronic alcoholic as was Tom Ziegler, and really fucked up, and as usual with one of the most beautiful girls I'd ever seen, all of about twenty-one, French, but exquisite, a French model is what she looked like. Totally devoted, 'Oh, John!' and he was a mess, a wreck. He always had that touch. I think Kristina's theory was that he was so dangerous, certain types are very masochistic, beautiful women are attracted to men that they think might kill somebody, might kill them. I don't know, who knows, he was always with incredible beautiful women. Tom Ziegler always was, but was a real ladies' man and was very good looking. John Mitchell was this little swamp rat.

"There were always a lot of fights at the Figaro. The Figaro was famous as a fighting place. Ziegler would beat people up. None of his friends, but if a customer pinched a waitress and the waitress said, 'That guy's really annoying me,' Tom would go over and knock him out."

"He became a karate expert after he moved the Figaro to Los Angeles, Mickey Ruskin told me," I add. Ruskin, owner of Max's Kansas City, was an admiring rival of Ziegler in that both the Figaro and Max's had excellent competing softball teams.

"He didn't even need that. Tom said the best karate is hit the guy before he thinks you're gonna hit him. We used to pull him off of a lot of people. There were a lot of fights there but not over issues, it was like against outsiders, or Tom wanting to let off steam, things like that."

By the late fifties, the influence of books like *Howl* and *On the Road*, and media coverage of the life style that produced them, was such that the Village belonged to the Beats. Within a couple of years Mike Wallace would be interviewing people at the Gaslight for a special on the Beat Generation.

The action in the coffee shops was a big change from the bar scene in the Village, partly reflecting a switch from booze to drugs among younger subterraneans, and partly the fact that it was cheaper and easier to start a coffee shop than a bar. But whether they served alcohol or coffee, the café explosion in the Village provided gathering places and performance spaces for a new generation of writers and musicians, especially folk singers. At the Figaro, Ziegler opened a basement for music, but since he didn't have the right city permit for the kids who came to dance, he devised a solution whereby the kids were strapped in their seats to prevent any spontaneous violations.

Some of the places on the circuit were Rick Allmen's Café Bizarre; the Café Rafio, in front of which its manager was shot by a tenant in the building; the Rienzi, started by five or six writers and painters, above which Ted Joans would hold rent parties in his apartment; and the Limelight.

Poet and intermedia artist Dick Higgins's old route for poetry readings, which they used to call "the Elephant Walk," ended west of Second Avenue in the days before the East Village blossomed. "I used to read in the coffee shops with the Beat poets. I never knew how the Elephant Walk got its name, it wasn't my name. It was a circuit, and it started at S and G Corner, Sodom and Gomorrah Corner, which was the corner of Sixth Avenue and Eighth Street, where a lot of the hustlers hung out, so that's how it got its name, and then one used to walk in on Eighth Street, go along MacDougal Street past the old Meat Rack—which was more strictly homosexual—on the Park, it was the metal railings that used to be cruising grounds. And then you'd get into MacDougal Street proper, the coffee houses, and particularly the folk coffee houses. For example Leonard Cohen used to read, that was the City Lights, that was quite a strong coffee house, it had quite a following. And then when you hit Bleecker Street it would turn east again to the Epitome coffee shop," which was managed by painter Larry Poons and had art exhibitions. There they held readings and "sort of miniature performances, what we would call art performances today. That was the center, that was where we hung out for about two years, about '58 and '59. Poons got involved for a while with Dick Bellamy, who had the Green Gallery, and had his first big shows there. The Elephant Walk ended where West Broadway and Bleecker Street met, which is what's now called La Guardia Place. Past that, there were no coffee shops, there was like a no-man's-land between those areas and the Second Avenue scene."

"The Limelight, remember where the Limelight was a few years ago over on Seventh Avenue South?" asks Howard Smith. It was opened by Helen Gee. "No liquor license. One of the reasons she didn't want a liquor license, she didn't want the Mafia to give her trouble. She had never run a place. The only reason she opened it as a coffee shop–restaurant, she was obsessed with photography. Those were in the days when one of the biggest arguments hanging out in the bars and coffee shops was, was photography an art or wasn't it? There'd be fist fights over that. I remember vicious, all-night battles, groups, people screaming at each other."

"It was a big hang-out, the Off-Broadway crowd especially hung out there, the actresses, actors, all the photographers who were anybody hung out there. Jean Shepherd eventually did his radio show live from there. The Mafia tried to get control of her place many, many times and she eventually sold it years later. She kept her photo collection going, and in recent years her collection's been shown in many museums all over the world. She's now worth a lot of money, because eventually those photos were worth a fortune—Westons and Ansel Adams. I think she told me once the most expensive photo she ever bought was twenty-five dollars. Her place was one of the most intellectual of all the hang-outs. People who weren't just full of shit but really did things. There was a little of everything, writers, actors, a lot of the *Voice* people."

One of the more interesting places to open in the second half of the fifties was Johnny Romero's, because it was a sign of changing times. Romero was a West Indian, and his bar was a racially mixed scene—that is, Black guys and white girls. It had its happy side and its sinister side. "It was the first bar, the only bar that I knew of in the Village that had interracial dating," says David Behrens. "And it had a calypso jukebox and it was probably the most happy place in the Village. I think to put it into perspective also is that Harry Belafonte was new that year, I mean that was the year that calypso was big in New York. I think that there were a lot of people who went there who were very proud to be there. It was a place you went to to support, I mean I remember feeling that way. You were glad that this was what was happening in America. Although it wasn't happening anywhere else in America. It became a political gesture to go there."

I first meet Romero in Paris, I think with Ishmael Reed, years after his place has closed. Then another time I recognize him in Rue Saint-André-des-Arts in the Latin Quarter and catch up with him in a little *tabac.* I want to talk to him about his bar and how much I enjoyed it in the old days. Ishmael has told me that he's a strange, bitter guy. Romero doesn't want to talk about it. He's sullen and offish. Maybe he thinks I'm a cop. Or maybe he doesn't like white people, especially if they're Americans. At the time I don't know the story about what happened to his bar.

Romero's was in Minetta Lane, a narrow alley that runs between Bleecker and Sixth Avenue. Fielding Dawson describes it in one of his stories. "The jukebox was to the left of the door, and beyond it was a small rectangular wooden table, which fit into a small corner, fitted with an L-shaped bench, and beyond that on the left still, were a lot of posters most of Negro guys and women. . . . The bar ran the length of the place, opposite the jukebox." There was a small garden out back with three or four tables. "Most white cats including myself spoke a spade musician's lingo and it was (embarrassing) strange, me talking to some spade cat imitating his jive. Hi man, gimme some skin! . . . What not many people knew was Romero's was an essentially middle-class place. Black guys and their chicks drove downtown in their big cars, or their sports cars . . . especially on weekends. It was the downtown place to go. I guess there were black gangsters and black detectives, too. . . . People were friendly. . . . It was Johnny's effect. He was a popular guy. Everybody liked him; he was very friendly. . . . The black guys who went there were *big,* big guys, and some of them must have been prize fighters." Dawson mentions meeting Roberto Clemente there.

Howard Smith's take catches the other side of Romero's.

"Do you know the story about Johnny Romero?" I ask him.

"Yeah."

"What was it?"

"That was one of the weirdest places I had ever been in in my life. Those were the days when the Village was a little known for interracial relationships but very few, I mean it was still dangerous for a Black guy to walk with a white girl in the South Village, he'd get beaten up. Johnny Romero was known on the scene as somebody who only went with white girls, and word went around that he'd opened this incredible place, like something you'd read about in novels about Paris in the twenties. I went to the place, I'll tell you it looked like the real McCoy to me. I'd never been in a place up to that point in my life that looked more dangerous. Wooo! Especially to an innocent Jewish kid from New Jersey, I'll tell you. And the Black guys in there did not look like they were fooling around, either. I mean they looked like they'd just as soon cut you up. They looked like guys fresh out of Harlem who heard that you could get white girls and they were there, but they didn't care about the Village, reading books, they didn't care about anything, they were there for poontang. That's what they were there for. And that was one of the few places that I saw where people smoked joints out in the open. In those days you didn't even smoke a joint out in the open at a party. You remember those days. It was real weird, some nights there'd be almost no one in it, and the next night it would be packed to the walls. I never felt safe in there. But like everyone else I was drawn to it because this was really different from any other place."

"And then there were rumors around that he was going out with Carmine de Sapio's daughter. That was the story. And that word went around and everybody said, God, they'll kill him. What are they gonna do? They're gonna kill him. Carmine de Sapio was a national political power, and certainly in the Village, my God. He almost made Harriman president. He and Richard Daley had equal power in backroom Democratic politics, and when the conventions would come around reporters from all over the country would ask de Sapio what he thought. We in the Village all felt he was a Mafia crook. So when everybody heard this it was like, what is he, crazy? You don't fool around with that. And then there were stories that they threatened him, that he was shot at, and then all of a sudden the place would close for a week or two, then it would be open again, and rumors would fly, what was going on? And all of a sudden it was closed, never to open again, nobody knew where he was, and then the rumors started that what they did was that they warned her, they warned him, they threatened him with everything possible, and finally they basically said, 'If you don't leave immediately this country, not the city, this country, and never see her again, you're dead.' And God knows what else they threatened him with. And also there was a story they also paid, they also gave him money. And he split. And that was the end of the relationship and it was the end of the place. That's the story."

De Sapio, who had been a Tammany liberal in his time and whose power base had been the old Italian Village and, supposedly, its mob connections, was later forced out of power by the new sophisticated gentry of the Village led by the Village Independent Democrats in a reform movement that helped launch Ed Koch's career. It's probably no accident that the man now Mayor Koch's chief adviser, Dan Wolf, was co-founder of *The Village Voice*. Some of us who were hot-under-the-collar reform sympathizers in those days now look back at de Sapio with a certain nostalgia.

Around the same time the underground began drifting over to the Lower East Side, subterraneans began to occupy old industrial lofts in significant numbers. There had always been a certain amount of loft life, especially among the painters, who needed the space. The lofts were scattered in various locations downtown, from Chelsea to East Tenth Street to Canal Street. Bond Street had some "very, very rudimentary lofts," says Gloria, "I mean but so rudimentary like, I mean Tony Frusella was staying with some people that had a loft in one of those buildings on Bond Street. It was really a junky loft. They had a fire place with huge gigantic logs and no furnishing at all and the sanitation and the plumbing was rudimentary if at all. Stanley Gould moved to a loft on Second Avenue over the Anderson Theater, below Eighth Street, there were lots of early lofts in those buildings. Romey Beardon used to live on Canal Street, that was the other loft scene. Romere Beardon, he's a painter and he's showing a lot now, he's a Black painter. That was kind of the beginning of the SoHo thing. Louise Nevelson had a loft on Third Street," as did Gloria's friend Chuck Mangrovite, who was building Wilhelm Reich's orgone boxes. A bit later, when the loft scene began to get a little more homey, the lofts provided the space for often enormous parties, which writer George Dennison used to refer to as "parties that changed people's lives." Westbeth, the low-rent creative artists' residence in the West Village, eventually came out of the loft movement when the painters finally got organized in response to loft harassment by landlords and the city.

Gloria's loft in Chelsea, one of the areas the subterraneans moved into, cost $51.75 a month for a whole floor, fireplace, and use of the roof for sunbathing. Other economies were possible. "Chuck had showed me how to turn the gas meter facing the wall so that it would tick backwards. One day the guy came to read the meter and it was facing the wall, and I panicked, I thought I was going to be thrown in jail. And he goes in the back and my heart is thumping, really it was like total panic. And like he looks at me and I'm panic stricken and he says, 'You know, there's something very funny I notice a lot on this block, the meter is facing the wall where it's very hard to read. Do you have a mirror I can use?' "

While the Beat style was coalescing and spreading through the bars and coffee houses of the Village, another style was being promoted by Norman Mailer, through his role in the early *Village Voice*, as well as through his writing and what might be called his socioliterary behavior. Mailer, in the mid-fifties, set about trying to shape his life as another might shape a novel. "If Mailer the failed novelist could not move the culture with his fictional imagination," according to Hilary Mills, his biographer, "he would make his own life a story that others would have to follow. It would inspire the underground army of similar souls which Mailer suddenly envisioned around him."

For Mailer, the *Voice*, which he helped start, was a public platform in an ideological campaign. "Norman felt that we were much too conservative on an ideological level," says Ed Fancher. "They wanted a straight paper that was going to make some money," says John Wilcock of Wolf and Fancher, "and Mailer was too far out for them." Mailer's break with the *Voice*, however, came ostensibly on a writer's issue—a typo that distorted a sentence in one of his columns.

But if Mailer was too radical—or maybe just too erratic—for the newspaper business, it was evidently as much in the direction of the political intellectuals as in that of the creative artists. Mailer spoke the language of the intellectuals as well as that of the artists, was in an intellectual as well as a creative tradition, which possibly helps explain why Mailer never attracted the animosity that the Beat writers did, and continues as the aberrant darling of critics and intelligentsia. Back at Brandeis, for example, Philip Rahv keeps urging Mailer's

Barbary Shore on me enthusiastically. So finally I go read the novel, fail to be thrilled, and ask Rahv what's so good about it. Rahv looks miffed. "It's written in a secret code," he answers evasively, referring to the Trotsky allusions in the book, thereby invoking an intellopol lingua franca I supposedly don't understand. But it's not that I don't understand. It doesn't turn me on.

If Mailer gets plenty of flak from those who consider themselves in an adversary relation to the establishment, in part it's because he is so easily indulged by it. How many times have I heard, on asking one of Mailer's intellectual acquaintances about something foolish he's done, the comment, delivered with a shrug, that "Mailer is Mailer"? As if he were the exception that proves—what? That smart Jewish boys can be just as crazy as macho goys? "The secret language of the dirty little secret of success," writes Norman Podhoretz in his autobiographical *Making It,* "as I was discovering from the images in which my own fantasies of failure, renunciation, and salvation were spontaneously cast, was the language of Christianity." It's fascinating that Podhoretz, editor of the Jewish *Commentary* magazine, yet whose career, if one is to believe his autobiography, seems to have been driven by a flight from Jewishness, originally wanted to write, instead of an autobiography, a biography of Mailer.

There has to be an element of self-contempt in the admiration of intellectuals and academics for Mailer's daring to be what they are not, could not be, and in many cases would not want to be. Podhoretz considers Mailer's pursuit of money and celebrity in addition to intellectual influence a noble public "experiment," rather than the normal behavior of an American who has bought into the familiar Horatio Alger syndrome. Mailer "would 'settle for nothing less,'" asserts Podhoretz, "than making a revolution in the consciousness of his time, *and* earning millions of dollars, *and* achieving the very types of American celebrityhood." Mailer's exercise of ambition may be illuminating for the unworldly, but is hardly a brilliant spiritual adventure.

"Norman has enormous ambivalence," says Ed Fancher of Mailer. "First of all, he's in opposition. Second of all, he's a multimillionaire.... He's very interested in money. He's very money oriented, he goes crazy." Let Mailer be Mailer. He is compelling because of his ambivalence as he enacts for us a painful duality in our culture, expressing tensions between intellectual excellence and ambition, between justice and success. Because of this Mailer, as an artist, is able to become one of those figures whose vices are also their virtues. And in opposing so emphatically the underground cult of failure with the middle-class cult of success, he has inadvertently called into question the legitimacy of both.

In a "footnote" to "The White Negro," called "Hipster and Beatnik," he explains of the Hipster, "that in a time of crisis, he would look for power, and in the absence of a radical spirit in the American air, the choices of power which will present themselves are more likely to come from the Right than the moribund liberalities of the Left." Mailer is a Hipster, as he conceives the term. It is easy to see how, "in a time of crisis," he might gravitate to the right. "One is a rebel or one conforms," writes Mailer, "one is a frontiersman in the Wild West of American night life, or else a Square cell, trapped in the totalitarian tissues of American society, doomed willy-nilly to conform if one is to succeed." Mailer is both a frontiersman and a conformist, both an explorer of the Wild West and trapped in the tissues of American society and its compulsion to success.

In fact, in the dialectic Mailer sets up, the frontiersman must become the settler, the Lone Ranger must become Horatio Alger, because the loner, the outsider, the explorer, is always doomed to fail, dooms himself to fail in conformist terms. And the one thing Mailer absolutely cannot do is fail. Poet William Carlos Williams, in his account of American history, *In the American Grain,* describes a type of outsider, doomed to failure, Columbus, Daniel Boone, who nevertheless is essential to the ongoing discovery of America. "It is my earnest desire," wrote Melville during the composition of *Moby Dick,* "to write those sort of books which are said to 'fail.'" In failure Melville was a brilliant success. Mailer's ambition is not of that kind. He insists on the claim of talent to mainstream success.

"I was just reading Kerouac's *The Subterraneans,*" I remark to Judith Malina, talking in her Paris apartment. "And it gets very annoying finally, the business about who's saintly and who isn't saintly and how saintly he, Kerouac, is, especially in that book where there are some unpleasant sexist sides. And just after that I read Norman

Mailer's book *Armies of the Night* and the thing that I then noticed is that he insists on the fact that he is not innocent, that he likes sin and assumes a diabolical pose, and after Kerouac it was a kind of relief."

"I'm a moralist," responds Malina, a stagy magnetism and emphasis evident even as she talks informally. "I think morality is really it. I think saintliness is the thing that we want. . . . I'm a Gandhian in that sense. I think that there is purity and I think it is available to us and I think we should strive for it every single second including this one. And I think Kerouac was brave and good to say it. I *despise* Mailer for his male cowardice, his fear of goodness, his fear of purity, his distrust of honesty and honor, I despise him because he's a coward. He thinks he's such a brave macho man, he stabs his wife and he's proud of it, he defends murder as murder—not to defend the murderer, of course I approve—but to defend murder as justifiable, to defend toughness of attitude, to defend hardheartedness, I mean I find him a pathetic devil's advocate, I don't think he can help himself."

"Mailer once said in my presence," says Seymour Krim in a café in the West Village, "that he loved Allen Ginsberg but he thought he was a damn fool. In other words, by being so exposed, and so bizarre." Krim's granny glasses and considered phrases give him the air of an intellectual Bohemian, a role that, in his writing, he has rebelled against as out of step with American culture. Krim's influential 1959–60 essay "Making It!" is the classic, if ironic, sneer at the underground cult of failure: "Middle-class ideals of success once curled the lip of the intellectual; today he grins not, neither does he snide. . . . You've got to move, hustle, go for the ultimate broke or you'll be left with a handful of nothing. . . . *Baby, that world went up in the cornball illusions of yesterday!* . . . The only enemy today is failure, failure, failure, and the only true friend is—success!" But what Krim perceived with irony, Mailer acted out in his career.

"I think the Beat Generation offered new possibilities to Mailer but he would never adopt that style," Krim tells me. "It was just alien to him, it seemed naïve. It seemed like Moondog on Broadway wearing a big blanket. Norman would never do that. . . . I think he regarded them with a twinkle in his eye. He was always interested in money.

And that kind of idealism, rank idealism, I think was something he couldn't relate to."

"What about selling out?" I ask. "Was that a concept that would have meant anything to him?"

"After *The Naked and the Dead,* unlike the rest of us, he was always conscious of having been a best-selling writer, and will always be conscious of it. It became some kind of standard for him. I mean you could talk literature all you wanted but he was very conscious of the power, of the reality of that, which does not come to most literary writers. So he always wanted to straddle those two worlds."

It is not surprising that Beat attitudes would be alien to Mailer as White Negro Hipster. Despite Herb Gold's 1960 contention that a Beatnik "is the hipster parodied and packaged as a commercial product," and promoted by his Columbia schoolmate Allen Ginsberg, "the greatest publicist for literary fashion since Ezra Pound," there are important differences between Hip and Beat. Not that Gold's quip that the Beatnik "bears the same relation to the hipster as the cornflake does to a field of corn," is completely off the wall. Noting the commodity component of the Beat movement, its association with the promo techniques of the advertising world, in which Ginsberg briefly worked—as of course did another art publicity genius, Andy Warhol—is not unjust. But there is more to the Hip-Beat distinction than that.

"Kerouac," says Allen Ginsberg of the Hipster, as opposed to Beat, underground, "thought that the cool element, especially Mailer's interpretation as a psychopathic knifer, and John Clellon Holmes' as a juvenile delinquent, was an idiot misinterpretation of a yea-saying, Dostoyevskian, healthy colossus like Neal Cassady. Kerouac was warm. Warmth, tenderness. Burroughs was very tender-hearted. Kerouac was really strong about that view, from Lawrence Lipton's *Holy Barbarians* on, that the ideologization of the Beatnik thing diverted it entirely from the open mind and universal intelligence, Shakespearian intelligence, Burroughsian intelligence, to an angry and violence-prone, antifamily, anti-middle-class attack, and demeaned the whole scene, and diverted all the energy into materialistic fighting and arguments and anger, whereas there should have been a much more angelic and lamby politics all along. With the introduction of Mailer's 'White

Negro' he was praising psychopathy instead of the Holy Lamb and the second religiousness, the psychopath who was sticking a knife into the white middle class. So that white-middle-class contempt wasn't from Kerouac, that was from Mailer. And it was only a phase for him, I think. I don't know if that was his term, it might be unfair, but the notion of emotionless rather than emotional, as cool, the Hipster being cool, that's the Mailer–Anatole Broyard branch. Then that developed through Lawrence Lipton's book, interpreting it as holy barbarians from a Marxist point of view, which Kerouac *hated,* see, and to try and take what we were doing and make it into political aggression, till by the time 1968, Chicago, he said, 'Those Jews Ginsberg, Hoffman, and Rubin, all they're doing is finding new reasons for spitefulness.'

"The demonstration in the park [at the 1968 Chicago Democratic convention] was supposed to have been a festival of life. It would have been great if they had done that but instead they sabotaged it. Wolf Lowenthal the first day was teaching karate when he should have been teaching t'ai chi. He's now teaching t'ai chi and he says, 'Oh what a mistake, my God, who sent that signal out?' ... Revolutionary aggression fantasies. I went there and I complained to Tom Hayden and Rennie Davis about a month before the thing, because we had started, Ed Sanders and Davis and Dellinger and Rubin and Hoffman and myself and a couple of others, the original signers of the Yippie manifesto, and made the press conference that announced, quote, 'festival of life.' And it was supposed to be rock 'n' roll bands and present something that would overjoy people compared to the drag of the war convention. And the political radicals by then were interested in confrontation to show how bad the fascism was."

It's fairly obvious that Kerouac's point of view, with its stress on poverty, antimaterialism, fellow feeling—"the fact that everybody dies makes the world kind"—and pacifism, with its insistent imagery of saints and angels, with its pervasive visions, is deeply allied with a primitive Christianity, which may partly account for its apparently instinctive populist appeal. Populism and primitive Christianity intersect in the sanctity of the common man. Kerouac once described the ambience of the Beat state of mind as "the strange talk we'd heard among the early Hipsters of the end of the world and the Second Coming, stoned-out visions and even visitations, or believing, all inspired and fervent and free of bourgeois Bohemian materialism, such as Philip Lamantia being knocked off his chair by the angel in his vision of the books of the fathers of the church and of Christ crashing through time, Gregory Corso's visions of the devil and celestial heralds, Allen Ginsberg's visions of Harlem and elsewhere of the tearful divide in love, William Burroughs' reception of the word that he is the one prophet, Gary Snyder's Buddhist visions of the vow of salvation, peyote visions of all the myths being true, Philip Whalen's visions of the mellific flashes and forms of the roof flying off his house, Jack Kerouac's numerous visions of heaven, the golden eternity, bright light in the night woods, Herbert Huncke's geekish vision of Armageddon experienced in Sing-Sing, Neal Cassady's visions of reincarnation under God's will . . ."

But Kerouac's view also has ties with classic nineteenth-century American Transcendentalism. "Beat" for Kerouac meant, as he has written, "characters with a special spirituality who didn't gang up but were solitary Bartlebys staring out of the dead window of our civilization." Whether you take the withdrawn hero of Melville's "Bartleby the Scrivener" as a parody or celebration of the Transcendentalist character, the reference is both clear and appropriate. The split between the politicos and the Beats on the question of activism is much like a similar schism concerning the Transcendentalists that can be found in Emerson himself, and reminds one of the perhaps apocryphal exchange between Emerson and Thoreau when the former went to visit the latter, who was in jail for civil disobedience. "Henry, why are you there?" Emerson was supposed to have asked. Thoreau supposedly responded, "Why are you not here?"

Throughout the sixties, with the increasing tempo of activism, of the cultural-pacifist variety that Ginsberg favored as well as of the hard-edged ideological-political kind, Kerouac became increasingly conservative, anti-Semitic, withdrawn, and alcoholic. You have to wonder, why was Jack not there?

If Kerouac seems to have been the inspirational spirit of the Beat movement, in death he has become the Holy Ghost to Ginsberg's Apostle Paul and a multiplying series of gospel accounts. Ginsberg likes to stress Kerouac's gentleness and the view that the antagonism surrounding the Beats was initiated by the hostility of those reacting to them. "I wasn't interested in working in the system or outside of the system," Ginsberg tells me. "I didn't think that was the point at all. That's a Marxist-ideological-conceptual thing. The whole idea of Us and Them is obsolete. One, it's vanity and self-righteousness, and two, it polarizes unnecessarily."

What the Beat shared initially with the Hipster was withdrawal from the political and cultural struggle as defined ideologically by contemporary intellectual polemicists. John Clellon Holmes, introducing the Beat Generation in the mass media, wrote that even in "the wildest hipster, making a mystique of bop, drugs and the night life, there is no desire to shatter the 'square' society in which he lives, only to elude it." It will be Norman Mailer, both in ideological essays like "The White Negro" and in his media persona, who will repoliticize the Hipster, reengaging him in a hostile way with society and, paradoxically, putting his mystique at the service of social and economic ambition. But as there are differences between Mailer and Kerouac, so Kerouac and Ginsberg evolved in different ways.

"What was *Howl*," asks Nat Hentoff, speaking to me on the phone about Ginsberg, "but, in a very powerful, distilled way, an indictment of what was going on in the flat fifties—not only the end of ideology, but the end of real feeling. It was quite a howl then, and so of course was *On the Road* . . . as a rebuttal, or as an indictment of the kind of conformity, you know. . . . These were political attitudes, as I understand politics. Because on the other hand you have people like Daniel Bell, and Norman Podhoretz at the end of the fifties writing that collection of essays in which he essentially said what Bell had been saying—you don't need much ideology anymore, because, he was saying, we've solved all of our problems pretty much. And what Ginsberg and Kerouac were saying, and they weren't radicals politically in the sense that we use the term, but they were looking at things radically, getting to the root of things and saying the root, my God, is diseased, it's so shrunken as to have no feeling. It wasn't so much a call to action as a call to consciousness. And whatever Allen says now, he certainly was against the establishment.

My God, the establishment in those days thought of him as some kind of crazy, homosexual idiot, or somebody who had burned his brains out."

"Y'know the ball game they put on him?" says Corso, referring to Ginsberg in the fifties Remo. "The so-called early Hipsters? Him and Kerouac, this is what they laid on these two guys. Me and Allen or Jack would have heated, loving conversations. Their so-called sharp hip talk was this: 'Dig that aggression.' Can y'imagine that, they called us aggressive because of the way we talked. Maybe they were right."

Though Ginsberg denies that *Howl* is an angry poem, making a distinction between anger and "wrath," maybe part of the thrust of the Beat movement was that it released aggression suppressed by the cool of the Hipsters and by the general withdrawal of the underground as an adversary movement. Maybe it is Ginsberg's willingness to confront the commercial culture, immerse himself in impurity, and "turn shit to gold" that distinguishes him from the later, declining Kerouac. Maybe Mailer's ideologized, politicized, hostile version of the Hipster is in some ways not so different from Ginsberg's "angelic and lamby politics" in its release of subterranean aggression, permitting the underground once more to grapple with the system, even if —far more than Ginsberg's approach—on the terms of the system. Besides, Ginsberg is not universally considered angelic and lamby even by those who admire him. Some talk about his apparent need for recognition, his desire to be universally liked and admired. "He's very competitive," says poet and photographer Ira Cohen. "I don't think that I know a more competitive person. Anyway, what's the big deal? Allen Ginsberg is a very complicated subject, and depending on my mood I could say almost anything about Allen, and I think that's one of the things that's probably in the end the most provocative and interesting thing about Allen." After all, Ginsberg's Beat angelicism and Mailer's Hip diabolism are both part of the same Christian mythology, and the first primitive Christians were all maverick Jews.

In any case, how far is Mailer's conception of "advertisements for myself" from the billboard advertisement *Evergreen Review* ran in the subway, of Ginsberg in an Uncle Sam hat with the caption, "Join the underground"? And how far from there to the thriving business developed by underground photographer Fred McDarrah, called "Rent-a-Beatnik"? While there were differences in intent in these three phenomena of the late fifties and early sixties, they all portended a movement away from the isolation of the underground and its cult of failure, using the methods of the mainstream business culture for its own ends, and even adapting some of the ends of that culture to its own needs. Suddenly the Bohemian need to keep a critical distance from the establishment seemed to be evaporating, and the ideological distinctions on which that distancing had been based were becoming irrelevant both to the Beats and to their bitter polemical opponents like Norman Podhoretz, once Ginsberg's fellow student at Columbia.

"It was McDarrah's idea, it was McDarrah's business. McDarrah needed a poet that could communicate with the bourgeois, so that was Ted Joans," says Ted Joans. We're talking about Rent-a-Beatnik in his Latin Quarter apartment, five flights up on Rue Montagne Sainte-Geneviève. "Because he had heard me read, he watched me in those coffeehouses, how the people responded, so he said, 'Ah ha, this guy, along with the Beatniks I pick up on MacDougal Street, will be perfect.' "

"Yeah, but this was merchandising, right?"

"You see now, Corso was against me to be involved in the Fred McDarrah thing. He was talking about 'Look, you got to read to creeps and squares. . . .' But I told him, I said, 'Take it to the enemy.' I said, 'For example, Christ. Did he just preach to the Christians?' I said, 'It'd be a drag. They'd say, "Yeah, we know that, man, you preached that last week, we all hear that, you know. Shit, we all right. Lay it on people who don't know." ' I said, 'When I was brought up, a guy was in this church, a preacher, the preachers that travel around from church to church, he'd say, "All of you here that've seen Christ raise your hand." He's disappointed if all those hands were all up.' I said, 'But he was glad when he saw a whole bunch that were not up, cause that was the reason the church brought him in, brought him in to get those who couldn't raise their hand up.' You see, so that's it. In other words, to get to the so-called squares."

"Was Rent-a-Beatnik successful, by the way?"

"It was successful till the Internal Revenue stepped in, and that was the end of it. Because money was coming in. I don't know what Fred was making, but I know what he was paying me, and I know what he paid some of the Beatniks. They got something like five dollars an hour. Five dollars an hour was a lot of money. Five dollars an hour and all they could eat and transportation there and back. And I would receive from seventy-five up to two, three hundred dollars."

In Paris, eighty years before the Bleecker Street café scene started attracting a large enough middle-class audience to make an enterprise like Rent-a-Beatnik successful, there was a development in Bohemian circles similar enough to be instructive. Till the end of the 1870's, the Bohemian cafés were meeting places for creative artists, serving them as, in the words of historian of the café scene Georges Bernier, "rallying points, ideological workshops, springboards from which their artistic concepts spread." The most important café at the time was La Nouvelle Athènes, of which writer George Moore could say, "I did not go to either Oxford or Cambridge, but I went to La Nouvelle Athènes." But at about that time, a handful of clever entrepreneurs started a series of Bohemian cabarets whose function was basically to vend Bohemia to the middle class. The most famous of these were Le Chat Noir and Aristide Bruant's Le Mirliton, cabarets of the sort that in fact, to this day, provide the dominant image of Parisian Bohemia through the work of Toulouse-Lautrec. But contrary to those who prefer to think that such adversary movements are pre-destined to be assimilated by the bourgeoisie, the artists' meeting places did not disappear. La Nouvelle Athènes continued for years as an important Bohemian rendezvous, and other such cafés evolved elsewhere.

In the Village also there were artists' bars and cafés that proved durable, but the merchandising that was taking place along Bleecker Street pushed creative people toward the Lower East Side, if for no other reason than that the influx of middle-class money forced up prices. Art is the avant-garde of real estate, writer Andrei Codrescu has quipped. And real estate in Bohemia seems to follow an ineluctable evolution from artists to gays to the middle class. "Julius's was a big hang-out and I remember the night it turned gay," recalls Howard Smith. "They turned it gay in one night. You remember Julius's, it's still there. Sawdust on the floor. It was famous for its hamburgers, it was a big Bohemian hang-out on the corner of Waverly and Tenth Street, and it was a bar we all hung out in. There were very few hang-outs. The scene was so much smaller. There were maybe five bars and you'd make the circuit during the night, a few coffee shops and a few bars. So I remember one night we went into Julius's, there were four of us, myself and a friend and both of us had girlfriends, and we walked up and there was this bouncer at the door. They'd never had a bouncer at the door, and he said"—Smith assumes a gravelly baritone—" 'Where are you goin'?' We said, 'We're going in, what do you mean?' He said, 'No, we don't want youse in here anymore.' 'Whaddaya mean, we been hanging out here for the past two years, every night, whaddaya mean?' And he said, 'I don't think youse wanna come in here anymore.' We said, 'Well, why not, what's the problem?' He said, 'All right, one a ya, c'mere.' He grabbed me and said, 'Take a look.' I took a look. It was gay. They had hired gay bartenders, they had decided to make it a gay bar. That was the first time I'd ever seen that happen to a bar. We couldn't believe what was happening. That was the talk of the Village."

Some years later, in 1965, in a gesture that came to symbolize the surfacing of the underground, Bob Dylan, one of the many descending from Woody Guthrie's radical minstrelsy, turned his back on the ambience of Club 47, the Gaslight, and Gerde's Folk City, and at the Newport Folk Festival went electronic. Dylan's "band got onstage and started to play," says one who was onstage at the time. "All of the old folk mafia were saying, 'Get them offstage! This is a violation of what this festival is all about! This is pop music! This can't happen!' . . . Pete Seeger was livid. He ran back somewhere and came back with an ax, and he said, 'I am going to chop the power cables if you don't take them off the stage right now!' . . . There was a fight going on at the sound board where they were mixing, over the volume, trying to cut off Dylan. The first song was 'Maggie's Farm.' A lot of people were booing. The second song was 'Like a Rolling Stone.' Half were applauding, half booing."

Dylan, says Nat Hentoff, "is such a hustler, and has been since he first came to New York, and I knew him pretty early on. He's like some underworld people I know, who has been lying and hustling and playing parts for so long that it may be, and I think in his case, it finally did come to be, though I can't prove it, that he doesn't know who the hell he is anymore, that the masks keep coming off and on and whatever the thing is down at the last one below the final mask, I think he's lost that entirely. I don't believe anything he says anymore. At one point he told me back in the sixties that all the stuff that really got him catapulted into renown because he was riding the *Zeitgeist*—'The Masters of War,' you know, the initial songs, the civil rights songs—he said, 'I just made those up because I knew people wanted to hear it and I figured that would be the quickest way to make some money.' Now I don't think that's true. I don't think it was true at the time. He may well now believe it was true."

"Do you think he was putting you on?" I ask

"He could have been, I mean he's a master of that. My guess is he went electric the same way Miles Davis went electric. When Miles, I guess it was the early seventies, saw that there was this large rock audience, not only here but around the world, and he didn't see why he shouldn't have some of it, and he knew he couldn't do it with his regular instrumentation. And people said that Miles had sold out then too. I think that Dylan was after the biggest possible audience he could get, and he saw where rock was going and he too wanted to be part of it."

"So by the standards of Seeger this would be a sell-out," I say, "even though the music might, in fact I think in Dylan's case the music did, get better."

"I think it did get better. He really was of another generation. Pete could never be electric, so if Pete and the others made it an ideological or a virtue-testing thing, they were wrong on the face of it. The motivation was simply that Dylan always wanted a big audience. And anybody who knew Dylan should have known that. And Pete certainly did."

Allen Ginsberg goes further in support of Dylan, praising his changes as a paradigm of fluidity in contrast to the crippling ideological rigidity of the old radical left. Selling out, says Allen, is "one of those cornball ideas that people who didn't have anything to do got hung up on. I wouldn't have minded doing it if I could find what to sell out to. Geniuses don't sell out, in the sense that genius bursts the bounds of either selling out or not selling out. When somebody has real inspiration like Dylan, the move to electric is just simply the expansion of his genius into more forms, wilder forms. He's got that sense of negative capability being able to go all the way in, without necessarily losing himself. Committing himself and at the same time doing it like a poet, landing like the cat with nine lives."

In 1962, Ted Joans, a painter friend helping him move, went down to the Brooklyn docks "where I put my things on a Yugoslavian freighter and headed for Africa. And what did he move me in? An old, obsolete Cadillac hearse. Ha ha ha ha ha!" Ted guffaws—hilarious. "Isn't that great, to leave America in a Cadillac hearse? You know, alive! Alive too, alive. You know, it was a old big white one too. That's it." Ted, who ended up in Timbuctou, didn't come back till '68.

By the time Joans leaves for Africa, I've already been living on the Lower East Side for two years. It's cheap and it's peaceful, but grinding, and the changes have been coming fast. The neighborhood is starting to jump. In the old bar across the street, on Twelfth and Avenue B, you can find almost as many subterraneans now as local Polacks, and if you go there every afternoon as I do, you're on talking terms with Stanley, the owner. But there was a movement abroad between 1958 and '62, led once more by the Beats, who eventually settled in their now-famous grungy hotel off Place Saint-Michel in Paris around the same time as my first European trip. I think everybody felt the need for a break somewhere in there, a chance to cool out, feeling lucky to get out alive. I leave for Europe about the same time as Ted for Africa. In Torremolinos, southern Spain, sometime in 1963, I find such a dense colony of hip Americans that when I ask someone for the location of a place I'm thinking of renting, she tells me, "Oh, that's over in Spanish Town." And some guy tells me he's just gone through New York, and the Lower East Side is *the* scene. Especially this old bar on Twelfth and B that's so jammed wall to wall with Beatniks every night, you have to fight to get in. He's talking about Stanley's place.

4

STANLEY'S

You catch the bus down to Chatham Square in the lowest Lower East Side, a neighborhood of various but distinct populations, East Side ethnics, Chinatown Chinese, cops and lawyers from the nearby courts, Bowery bums. But at the hour of evening you usually go to O'Rourke's the streets are empty, no business being done in the area at night and many of the surrounding tenements condemned and deserted. A no-man's-land, and certainly a no-woman's-land, but inside O'Rourke's a never-never-land. I don't know how I'd heard about this place. It suddenly starts coming through on the grapevine and I finally go down there one night.

O'Rourke's is like a museum of old Bohemia, a revery by Saroyan, O'Neill purified by nostalgia, Steinbeck's Cannery Row in New York, so that even the Bowery bums in there metamorphose into some charming stage version of themselves. Ancient wrecked actors suddenly break into old-time vaudeville routines to enthusiastic applause. Drunk old washed-up good-natured whores dance around flinging skirts and ham sex innuendos. Cheap beer and happy drunks, boozy good-humored off-duty cops. Waves of spontaneous dancing sweep through the packed room now and then to polkas on the jukebox. Suddenly everything stops while some old guy does a juggling act, or everybody starts singing "Ta-ra-ra-boom-de-ay," believe it or not, followed by "The Sidewalks of New York," followed by maybe "When Irish Eyes Are Smiling." Local hoods, lawyers, and civil servants from the nearby courts. A sprinkling of artists and writers, an occasional face from old Bleecker Street scenes, and maybe a college kid now and then.

O'Rourke's was a scene long before Stanley's became a scene, but it was a different kind of scene. It had a "little old New York" kind of tone, strictly blue collar, heavily colored with the successive waves of New York's old immigrant generations. Though it was lowest east, on Pearl Street and Park Row where Police Plaza is now, it was a spectacular but typical sample of the East Side before we got there. And of what happened when we got there, especially after the "youth culture" moved in.

"No matter how much the hippies beg for dimes and quarters from obvious non-hippies on avenues B, A, and 1st, in Tompkins Square Park, on St. Mark's Place, and on 7th Street," writes author Clarence Major in an article from 1967, "that bright middle class glitter in their eyes and the underneath glow in the personalities speak of a security these natives can never know."

"It was a wonderful place," says actor and journalist Al Amateau, one of the first among us to stumble on O'Rourke's. "When we went there it was before it became fashionable. Maybe 1959, '60. It got popular toward the middle sixties," whereupon it also got pretty rough. "It got awfully rough. Very, very violent. I mean it used to be the place where cops would come. There were a couple of cops from around police headquarters who were incredible singers."

"What types?"

"The cops looked like cops. One guy was gray-haired and slightly effeminate, and the other guy was stocky, rough. And the guy who ran the bar was a Swiss German who worked at times in a dairy in Brooklyn. It was a remarkable place, and it changed, I mean the gentrification. We were gentrification. We were the death of that place." Before we got there the only fights were among the local wise guys against one another.

"As a matter of fact," Al goes on, "I had stopped going there soon after it became ultra-chic. I remember I saw one of our writer friends and a whole bunch of people who I had never expected to see in my life there. And it was a pleasant surprise, but then I got to figure it was no longer a place to go and get drunk and to listen to, quote, 'interesting people,' that is, people I wouldn't see elsewhere."

It was a beautiful bar. "Very open, very light. Old. Damn place was extremely old. The jukebox had a disk cut in the place and the emcee on the cut announced the place, 'O'Rourke's Bar, Pearl Street and Park Row,' with an appalling wonderful New York accent," says Al, who himself has the remnant of a tough-city-boy accent. From the 1880's or '90's, pressed-tin ceilings, a lot of mirrors, ornate wood. There was a time at O'Rourke's when every night, if you stayed late enough, was like New Year's Eve.

Then the middle class hits, first in the form of drop-outs from the middle class. Then college kids from NYU in increasing numbers. Then college kids from out of town and young professionals slumming. One night suddenly there's a large group of kids just graduated from Antioch standing in the middle of the bar, looking conspicuous. This doesn't happen in O'Rourke's. The place could accommodate a few college kids here and there in a good-natured way, but that was about its capacity. And these kids are all together in a group that sticks out like a peeled banana.

I can already see what's going to happen. O'Rourke's is based on a kind of camaraderie, the camaraderie of people who are never going to get anywhere and know they're never going to get anywhere, who don't even want to get anywhere. Suddenly the middle class makes an appearance in the form of a bunch of kids rebelling against the middle class and looking for something valid and real and so hip it's not even hip yet. But they emit the unmistakable vibes of acquisition, everybody there can smell it and it smells like a kind of spiritual BO their best friends can't tell them about because they have it too, but here it's neon, you can see it register in the bleary eyes of the old types when they notice the kids, in the red eyes of the bums, in the narrowing eyes of the local hoods: They got everything else, now they want this too. It's only a question now of this reaction reaching critical mass, nobody can stop it. I edge toward the door. What's going to happen is some little incident, some college kid being polite in a way that sounds too condescending, one of the girls getting uptight about someone feeling her ass, some last drunken straw.

What's going to happen is folk songs. It's already starting to happen, and when it happens it's as if present and future telescope into some dimension faster than time. The college kids are in a circle and they're going to start singing folk songs, they don't seem to realize that Pete Seeger is not one of the folks here. Even worse, some of them are going to break out guitars, it's proletarian night in summer camp, we're going to have a few songs about the toilers while toasting marshmallows. Worst of all, the singers are going to be in front of the bar, getting between the drinkers and the drink, always a big mistake when there's serious drinking going on, a mistake the singers don't even know they're making, won't have a chance to know, because before they have a chance to get through one chorus of "I dreamt I saw Joe Hill last night," and without warning of any kind, one of the hoods is going to ram his fist right into the singing mouth of one of the guitar players, one of the other kids will say something hip and reasonable like "Hey, come on, man, cool it, like let's break it up," and the hood will pick up the guitar and break it over the kid's head, and the other hoods will think, *What the fuck are we waiting for?* and everybody will start swinging, women screaming, guys crumpling and going down, bottles breaking, this is in fact what will happen and it will happen when it happens with incredible speed, before anyone can think it's spilling out the door, but by that time I'll already be getting into a cab, blood and glass on the sidewalk, two guys kicking another down in the gutter, the last thing I'll see as the cab pulls away is one of the hoods punching a college girl in the stomach, hard, a really cute blonde.

Around that time I saw a sign chalked up on the Jersey side of the Holland tunnel that said, NEW YORK FULL, TRY PHILADELPHIA. You couldn't even find an apartment in the Village anymore. Lynn Gingrass arrived in sixties New York from the Midwest to attend NYU. Lynn is a writer who used to both tend bar and play simultaneous chess downstairs at the Figaro. Today he is also a private detective whose talents were already manifest in the way he found an apartment back then. He discovered that the only way to get an apartment in the Village was to get *The Village Voice* at the *Voice* office itself on Sheridan Square early in the morning the moment it came out and race to a phone booth to call the advertised rentals. "So I did that a couple of times, and it still didn't work for me." He then decided the only thing to do was to beat the system, and he got together with a friend.

"So what we did, one of us got in the line waiting for the *Voice*, and the other person systematically went to every phone booth in the Square, and removed a little gizmo under the mouthpiece. Without it, you can hear the person talking, but it's needed for the person to hear you talk back. So, I took those out of every pay phone in the Sheridan Square area and put them all in my pocket. And you should have seen it. The pandemonium. Because people would get their paper, and then *run* to the phone booths while ripping the classifieds open so they could pop their dimes in and start dialing. It was amazing, all these people screaming into the phone and nothing was happening. And they were pounding and yelling and screaming. They just stared in disbelief when somebody actually got a phone that worked—I'd surreptitiously slipped the thing on. And then sort of at my leisure I called three or four places and was obviously the first person to go to each one of them, and I found this incredible place," ninety dollars a month for two floors in a pre–Revolutionary War brownstone with a circular staircase on Leroy Street.

Gradually, however, a new generation of scene-makers started finding one another and, simultaneously, friendly places where they could congregate. Poet Diane Wakoski came to New York from Berkeley in the fall of 1960 with composer Lamont Young. Young, probably through Richard Maxfield, an electronic composer who taught at the New School, met a Japanese electronic composer named Toshi Ishinagi, who was at that time married to Yoko Ono. Young and Yoko got together and started the 112 Chambers Street loft concerts.

"I was interested in poetry," says Wakoski, "and so I read *The Village Voice* the first week that I was there to find out what was going on in poetry." We're eating Creole food in a restaurant in Boulder, or she is, since I've just returned from reading my fiction around New Orleans the night before burned out on cayenne. Wakoski, who grew up in southern California, still has something of that blond California look. "I found an ad for a coffee house called the Tenth Street Coffee House that was having poetry readings, and I went there. That was Mickey Ruskin's first place. He had just gotten out of law school and decided that practicing law wasn't the most exciting thing in the world and wanted to do something interesting."

At New Year's, Wakoski went to LeRoi Jones's New Year's Eve party with someone who was being so bitchy-gay that she got very unhappy, whereupon someone invited her to another party at poet Armand Schwerner's. And that's where she met several of the group of poets, all at once, that she is perhaps most identified with: Schwerner, Jerome Rothenberg, Robert Kelly, George Economou, Rochelle Owens.

"And probably if I had been my normal self I would have been very quiet and a wallflower, but I had been so unhappy at LeRoi's party that when Diane di Prima came by and said, 'Do you want a pill?' I said, 'Sure.' I said, 'What is it?' She said, 'I don't know, something good.' I never took drugs, I hardly drank liquor. So I took this pill, which must have been some kind of Dexedrine, upper, that just made me talk a mile a minute. I induced all those people to start coming to the Tenth Street Coffee House and read their poetry. They were like most New Yorkers, suspicious of these scenes. The people who were serious poets and had college degrees and stuff didn't go to MacDougal Street or any of those places, even LeRoi Jones was very suspicious of that whole world."

The Beats, of course, were well established in New York thanks largely to their readings in the Village. The Tenth Street Coffee House, however, was in the East Village, as that part of the Lower East Side was coming to be known. It was significant that these newer poets on the scene were slightly suspicious of poetry readings.

FRED W. McDARRAH

Louis' Tavern and the Circle in the Square theater in 1959,
before demolition

FRED W. McDARRAH

The Remo

WIDE WORLD PHOTO

Maxwell Bodenheim selling his
poetry on the fence of Judson Church,
Washington Square South

FRED W. McDARRAH

Moondog, 1967

Allen Ginsberg, 1966

FRED W. McDARRAH

Fred W. McDarrah

David McReynolds of the War Resisters League speaking to a crowd at the 8th Street Bookshop

Fred W. McDarrah

Closing of the original Cedar Tavern, March 3, 1963; poet Frank O'Hara, *center*. Others include poets Jack Micheline (*left*, at bar) and Barbara Guest (next to O'Hara), sculptor Abram Schlemowitz (in front of Guest)

Fred W. McDarrah

From the terrace of the Café Figaro,
Bleecker and MacDougal

Ted Joans reading at the Café Bizarre, 1959

FRED W. McDARRAH

Mickey Ruskin
in his Avenue B bar,
the Annex, 1964

Stanley Tolkin,
owner of Stanley's, in
kitchen of his bar
the Dom, 1964

FRED W. McDARRAH

Fred W. McDarrah

Stanley's, at Avenue B
and Twelfth Street, established
in 1890

Crowds waiting
outside the Dom
(downstairs) and
the Electric Circus
(up a flight of stairs)

Fred W. McDarrah

Fred W. McDarrah

Ed Sanders's Peace Eye book store
on Tenth Street, before its move to Avenue A,
with the "strictly kosher" sign
from a previous tenant

Fred W. McDarrah

Listening to a reading
at Le Metro, 1964. Poets Ted Berrigan (*left foreground*),
Ed Sanders (*center*), Paul Blackburn (*extreme right*)

Andy Warhol and
friends in Max's Kansas City,
including (*left to right*) Brigid Polk,
Paul Morrissey,
Viva

FRED W. MCDARRAH

Marilyn at the
Mudd Club

JOE BATTLE

"What may be thought of as Public Poetry hit a pinnacle in the summer of 1960 on MacDougal Street in west Greenwich Village," states the foreword to *Seventh Street*, an East Village poetry anthology of 1961. The foreword is unsigned, but was written by poet Howard Ant, one of the two initiators of the seminal readings at the Tenth Street Coffee House, according to the editor of the anthology, Don Katzman. "The Beat movement, moulting from metamorphosis to metamorphosis, had clambered—or been ferried—to its latest stage, the Strident Commercial. Up and down MacDougal, all that summer, beat poets played to the tourist hordes of habitats from Dubuque to the Bronx. . . . Their audience was essentially a cluster of sensation-hunters who had come to Greenwich Village to See The Beatniks and report on them to the folks back home."

The attitude toward the Beats of many of the east side art/lit crowd can be seen by the reaction of the hero of Bill Amidon's novel *Charge . . !,* sitting in a bar called Shondors that is obviously Stanley's, when Allen Ginsberg comes in. "Jesse feltlike a fantastically ridiculous subject because Allen Ginsberg had just entered the bar and walked past their table—out of thousands of *TimeMagazines* and freakscenes allover the world and past their table!"

"The Beats weren't really considered avant-garde," says Wakoski. "They were the new fashion in a funny way. Once Ginsberg's trial [attempting to suppress *Howl*] made him a subject for *Life* magazine, that was something you could dislike not because it was avant-garde but because it was trendy in an arty sense, and I think a lot of poets reacted against that."

Lamont Young knew musician–choreographer–performance poet Jackson MacLow, putting Wakoski in the position of being able to cross-fertilize the poets with the avant-garde performance people. The first reaction on the part of the poets, however, was allergic.

"In '61 or '62 when Lamont and Yoko were doing the loft concerts, Jackson MacLow was performing that night and I persuaded some of the regular poets to come. And Jackson did one of his wonderful interminable performances that went on and on and on and on, which seemed normal to me, and at the intermission we all went outside. And I remember vividly Armand Schwerner pacing up and down in front of the loft on Chambers Street just in a fury of rage—'This is not art, how dare he expose us to this,' et cetera, et cetera, et cetera. Now Armand is the one person who's been deeply influenced by this and really moved over into it. I can so vividly remember that night when he would not accept that, even as an entrée into art."

"Jackson introduced chance-method poetry at the Tenth Street, and I was there the night everybody walked out," says poet-novelist-editor Carol Bergé. "Oh, Diane was furious. Jackson changed my life that night, and I know damn well of at least four other people. He had a tremendous influence on an astonishing number of people. We all, I, worked in his plays and performance pieces, I can't even remember how many."

"I read a piece that's all plant names," says MacLow. "And so I was halfway through it and the master of ceremonies, named Howard Ant, said, 'Now I think that's enough of that.' I wasn't surprised because it wasn't like anything that any of the other people were doing. Diane got in a rage and went out. I was, you know, going to stay around and hear what everybody else was doing. Diane ran out in a rage and so Iris and I went out. In the middle of the week I got a letter from Howard Ant: 'We had this tremendous discussion, I was wrong, will you please come to our group?' So, that's when I first got to know that group of poets." Such is the almost organic evolution of artists beginning to make contact, root themselves, and develop a scene.

The chance methods that MacLow introduced into the process of artistic composition were, for him as for John Cage, allied with his interest in Buddhism and its injunction to bypass the ego. Talking with MacLow in his loft you immediately sense the congruity of his work with his personal style. Removed and self-effacing behind his beard, speaking in a quiet, restrained voice that is at times almost inaudible, amid piles of books and papers among which his cat is allowed free rein, underplaying his own role in developments where it was central, his main assertion seems to be his nonassertion. The influence of chance methods, in which both MacLow and Cage were seminal, was extremely important in maximizing awareness in artists of all kinds from the fifties on of the importance of using technique

—chance being but one instance—to move beyond cliché, formula, and preconception. The ideal was an autonomous process of composition, beyond the control of the ego. William Burroughs and Brion Gysin's cutup method in writing, or the collage/combine work of Robert Rauschenberg and Jasper Johns, who were influenced by Cage, are other examples of randomizing materials to arrive at unpreconceived results that surprise the artist himself, that move him from the known to the unknown.

Poet Paul Blackburn was the ubiquitous organizer and connection among poets for the East Side poetry-reading scene. Another was Carol Bergé. Such was Blackburn's commitment to the oral performance of poetry that he could frequently be seen hauling a large, heavy tape recorder in the days before miniaturization, to make sure the readings were captured for posterity. When I met him, Blackburn, now dead, lived next to and hung out in McSorley's Ale House on Seventh Street. According to Tony Weinberger, author of *Tales of Max's Kansas City,* a book that has little to do with Max's Kansas City, Blackburn and a painter friend would regularly alter the street sign for Hall Place, a short street that runs into Seventh opposite McSorley's, to read Ale Place. Maybe the city got tired of changing it back because it's now named, unalterably, Taras Shevchenko Place.

Around the middle of the fifties "the two forms of publishing, through books and through readings, were opening up at the same time, and, you know, the situation was there and the invitation was there really in effect to establish your own network," says poet Jerome Rothenberg who, with his beard, resembles a graying rabbi. "There was in fact an already developing network of book stores that would handle the work, you know, throughout the country, so at least you could distribute the books or the magazines."

"People came in who were not known," says Ted Wilentz, co-owner with his brother of the Village's key 8th Street Bookshop, which no longer exists, as we talk on his patio in Washington, D.C. "And we felt the writing, as we got to know the writing, was important, and we treated them with great respect. Some of them would probably be followed around stores because denims at that time were shocking, and the beards. So we treated them with respect. In fact I met Corso because he came in with some poetry, and said, 'Well, my friend wrote this poetry,' and we used to take stuff on consignment, and usually this stuff would stay on the shelves. But his stuff sold all the time. He kept coming back. So finally I said, 'Are you Corso?' He says, 'Yes, I'm a little shy about saying so when it's about my own stuff.' "

"I think part of it does have something to do with the economics of the fifties and sixties," continues Rothenberg. "For example, mailing costs were very cheap, the relation of the American dollar to certain foreign currencies was even more favorable than it's supposed to be now, and so, many of us coasted in on that discrepancy to print in places like Gibraltar and Spain, Ireland, London. There was a certain amount of printing going on in Japan. In addition, particularly by the early sixties, poets were much more willing, it seems to me, than today to use alternative and inferior methods of publication, like mimeo." Rothenberg did at least one book in mimeo, "the first edition of Rochelle Owens' play *Futz*, before it was performed. Finally I think it came out in La Mama with O'Horgan directing. Around the same time Diane di Prima was doing *Floating Bear,* and that was a sort of exemplary mimeo publication."

The easy interchange between the small-press world and that of Off-Off-Broadway seen in the career of *Futz* is characteristic of the commingling of the arts at the time. There were also close ties among Off-Off-Broadway and underground film people. According to Ross Wetzsteon, Off-Off-Broadway started in reaction to Off-Broadway, which was doing only the avant-garde from Europe, already confirmed as classics, so that there was no place for the contemporary American avant-garde to be performed. I remember when Wetzsteon, who is today just about the longest-surviving editor of *The Village Voice,* mostly in the theater section, came to my apartment to tell me the paper had just offered him a job. We're talking now in his *Voice* office. "This is where the real underground started," says Wetzsteon, aside from the Living Theater, which as a largely political group was sui generis. "There were four elements to it. The Judson Poets' Theater, whose first major Off-Broadway hit was Gertrude Stein's *What Happened.* Then around '62, Ellen Stewart's La Mama got started, and the thing about La Mama was that they would do a play every week. Café Cino started in, I think, '63. That was a very gay sensibility, very campy, transvestite. When Joe Cino committed suicide, the theater split," and one branch became Charles Ludlam's Ridiculous Theatrical Company. According to playwright Ronald Tavel, the original Theater of the Ridiculous actually started in a gallery on Tenth Street when Tavel split from Andy Warhol, for whom he had been writing movies. The fourth element "was Theater Genesis at the St. Mark's Church. Ralph Cook was a friend of Sam Shepard, they'd been waiters at the Village Gate together. Basically the center and focus of that group was Sam Shepard. They did all his early plays there."

Composer Steve Reich became conscious of an initial core interarts community of film makers, dancers, composers, painters, and sculptors, both around the San Francisco Mime Troupe, with which he worked for a while, and around the Living Theater in New York. "It was in San Francisco that I began to reach that audience and became part of the artistic community with the accent on the painting and sculpture end of it," says Reich. He speaks quickly and very precisely. Reich marks 1966 as the beginning of his professional life, largely "as the result of a concert that I gave at the Park Place Gallery, which was a Minimal Art gallery, run by Paula Cooper in those days. They showed Smithson, they showed LeWitt, they showed Charles Ross."

"You know, I think I went to those concerts," I say, laughing as I remember.

"There was white paper on the floor because someone did an electronic piece, you remember that?"

"Yes, right."

"Chuck Ross's prisms were there, and John Gibson played in back of those prisms."

I would get ideas about writing from listening to music in those days, modern classical as well as jazz. Reich himself had been a jazz drummer. "When I was at Cornell I basically studied philosophy during the week and played jazz on the weekends. My idol in those days was Kenny Clarke, and in many ways it still is, a minimum of interference and a maximum of just fantastic—time, very easily, effortlessly produced, floating, buoyant, endless time."

Reich developed his own group to play his music, which became Philip Glass's ensemble, according to Reich. "I offered those musicians to him to use." However, Reich points out "that both of us have founded our own ensembles" in a 1978 interview with Glass. There has been a certain competitiveness between the two in later years. "I criticized the work," says Reich of Glass, "you know, by saying, 'This is working, this isn't working.' And in February '68 he wrote a piece called 'One Plus One,' which was knocking on a table top adding together twos and threes, and that was his original insight and began his work. His next piece was called 'Two Pages for Steve Reich,' and now it's called 'Two Pages,'" Reich observes drily. One of the things characteristic of the sixties arts ambience was the sense of the creative world as a community rather than, as now, an arena of entrepreneurial gladiators. "It was really our isolation from everyone else that threw us together," says Glass in the interview with Reich quoted above. "It was this isolation, this feeling of banding together to escape the indifference and hostility of the outside world that created a kind of community.... This was as much a social environment as an artistic one.... In those days, Lower Manhattan was a mixed environment of dancers, sculptors, and musicians, all able to discuss each other's work in a fashion that was not at all academic or historical but real, alive, and very rewarding."

The first time I go to the Five Spot on Cooper Square to hear Ornette Coleman play is also the first time I'm stoned out of my mind. The friends I'm going with turn up at my apartment early with some very strong pot, and by the time we get to the Five Spot I'm in the fifth dimension. At the Five Spot I discover a group of super-intense musicians, at least one of them playing a plastic horn. I mean plastic, first of all, is supposed to be middle-class sleaze, and they're producing these ugly, savage sounds and it blows me away. Years later, hearing the same music, I can't help but notice how time and musical developments have rendered it lyrical, almost pretty. But that night I'm staggered by its audacity, for me it's like Parisians being shocked out of the Belle Epoque by Stravinsky's *Rite of Spring* in the Théâtre des Champs-Elysées.

Ted Joans, who had a mural up behind the stage of the Five Spot, remembers Ornette Coleman playing there when Charlie Mingus, who didn't like his music, started hassling him. "Mingus came up while they were playing, man, you know Mingus was always a bully. And he came up while they was playing and started clomping on the piano. Ornette took his horn down and, you know, and stopped and sort of looked at him, and Don Cherry was taking a solo, man, Don just ignored him but Ornette, you know you could see he was disturbed. Now see, Mingus did that with Ornette—if that had been Sonny Rollins or Miles Davis you don't do that shit, they come over and shove your ass off the stage, see, but he did that, Mingus was that kind of person. In fact with Mingus's attitude Miles Davis took up boxing. He started taking boxing lessons."

"Because of Mingus?"

"Yes, he knew that he'd perhaps have to deal with this man."

Amiri Baraka, in *The Autobiography of LeRoi Jones,* tells about getting slapped by Mingus outside the Five Spot and then fighting him off: "I was defending myself as best I could against some two- or three-hundred-pound nut." Tuli Kupferberg tells a story about Mingus playing at the Half Note during a jazz and poetry evening. "Mingus was playing for a while and someone gets up in the back and says something like "Aaah, poetry!" So Mingus looks at the guy, and the eyes go back and forth, and it ends up with Mingus—I think they were standing on the bar actually and playing something—skipping from the bar and running on the tops of the tables all the way to the front and the door, chasing this guy out of the bar."

The audience of artists and writers of which Reich speaks was gravitating around other centers as well as the Living Theater and the jazz clubs. The Tuesday night gallery openings, along Tenth Street and elsewhere, were always an interesting itinerary of parties. And the Judson Church, on the south side of Washington Square, was growing increasingly important. Al Carmines of the church was, according to Carolee Schneemann, "like Ruskin. He opened the doors, he gave us the place, he said, 'Come in and do what you wanna do.'"

Schneemann, who was basically a painter, but had begun working with actual time and space, made contact with Claes Oldenburg's Happenings scenes around 1961 through a connection involving her husband, avant-garde musician Jim Tenney. His best friend was film maker Stan Brakhage, who was friendly with poet Robert Duncan, painter Joseph Cornell, and film maker Maya Deren. "They all knew each other. That's part of the scene, it was a community." As a result she started working with dancer Yvonne Rainer and got involved with choreography as a participant in the Judson Dance Theater, which also included Trisha Brown, among others. "There's only three hundred people anyhow, right, and they're all your friends or they're my friends, and we keep having a party so everybody's there sooner or later."

"The dancers were a separate scene or not?"

"No, we were all mixed up together. I mean they were defined as dancers but we kept interrelating, interworking. The influences were going back and forth so fast, that's what was so vital, right, you remember that."

The Charles Theater on Avenue B, just across Twelfth Street from where I was living, which showed underground films, was another center for the underground community. A showing of Stan Brakhage's marathon narrative film *Dog Star Man* would turn out a good proportion of East Village subterraneans. That was the first big underground film scene, dating from 1961–62, according to Jonas Mekas, film maker, archivist, underground impressario, and film critic for *The Village Voice* from 1958 to 1973 or '74, who was, you might say, the head of the underground film community. At the Charles, Mekas programmed first some of the commercial films, "and then the independents immediately, in the midnight shows, special shows, and we used to run on regular programs the independents."

The scene at the Charles was the crystallization of a movement that had broken away from an earlier Bohemian cinema, perhaps best represented by Maya Deren. "Maya Deren was very much opposed to this type of film making, to this direction. Maya Deren was very formal, she came from the twenties, thirties education, background— very classical, very formal, and very intellectual—and she thought that everything must be controlled. She attacked me why I praised *Pull My Daisy* in *The Village Voice.*" Mekas's English is phrased with the accent and syntax of a Baltic language that few people in the world can speak.

The newer movement was deformalized and favored a candid, improvisational quality whose precursors included Helen Levitt and James Agee's film about Harlem, *In the Street*, Sidney Meyer's *The Quiet One* (written by Agee), John Cassavetes's *Shadows*, and the Robert Frank –Al Leslie production *Pull My Daisy*, involving the central Beat figures. Such films, which also influenced the French New Wave film makers like Godard and Truffaut, were moving toward a democratization of the medium, both in the way they freed up what was considered fit subject matter for film, and in the deemphasis of technique and the use of cheaply available equipment. This was in face of a situation where the enormous costs and high value placed on polished production had made Hollywood a commercially elitist industry claiming populist sanctions only because it could control a mass market. In this respect, the underground film movement was in the vanguard of the thrust of the sixties cultural revolution, which, if it did not "seize control of the means of production," at least managed to find affordable ones.

As with mimeo and offset in underground publishing, it was the availability of a cheaper technology that gave underground film part of its push. In particular, says Mekas, the Signal Corps of the U.S. Army played a crucial role in the movement by deciding "to get rid of all their little Eyemo cameras and film stock, they are portable army battlefield sort of, uuuh, you can drop them, nothing happens to them. They put all those materials on the market and was made available in various little stores around the city here and in San Francisco for very, very little money. Most of the films shot by the independents between 1955 and '65 were shot with those cameras on those outdated stocks. You could, you know, buy one of those cameras for a few dollars, so that helped a lot, that helped a lot. So then, Ron Rice made *The Flower Thief* on that kind of stock, and Jack Smith made *Flaming Creatures*, and down the line."

It's significant that though there was a fairly strict censorship system in force against underground films regarding erotic content, and Mekas was prosecuted and convicted for showing *Flaming Creatures*,

145

the film makers went ahead and made their films without paying any attention to it. Exhibiting was considered a separate problem. If they had started worrying about accommodating to censorship so their films would get shown, the whole movement would probably have been stillborn. "None of the people who made films that later had some sort of censorship problem talked in those terms that they should restrain, they just did what they wanted," says Mekas. "Or that they said, 'Oh no, I won't do this because then I cannot show.' That kind of thinking did not exist."

The interchange common in these years among different kinds of creative people, especially pronounced around the artists involved in Happenings, was itself the basic thrust of the group known as Fluxus. This group was a fluid association of creative people oriented toward the intermedia rather than any one artistic discipline, which started at the end of the fifties and crystallized under the name of Fluxus in 1961. It was, and is, a communal kind of grouping rather than a programmatic movement, and as such was an extension of the underground community. Dick Higgins, for example, who describes himself as something like the ideologist of the group and attended John Cage's course at the New School in the fifties (as did the non-Fluxus artists Jackson MacLow and Allan Kaprow—one of the originators of the Happenings movement) has deep associational roots in the Downtown avant-garde.

The Tenth Street Coffee Shop was in no-man's-land, "between Broadway and Fourth Avenue, it was really out of the way, I mean it was a dark, a very dark street," says Don Katzman, one of the founders of the underground newspaper *The East Village Other,* known as *EVO,* and a poet and playwright who looks like a tough guy from Brooklyn, which he is.

Carol Bergé, a writer who, small and dark-eyed, is not French but looks it, had an art gallery right next door. "At that time Tenth Street was the hottest place in New York for art," she says in her flat, quick voice. "And so Mickey Ruskin opened a shop there. I had a shop right next to there, see. It had originally been a machine shop. It was covered with oil and dreck and old wood and oh God. And I and several friends cleaned it up and made a gallery out of it."

"It wasn't an extension of the old Tenth Street gallery scene."

"Not at all. That was all Abstract Expressionists. Hilda Carmel was on that block, she had the Carmel Gallery. The Brata brothers, they had wonderful openings. Nothing but wine, but"—she snaps her fingers—"that's part of seeing this incredible art, you know, the new stuff that was happening. Nancy and Bob Ellison were renting de Kooning's apartment from him. And he left his paintings in it. And he used to come and visit them and visit his paintings. This was all on Tenth Street. Mickey picked where it was happening. He knew, like I believe I knew, but you can't spell it out to anyone. You go there like magnetism. Like I picked that place on feel. I knew that's where it was happening, I felt it."

"The readings that were held down there," says Katzman, "you were open to criticism, which meant that if you read a poem, after you read anyone could get up, right, and the reason I remember this was I read my first poem there and Chester Anderson laced into me. Chester just tore me apart. . . . When Mickey bought Les Deux Mégots, on Seventh Street between Second and First, it was a much larger place."

"Why did Mickey call it Mégots instead of Magots?" asks Bergé, who used to date Ruskin, "very uneventful dates," she says pointedly. "It means cigarette butts but Mickey wasn't qualified enough to know that. He had no French at all."

"No, what I had heard was they misspelled it," says Katzman, "then Mickey learned later what it meant."

"He had to move from Tenth Street to the Deux Mégots because there were too many of us," says Bergé. "There were a hundred by then."

"We had our own clique," says Katzman. "That's the truth. It was a Wednesday night we would meet."

"In people's houses," puts in Bergé.

"Yeah. Or upstairs. The reason we did was that the Deux Mégots readings got so large it was not homogeneous anymore. This group favored that type of poetry, that group favored that type of poetry. The other reason we did that was because we could no longer comment or criticize each other's works. The Deux Mégots was just too large a reading. The important thing about the Tenth Street was that we did criticize. As vicious as sometimes it did get, it was a good thing. Because it opened your eyes.

"The Deux Mégots had tremendous energy," Katzman continues. "The reason it had tremendous energy, though, was there were so many different types of poetry. Deep Image, Black Mountain, Beat, 1920's—that was even interesting, it gave you such a historical perspective on the Village, East and West."

"The funny thing is it's a family," says Bergé. "You have to get that feeling. It's something so tribal that even now, supposing I should say that I don't like somebody's poetry, it wouldn't matter. That's family. We didn't think about who was going to make it and who wasn't. I don't think anyone did."

I too remember a sense of community during those days on the East Side. Once during the sixties I was on a television program with Howard Fast to discuss a Utopian novel he'd just published about a group of children who are brought up with the ability to read one another's minds. We had something of that empathy on the East Side, so that sometimes the barrier between the subjective and the social world seemed to shimmer on the brink of evaporation. And the empathy was not limited to the creative community. The neighborhood was for a while the model of the American melting pot, polyglot with Poles, Jews, Ukrainians, Blacks, White Russians, Puerto Ricans, Italians, and us, all willing to live and let live with, even, a certain amount of neighborliness. I was always surprised when the Blacks from my building, with whom I often lounged on the stoop, would nod tensely at a passing patrol car with the phrase, "Here come Whitey." Or when some other ethnic neighbor would be picked up in Tompkins Square Park for drug peddling or for rolling someone like me.

One time my then wife, writer Lynn Luria, and I are having a big party in our small apartment. I don't remember much about it except that a couple is screwing in the tiny bathroom and nobody can take a piss for what seems like hours. Irate banging on the door is answered with moans and curses and the crashing of medicine cabinet shelves. Poet James Wright is there drinking and endlessly and magnificently reciting Georg Trakl's poems, which he has translated, from an apparently photographic memory. It's hot and people are drinking and groping and grooving out on the fire escape. Wright is becoming highly emotional in his Trakl recitation in the front room and suddenly there's a knock on the door and three strangers are standing there. My first thought is it's neighbors who don't like Trakl's poetry, but no. They're guys who noticed the festive fire-escape scene from the bar across the street and want to crash, so I say sure, come crash, and they're the ones who first tell me about Stanley's across the street. Later, after Wright begins sobbing over Trakl and after the party breaks up, I go down to Stanley's and I like what I see. For the next five or seven years I'm there sometimes every day.

When I start writing my first novel, *Up,* a book about the East Side that is a combination of autobiography and invention, I realize that that place and time is one in which we can in fact partly invent our autobiographies, in which life is not something imposed on us but a process in which we are creatively involved. The distinction between art and life in the book is reduced to a quibble of form only partly out of theoretical considerations. It's also a consequence of the kind of life that, after decades of alienation, we are finally positioned to lead. What critics don't realize when they foam, or even effervesce, about "Postmodernism" in fiction is that it did not come out of arbitrary literary considerations but out of a kind of life. It is a way of living in which you participate in a communal imagination, rather than having to struggle continuously with an intrusive public vision imposed by the mass market. "Use your imagination," I like to tell my students these days, "or someone else is going to use it for you."

Dissolving the boundaries between art and life was part of the tide of the sixties, and it brought its problems too. Of course, it is impossible to actually lose the distinction between art and life, despite the panic of certain critics, unless you're insane or stoned, naïve, or hopelessly enmeshed in the coils of folly. The problems derived from the fact that, during this period, there were many citizens who were. In the hands of an artist familiar with the ways of the imagination, the breakdown of conventional limits for the imagination places art in the service of the actual, to the enrichment of both. In the hands of a skilled social critic an analysis of the part imagination plays in what we call reality helps demystify our experience. In the hands of an untutored teen-ager zonked on acid, or a monomaniac theoretician trapped by an idea, the results will be predictably vulgar.

Calling into question the prescribed boundaries between art and life was not, of course, simply a literary affair. From an emphasis on process to reunite art with the flow of life, to the use of collage to incorporate the commonplace, from the use of random sound by John Cage to the use of aggressively nonartistic objects by Rauschenberg in his combines, from the Living Theater's strategy of having the actors, clothed or unclothed, interact with the audience and environment to the preference of underground film makers for a candid, home-movie quality and cinema verité, from the use of everyday movements in dance to Kaprow's substitution of participation for audience in Happenings, from the insistence on subjectivity in the New Journalism to Frank Stella's play with the edge of the canvas, an effort to desacralize art, to knock it off its pedestal and out of the remoteness enforced by its frame, to get it out of the quarantine of the museums and into normal secular experience, was part of the push of the creative community to democratize high culture. Pop Art was only one phase in this development. If nothing else is clear about Postmodernism, it is glaringly obvious that it is impelled by a passion for reengagement with common experience, including the experience of the citizen in process of helping to create his environment through the imagination. In one of his essays, Robert Creeley, quoting Yeats, asks, " 'How can we tell the dancer from the dance?' " and responds, "Who was it that wanted to?" thus emerging from the ironic distancing characteristic of Modernism and the New Criticism's quarantine of art from life, and especially from the artist's life. At best, a need for a new realism, more available and inclusive, was being expressed by the art originating in the Lower East Side and elsewhere.

On the west coast at the time, Steve Reich was doing his early tape-recorder pieces in this spirit. His "Livelihood," which he now repudiates, "was a collage piece, a three-minute piece, based on, I don't know, maybe twenty hours of material recorded in a yellow cab that I drove for a year. It was totally bugged, I mean nobody knew about it. And besides, without a voicegram of your voice no one could've been recognized. I was using fragments of speech, slammings of doors, people calling out prices, and things that were totally impersonal. In '64 I began working more in tape loops, which obviously led to 'It's Gonna Rain,'" which used a fragment of "the voice of a Black Pentecostal preacher preaching in Union Square" in San Francisco for theme and phased variation.

The imagination can operate on life in more ways than one, and one way is in promoting the imaginative work itself, something that was perhaps naïvely taboo in earlier American Bohemia but raises questions about the distinction between art and publicity. The trick, evidentally, is not to allow the work to be identified with the promotion, either unintentionally, as in the case of Kerouac, or intentionally, as in the cases of Mailer and Warhol.

"The history of the whole Modern movement is filled with examples of conscious manipulation and of the propaganda side," I point out to Dick Higgins as we talk in his loft on Spring Street in SoHo.

"Oh sure. That's how we launched Happenings and Fluxus, and even Something Else Press. I could do it because I had a body of material. But I lost the ability to do that the moment I was concentrating on my own art rather than on other people's art and on a body of material. Sure, even when Happenings were first appearing one of the first things I did was get it on the Henry Morgan television show. I knew how to do that kind of thing because I had had a job for a little while in a public relations firm. I knew how to send out press releases and that kind of thing, and I could do it again with Something Else Press.

"I used to pose as a millionaire," says Higgins, "although my house was always in hock and that kind of thing, during Something Else Press days, because it was good for business. It made it much more easy for me to sort of get media coverage for the books that we were publishing and that kind of thing. Oh sure. Grace Glueck misunderstood something that I'd said in the course of an interview and made me out to be a steel heir. I used to use that clipping when I wanted to go and get bank loans for Something Else Press. Between that and my prep school accent I was always able to do that kind of thing. Let me just give you a nice statistic. When Something Else Press went out of business it owed various people more than a quarter of a million dollars." He laughs.

By 1963, Mickey Ruskin had given up the Deux Mégots to open the first of his widely known restaurants, the Ninth Circle in the West Village. The Deux Mégots became the first hip macrobiotic restaurant in town, an Osawa joint called the Paradox, where you paid fifty cents for a bowl of good, filling vegetable soup, and the main reading scene moved over to Café Le Metro on Second Avenue. Despite harassment by the city on ostensible grounds of such things as fire laws and entertainment regulations, the readings continued through 1965 and became so popular, not only with an expanding group of poets but with the public as well, that there was often a crowd outside waiting for admission. Paul Blackburn, as so often, was the guiding spirit of the readings.

The Metro was both a coffee house and "antique" furniture store, with bare brick walls, spare and dark. Coffee was a quarter, which was a lot at the time, but served as the cover charge for the readings.

"All of a sudden I found myself involved in the Metro Café," says Gerard Malanga, a Roman-looking blond poet and photographer who has been closely associated with Andy Warhol, "and not so much because I wanted to get up and read a poem, but because I found a need to socialize with fellow artists, and the Metro café was a kind of opportune moment where—I'm sure there were other poets who felt the same way I felt—that we just wanted to, you know, chew the fat, as it were, sit down, have a drink, whether it was cappuccino or whatever. When I look back at it I realize that the Metro café, as with a lot of cafés that generated a reading series, was a great educational opportunity because it allowed a lot of poets, whether they were conscious of it or not, to become educated in terms of reading each other's texts."

One of the main groups at the Metro was the second-generation New York School, which was no more from New York than the first Cambridge generation; in fact it had largely come from, or through, Tulsa, Oklahoma. Poets Dick Gallup and Ron Padgett had lived across the street from one another in Tulsa as kids and communicated via tin can telephone until a car came along and wrapped the string around its hood ornament. Nevertheless they stayed in close communication once they got to New York, going to museums and galleries, and sharing one MOMA pass among about ten people, each writer, according to Padgett, slipping the pass back through the gate in the sculpture garden to a friend once he got in. Padgett, who looks like he could have done a part in *Grapes of Wrath*, attended Columbia, where Kenneth Koch, whom Padgett considers an extraordinary teacher, became an important influence on him. Ted Berrigan was the *chef d'école.* "Ted's deal with life was 'Live hard and die young,' " says Padgett. He did. "He knew it was going to happen," according to Padgett. It was a deal made by many subterraneans.

Despite the success of the Metro readings, it was perhaps not till the readings moved to the St. Mark's Church on Second Avenue that the Uptown literary establishment started taking note of what was happening. "I think when things started, for example at the St. Mark's Church in the Bowery," says Anne Waldman, who later became head of the church's Poetry Project, "then there was a focus, things could be sort of pigeonholed a little more easily." The move to St. Mark's came about in 1965 because of friction between the owners of Le Metro and members of the Umbra group of Black writers. The falling out was bitter. "The shopkeeper who runs the Metro," wrote Ishmael Reed in the new *East Village Other*—the East Side's answer to *The Village Voice*—of which he was then an assistant editor, "is a special breed of shaggy rapacious wolf. He does not have the fine combed fur of the Tartar wolf but is a scroungy raunch mongrel kind of wolf who maskerades [*sic*] as a benevolent sheep dog. . . . This constant friction and irritation causes him to blow his wolf cool and leads him to do weird handstands, like going after Archie Shepp with a meat cleaver, or cane whipping Don Harriman or flagellating a gentleman like Tom Dent, former editor of Umbra magazine. . . . The great Walter Lowenfels shut down 'murder incorporated' that night. . . . Lowenfels and his followers left as did the moderator Allan Katzman."

In any case, the move signaled a turning point in the literary underground. The audience was getting bigger, and one way or another, things had to expand. St. Mark's, which already had a tradition of hosting people like Isadora Duncan, Frank Lloyd Wright, and Hou-

dini, and had already been having poetry readings, with Paul Blackburn passing the hat for the readers, as well as jazz concerts,
underground film screenings showing Andy Warhol's first movies,
and Off-Off-Broadway theater, "before things became official," as
Anne Waldman says, got a grant from the Office of Economic Opportunity in 1966. A professor at the New School "had the bright
idea, as a sort of sociological project, to have this money go to artists
in the Lower East Side community to benefit alienated youth, and he
would do a study of the alienated youth." Poet and journalist Joel
Oppenheimer was made the first director, and Waldman was one of
the assistants.

"Everything was changing at that point," says Waldman, tough
and elegant veteran of Village scenes, "moving out of what was left
of the cafés into more official poetry programs that had become more
organized and institutionalized. You'd been passing the hat for x number
of years and you wanted to be able to pay the poet twenty-five dollars, and not just five dollars and twenty-five cents. And now it's up
to what? A hundred and fifty? Inflation. Now, what's a cup of coffee?
And you can't sit around the way you used to be able to. There are
too many people that are waiting to get your table."

"What has gone from the café scene," says Andrei Codrescu, "where
everybody paid for their own coffee and they felt that they could be
as obnoxious as they wanted to be"—like Ted Berrigan standing up
and disrupting the Metro readings, saying things to the readers—
"changed when it moved to a hall and people had to be an audience
and sit in a chair." Poets became more like performers, even enter-
tainers, rather than artists engaged in dialogue with other artists. In
fact, in the bars, the dialogue was sometimes an unwanted one with
the drinkers and drunks, which nevertheless also helped minimize the
performer-audience situation to elicit something more participatory.

"It's kind of like what Brecht was always talking about with an
audience," says poet-playwright-novelist Michael Stephens, "you let
'em smoke cigars and drink and fart and belch and eat, it makes
whatever the performance is better. If you go into a church, like St.
Mark's, it's still a church, no matter how great that place was, and
there's a certain reverence, whether you want it or not. Whereas

you're sitting in a bar and you have a reading, people get loose, they have drinks, and it's what cabaret is all about." However, at the more informal readings at St. Mark's as opposed to the official paid readings, as in the bar scene, "people would come in with their beers and their dope and they'd just sit around and if they didn't like something they'd heckle and talk out loud."

Partly as a result of the institutionalization of the reading scene, not only in halls like St. Mark's, but in the college reading circuit as well, and also because of the change in the cafés, writers tended to meet more in apartments. First of all, some of them now had apartments sizable enough to host biggish gatherings. It was out of the saloon and into the salon, so to speak. LeRoi Jones's apartment was for a while one such gathering place, as was, later, that of Waldman and Louis Warsh. "After every reading we would have a reception," says Waldman, where people could pretty much "do whatever they wanted. I remember the night when I was so shocked when Kenneth Koch took off his shoes. He was really getting down." Around that time there was "a lot of group work, for example, collaborative kind of work. I know in my apartment there were all these late-night sessions, you'd be writing collaborations, you'd be putting together a magazine, you'd be reading things out loud, you'd be reading your latest poem."

Another result of the poet's new identity as performer for an audience was a tendency, starting way back with Dylan Thomas, to move in the direction of show biz. However beneficial it might have been in the fifties and sixties for writers to become aware once again of the connection of language with voice, and even to create some poetry mainly for performance, there were some less attractive sides to this tendency. "I was brought up on the notion that you could always make a bad poem sound great if it was read aloud well," says Gerard Malanga. Whether performance poetry is a fruitful genre or a new kind of vaudeville, and whether it's good or bad, are other questions, but what is unquestionable is that in a time when writers are reaching out in an attempt to create a new popular audience, it is a useful technique.

Officially or unofficially, St. Mark's Church, like the Judson before it, quickly became a thriving center for the subterranean culture with a variety of activities, including a series of workshops taught and attended by many distinguished writers. It was not exactly a conventional institution. For one thing, books from the library bought for the alienated youth kept disappearing. There were other strange events. "I remember coming out of the church one night," Waldman tells me. "I'd been there mimeographing an issue of *The World*, and there was a deer carcass hanging from the trees. And then there were the grave robbers, who were junkies looking for loot, and somebody finding a skull in the garbage can. The typewriters were going, chairs. They had a Holmes system, and I tripped the wire at one point and these guys arrived with guns at my head."

The Up Against the Wall Mother Fuckers, a group of extreme left radicals, "were using the kitchens, and they were having these free dinners Thursday nights. They were so irritating, we were trying to accommodate them, you know, they would always leave the kitchen a mess. The Black Panthers were also offering breakfast for children out of St. Mark's. One of the major stories was the assassination of Kenneth Koch. During the Columbia riots, three guys, including Andrei Codrescu, when Kenneth Koch was seen as representing the establishment because he taught at Columbia, so during his reading one of these guys, a White Panther, came down the aisle with his trench coat and a gun, and Andrei was handing out this manifesto, and Kenneth was reading a poem called "To My Audience," and these blanks started going off and I nearly had a heart attack. It was the break, so I took Kenneth to the Orchidia and we had I don't know how many drinks and came stumbling back. I encouraged him to go on. And then a couple of people wrote poems about it. And Gregory Corso streaked during a Michael McClure reading, during the year when streaking was very popular, so he was the first poetry streaker. The John Wieners reading when he arrived in gold lamé with tiaras. One night he had one whole pant leg rolled up and a rope around his neck and a bandanna, losing his poems in midsentence dropped to the ground. The Robert Lowell reading when Gregory heckled, Gregory was saying, 'Don't be so condescending, do you have to be a professor around us?' I don't think Lowell knew who he was at the time, and then *The New Yorker* reported it as 'a young man' in the audience—forty years old?—heckling Robert Lowell. The Kesey event where he had everybody doing deep breathing in the balcony and the balcony almost collapsed because of the extra air"—we laugh—"and it was just overweighted to begin with, it was so mobbed."

Meanwhile over at Twelfth and B, I'm working on my first books, waking up late in the morning, writing through the afternoon, then staggering out onto Avenue B, my mind blank after hours at the typewriter, down the Avenue to Tompkins Square Park to stare at the many-ethnicked panorama, the swarming kids, the old chess players, the cavorting dogs, and the sexy subterranean women, especially after miniskirts and see-through blouses come into vogue, then over to Stanley's across the street for a beer or two and a little idle chat with Stanley or whomever, before the place gets jammed with its usual population of creative genius, Puerto Rican street guys, chicks on the make, hip tourists from the West Village or Uptown. Then dinner, and the prospect of meeting a friend or two and going over to some interesting place like Slug's on East Third to hear some great jazz or hitting the late show at the Charles Theater next door to see an avant-garde film. When I don't have to sweat some ill-paying job and am not getting robbed or mugged too much or getting too paranoid about getting robbed or mugged too much and the roaches and water bugs and rats aren't too bad and the heat is working in the winter or it isn't too hot in the summer and the pachangas aren't coming in too loud across the air shaft and the poisonous stench from Elk's furniture-stripping shop downstairs isn't seeping through the floor or the soot spew from the Con Ed stacks on Fourteenth Street isn't boiling through the windows, it's the best situation and schedule for working on a book I've ever had, before or since.

For five years, from about 1962 to 1966 when Max's Kansas City began to draw some of its subterranean clientele, and even after, Stanley's was the center for the East Village scene, the place you went before and after and sometimes during. A whole creative generation passed through Stanley's, people I didn't know by name then and have met since, but with whom I must have passed many a long boozy night. To go all the way over to the Cedar or other bars on University Place was a drag and the White Horse in the West Village was out of the question, and besides, why bother? To the real East Villager even St. Mark's Church over on Second Avenue was a trek, to be justified by some extraordinary event. The East Village is geographically isolated from the rest of the city. Manhattan is vertical, if you want to go somewhere you go Uptown or Downtown, but the East Village requires a lateral trip even to get to the vertical axis, and there are no subways and the crosstown busses aren't very convenient. Thus where the Village is removed from Uptown by long subway rides, the East Village is twice removed, and this perhaps accounts for the fact that for a while it became an underground underneath the underground. When Michael Stephens moved from the East to the West Village, he and Codrescu, according to Codrescu, "used to write letters to one another as if we'd moved to different countries. . . . It seemed like they were different worlds."

"I crossed the street to a bar," says my first novel, *Up* (1968), of Stanley's, "whose owner, a nervous modern version of Chaucer's canny host, had cultivated a lumpenintelligentsia clientele whose beards had totally displaced the red noses of indigenous Polack rummies. His name, an arc of small gilt letters, vowels obliterated, smiled from plate glass like the gold teeth of an impoverished immigrant. The bar was an old establishment, and he had taken care to preserve the woodwork and glasswork of the manly, mustachioed nineties. I moved through the beer-laced mist of tobacco smoke to find a place at the bar and asked for an ale . . . one foot on the brass rail and my elbow resting on the bar . . . filled with a comforting sense of assurance that seemed to inhere through the long mass of the bar by virtue of its solidity, by virtue of its age, by the beauty of its wood, by its sheen of long use."

It's late afternoon. Stanley's is shadowy and still quiet, a little like a cave opening on Avenue B but protecting you from the noise, dirt, and intense ghetto street life of the neighborhood. Stanley is there, Stanley's black cat is there, Stanley's wife is there, joking with a handful of the old palookas left over from the days preceding the bar's sudden blossoming as the hottest, hippest, and most packed

freak scene in the city. Stanley has long since replaced his wife behind
the bar with a set of regular bartenders, one of whom has a Franken-
stein imitation that eventually gets him into a Mel Brooks movie. Out
the plate glass window I see Bill Amidon heading in, sporting a vaguely
Chinese-looking diabolical mustache. He sits down at the bar and
scans the mostly empty tables in the long room. Amidon is very
speedy and likes to talk. He got out one unthinking energetic novel
called *Charge . . !* (1971), then literally ran out of energy and packed
it in. He just stopped eating, terminal anorexia. Domenick Izzo, later
a central figure at Max's Kansas City, who says Amidon died in his
arms, claims that Bill's father also died of anorexia.

Stanley comes over and puts a beer in front of Bill. "How's the
book going?" he asks.

"I'm writing a lot of pages." Bill probably shouldn't be drinking.
Diabetes. If you ask him about it he answers that he only drinks beer.
Stanley watches him sipping the beer, wrinkles flickering across his
high-domed, balding brow like fugitive hieroglyphics. You know
Stanley is smart as soon as he opens his mouth, he's one of those
people who's always thinking three things at once, often contradictory, and his speech, tentative and spare, reflects an effort of contain-
ment rather than an ease of expression. My private theory on why
Stanley died, as he did a few years later—they say of a heart attack
—is that he had too much on his mind and couldn't handle it. Stanley
was an East Side ethnic who built his nothing local bar within a very
short time into a huge success, followed by the even more spectacular
success of the Dom, a bar and one of the first hip discotheques, in
the giant Polish National Hall over on St. Mark's Place. "There's only
one trouble with this place," he once complained to me about his bar.
"It's not Uptown." It was shortly after he finally made it Uptown,
with a place called the Gymnasium, that Stanley died. On opening
night at the Gymnasium, to Stanley's consternation, eight free, open,
spontaneous types, probably from Downtown, appeared on the dance
floor and took all their clothes off.

I suspect that when Stanley opened a second level of his bar downstairs in the somewhat romantic style of a French *cave,* it was an
attempt to upgrade the bar socially as well as to increase capacity.

The downstairs was a vaulted room, formerly a cellar, with raw brick walls and wooden tables. On the stairway down there were nice wood sculptures, done by one of the patrons, with figures stacked in modern totem-pole style. "It was pitch dark," laughs soft-spoken, courtly poet Lorenzo Thomas. "And the attraction to it was that people would go down there and they'd sip a jug of wine and they'd sit there for hours. It was less crowded than the upstairs, where, of course, the bar was always five deep. It was like a train station, right? You had to shout to the person next to you to be heard." At times there were poetry readings and music down there. Thomas remembers a long, heated discussion downstairs among a group, some Black, some white, mostly writers, about racial attitudes at the time, that went on for hours and hours till closing time, that "to all intents and purposes" became a cover story that Calvin Hernton published in *Negro Digest*. "I think he probably went right home and wrote it."

I used to watch Stanley hooking the new hip population of the East Village, working them with free beers and sympathetic talk at a time when the rest of the locals regarded these strange guys with beards who didn't work, and their bra-less girls who looked like they wore nothing under their skirts either (and often didn't), with at best mild contempt. "What's going on over at Stanley's?" I ask a local Polish acquaintance one weekend night when the bar is just catching on with the hip types.

"It's a who house," he says.

"Two plainclothes cops once sounded Shondor"—Amidon's name for Stanley in his novel—"for 'harboring hookers'—because they saw girls leaving with different guys everynight. The cops hid in an unmarked car across the street and they peeked at those fine assed females leaving with roistering drunken painters skinny haunted writers with whom they would trade love (if only for a few moist rich intense days) and big black buckniggers who had nothing better to do than rape little blonde girls (like all cops virginal daughters): little blue-eyed sincere naive girls who wouldbe subjected to allmanner of strange erotic sexual punishments: gangfucked by naked old sculptors and 17-year old black faggots; whipped locked for days in a dirty room violated regularly by animals until they got hooked on it. Little innocent girls—who in truth hungaround Shondors mainly to get goosed greased graced gored and gobbled by those social miscreants. . . . The cops . . . couldnot understand . . . that a pair of funky paint-splattered levis and a three day growth of beard might just get another man laid."

Amidon in the *Voice* once published a short list of the various kinds of people who went to Stanley's. "In '63–64 at Stanley's (before anybody knew who they were) you might have walked in on any given afternoon or evening and encountered writers such as Ishmael Reed, Calvin Hernton, David Henderson, Ron Sukenick, Allen Ginsberg, Tuli Kupferberg, Ed Sanders, and Lennox Raphael; actors like Moses Gunn, Mitch Ryan, Lou Gossett, and Cicely Tyson; musicians such as Odetta, Marion Brown, and Richard Andrews; Khadejha the fashion designer, who was Afro before people knew what that meant; Tom Dent, one of the founders of the Free Southern Theatre; Walter Bowart, who tended bar there and later was the original publisher of *EVO*—and Clark Squire, one of the Panther 21."

Stanley liked us. That wasn't why every third beer was free at the beginning. The frequency went down as business went up, but he was still occasionally generous with the regulars. He liked having interesting, educated people as customers. He liked the girls with their new sexy styles. Stanley was all friendly host, as opposed to Mickey Ruskin, who after a while went into competition for the underground trade with the Annex a block or two down Avenue B on the other side of the street. Not that Mickey wasn't generous. His opening bash was a grand free party. And his place featured free peanuts, whose shells were left strewn on the floor like sawdust in an old-time bar. But Mickey's tack was to be cold, if not bluntly nasty, to outsiders. Mickey wanted to keep out the middle class to make space for the underground. To Stanley, the underground was the middle class.

Stanley doesn't yet have any idea of what the underground is all about beyond the fact it has money to spend for beers. Later, five, five-thirty, when the bar starts to fill up, Stanley gets busy but finds time to come over and point out a couple of freaks, saying confidentially, "See those guys, they make their living singing dirty songs."

The guys are the Fugs, led by Tuli Kupferberg and Ed Sanders, the crazy shrewd doctors of scatologic who are just beginning to make it as a singing group, but to Stanley a dirty song is a dirty song. Stanley is blue collar moving up, Mickey is a young Jewish lawyer dropping out. Their careers are defined by their attitudes toward the middle class. Stanley wants it, Mickey is trying to get rid of it. There's an edge of hysteria in the urgency of each.

On Avenue B their trajectories crossed briefly before they died. Stanley was one of the first merchants to recognize and exploit the commercial possibilities of the underground, Mickey was one of the first dropouts to make a business out of dropping out. In the course of those years, this being America, everybody began to discover they had something to sell, whether it was beers or drugs or novels or paintings or fashion or life style or even sex.

Stanley's jukebox is blazing away—a good box is one requirement of a good bar—"an endless symphony of BarbraStreisand-BillieHoliday sadsongs cooing guitarstrumming nuns Frenchmovie music and Birdizoot-Monk-Sonnyrunning together like notes on an endless Trane solo," according to Amidon, and when I look up three or four beers down the road it's dark out. I go pay a visit to the men's room, in Stanley's a john with character, cavernous, black-and-white-tiled floor, clean. The urinals alone deserve a sentence to themselves, massive shoulder-high thrones that, riddled with a geography of fine cracks, have the look of old crackled porcelain. When I come out there's a scene going on, the patrons piled up at the plate glass window watching Stanley, on the sidewalk, confronting a drunk, a Puerto Rican kid, wielding a switchblade. "You're going to cut me? Why are you going to cut me?"

"Because dju was lookin at me, man."

"I wasn't looking at you. Why would I want to look at you?" Stanley's patient projection of some superior state of equilibrium has a way of reducing such guys to a condition of ill-natured helplessness. This one isn't even serious. Soon he staggers off down the sidewalk cursing and muttering.

Others aren't always so lucky. Ishmael Reed reports in *The East Village Other* that Stanley's bartender was knifed at 4 A.M. closing time "while assisting a bar patron who had become involved in a brawl with fifteen neighborhood youths." The bartender, a painter, had a collapsed lung and needed to have a spleen removed, and had been not only knifed but repeatedly kicked "by the youths as he lay sprawled on the pavement." Stanley, who rushed him to the hospital, was of the opinion that the patron had been spoiling for a fight and started it by glaring at the kids through the window.

Fights were not uncommon in Stanley's. Sometimes they were over women, like the time a large fellow they called Tank standing next to me suddenly flattened a guy without blinking or moving anything but his right arm, when it became clear the girl he'd been talking to all night was going to go home with the sucker. Sometimes it was just to release tension in the neighborhood, like the huge brawl Amidon describes the night JFK was shot. Sometimes I would sit out on my fire escape on the second floor across the street and watch the fights pour out of the bar late at night. Stanley always managed to get them out on the street. Mickey Ruskin couldn't understand how Stanley handled the rough scene that began erupting in the East Village as heavy drug use and friction among neighborhood groups increased. The Annex, safe enough to take a child to at first, was soon killed, according to Mickey, by the mounting violence. But Stanley was not a dropout. He was of the neighborhood, and he knew how to deal with the neighborhood. Actually, Avenue B became a street of interesting bars for a while. On the corner up from Stanley's a place opened called the Old Stanley, which was newer than Stanley's but named after old Stanley, who owned it, or had owned it. During a certain period you could bar-hop along B practically from Fourteenth to Houston.

Later, Stanley started his other big project. "He took over a hall down St. Mark's," says Lorenzo Thomas, "the Polish National Hall, called the Dom. There was a big upstairs dance hall, and there was a downstairs, which in the original version, the downstairs section was where the food and stuff was prepared for the dances held up in the dance hall. Like, all the dance halls in Harlem, like the Renaissance and all those places, all had the same configuration. What happened, Andy Warhol rented the place. It was called the Exploding

Plastic Inevitable, and Warhol conceived it as an exhibit," Thomas claims, "but what it was, was a disco." Actually, it had live music at first, but it set the style for all discos to follow.

"We'd discovered the Velvet Underground," the group that was to be featured in the Exploding Plastic Inevitable, says John Wilcock, "by Barbara Rubin taking us all to that sawdust place, the Café Bizarre, where the Velvet Underground were playing in the Village, right, and where the management was trying to kick them out. And Barbara Rubin took everybody over there, and we sat right in the front, Gerard Malanga and Morrissey and the whole bunch of us, and Warhol instantly hired them, on the spot, immediately. Barbara Rubin thought they belonged with the Warhol thing, and Warhol took one look at them and agreed instantly."

Then, one day when they were having trouble finding a place for the Velvets to perform, they were sitting in the Figaro, and they were overheard talking about their problem by the people at the next table who happened to be Jackie Cassen and Rudi Stern, who did dance concerts with light shows. They knew about the Dom, which they had just rented from Stanley, and took the Warhol bunch over there, and a deal for its use was quickly made. "All these things were coming together," says Wilcock. "They got the Dom, and they walked in there and they saw the gallery thing at one end at the top overlooking it, you know, like a projection area almost, and all this enormous space with all the walls, and the thing that goes around with all the lights on it." Wilcock further describes it in his *EVO* story on the place: "A colored spotlight onstage focused onto the mirrored ball that revolved in the ceiling sending pinpoints of light on predictable circuits around the room. A plastic globe glowed in cycles of changing pastel colors."

"They put all these ingredients together," Wilcock continues, "and they put up lots of screens and they showed Warhol films on the walls and God knows what. And then, like, I'd be hanging around on the balcony where all the spotlights were, and they had spotlights with different color gels on them and some kind of thing where you could strobe it, basically, and I'd be standing talking to Andy, and some guy operating the spotlight would say, 'Oh, Andy, can you get somebody to take this? I've just got to take a pee.' And Andy would say to the nearest person, 'Would you do that?' or he wouldn't even say that, he would just indicate that's what this person should do. This person like a zombie would immediately go over and do it very tentatively, start to gradually discover the potential, and you could like do spots and zoom it around and change the colors, right, and, like, within thirty seconds Andy had created an artist. I was very impressed by that kind of thing, it was always going on around there, just constantly, nonstop."

"The hall was a frantic, frenzied fandango of action," Wilcock's article elaborates. "The lights flashing on and off, the fragmented pieces of movies, the colored patterns and slides sweeping the mirrored walls, the steady white beams of balcony projectors, the Sylvania strip lighting writhing on the floor, flashing on and off like a demented snake who's swallowed phosphorus, the foot-long flash lights of Gerard Malanga randomly stabbing the darkened hall as he danced frenetically in front of the group."

Warhol, says Thomas, "had Gerard Malanga running around dressed in black leather, and this band called the Velvet Underground," with Lou Reed, John Cale, and Nico, the deep-voiced beauty who previously had had a substantial part in Fellini's *La Dolce Vita* when she was fifteen. "This thing was set up for a week. Everybody went there. Every night. Then it was revived as the Electric Circus." Actually it was first revived as the Balloon Farm, without Warhol. Then, later, according to Thomas, Murray the K took an airplane hangar out in Roosevelt, Long Island, called it Murray the K's World, and installed all of this interior design on a mammoth scale.

"The downstairs section was taken over by Stanley Tolkin," continues Thomas on the Polish National Hall scene. "He made a bar out of it called the Dom. Now it already had a long bar in there, and there was a huge room next to it. He installed all these tables in there, and for the first night of the opening he leafletted Stanley's announcing this affair, and of course the word was all over the street, and the opening night he served draft beer for a nickel. So you can tell what the result was. The entire Lower East Side, all the painters, all the poets, everybody in the world showed up. There was no attraction except nickel beer. The place must have had about five hundred people in it. Interesting people were there, you know. Carol Bergé was there, Robert Creeley was in town so Carole grabbed him and took him over there. Ted Berrigan, everybody was there, every different magazine grouping or workshop grouping, all of the various painters, musicians, in other words it was like the entire East Side simply turned out in one place at one time for the opening of this new joint." The Dom–Electric Circus scene really made it big for a while. I remember one time as I passed by seeing limousines and hired buses lined up outside, and a police cordon. Later I heard the whole place had been rented by the Uptown jet set, Kennedys and all.

"Dancing came later," says Thomas. "There was no entertainment. It was just Stanley's and Stanley's basement enlarged, right? After that they began to do things like live music. They had jazz, they had bands that played back in the larger room for dancing. The Electric Circus was still going upstairs, and that changed from being a Jackie Onassis celebrity place, as it was when it opened, to being a kids' place—you know, kids that came in from the suburbs. The Dom became a jukebox disco place, and the population changed from the East Village people to mainly Black kids and the box was mainly soul music."

The Fugs were actually conceived at the Dom, according to Sanders and Kupferberg. "We'd go there after the poetry readings," says Sanders. "I remember after I think it was a Robert Creeley reading at the St. Mark's, we all went over there. There was Joel Oppenheimer and LeRoi Jones and I think Creeley was there, all kinds of people were there, Ted Berrigan. The place was packed and there was this strange music, you know, by the Beatles, this was late '64, so the Beatles had hit, there was Wilson Pickett, and all those Black dance groups. So anyway, we said, hey, you know. We used to go there dancing after the readings, and we'd think of all these weird dances and Stanley would rush out and break it up. He wouldn't let you do anything too off the wall, in terms of group dancing, you know. So Kupferberg was there one time and I said, 'Hey, you know. This is it. We'll set it to poetry and see what happens.'"

The East Village, that segment of the Lower East Side that begins with Fourteenth Street and ends at Houston Street, was in fact a world of its own, almost what used to be called a neighborhood. Tompkins Square Park was its center, and a local could just as well think of going east toward the East River to satisfy most of his or her culture needs as going west toward Cooper Square and the Village beyond. Slug's, on East Third Street between Avenues B and C, was a jazz bar that easily rivaled the Five Spot or any other hip jazz scene in the city. It was owned by Robert Schoenholt, a low-key, almost self-effacing man, who later had a well-known place in SoHo called the Spring Street Natural Food Restaurant, recently moved east along Spring out of now Yuppiffied SoHo to Little Italy.

Slug's was a "long room with different-color light bulbs and stretched nylon parachutes on the ceiling, and the stage at the end, a brick wall on one side and the other side lined with window bars," beautiful window grates scavenged from demolished buildings on the Upper West Side, says Schoenholt. "It was kind of funny looking, bars on a brick wall, but I liked it." We're talking many years later in another restaurant of his, called Laughing Mountain, since closed, down in the farthest reaches of Tribeca on Chambers Street, an establishment that, in keeping with the new Yuppie tone of that neighborhood— which Schoenholt laments—is much more posh than his other two places. As we talk at the bar, novelist Ken Gangemi is bartending. Schoenholt to start with was not involved in the music business nor, apparently, is he very literary. He had worked in Ruskin's Ninth Circle as a waiter, "a very turned-on place, everybody used to go to the Ninth Circle." Before he opened Slug's he used to go to Stanley's, where he knew Ishmael Reed as a very down-to-earth guy. "I couldn't believe, after knowing him all those years, I couldn't read his writings. He used to hang around in Slug's all the time. He loved music."

"Did it take a while to catch on?"

"No, it caught on right away actually, but there was a time when I first started the place it became a hang-out for very powerful drug kingpins from out of the neighborhood. So, like, they'd walk into the place, before it really came to be a music scene, and every table and everybody in the place was heavily armed, they were carrying weapons and their bodyguards were spreading around, it was a very heavy, electric atmosphere. That was one of the reasons that I encouraged music, I was very happy about it because the scene was getting very intense. It was out of my hands. I would just tiptoe around, I didn't want to disturb anybody."

"Were they doing business, or just hanging out?"

"Yeah, they must have been doing business."

"What were they dealing, heroin?"

"Yeah, it was probably heroin, yeah."

"So these were Black guys from Uptown?"

"Yeah. It sort of had just caught on. Before the music scene. That's what happened, that's why they came."

"So the drug people pulled in the musicians."

"That's right. It was amazing, when we first started music, all these people that I had heard about started to appear in person, and even though the names didn't really matter to anybody, it was astounding to me to see a famous trumpeter or saxophone player, so I'd talk to them and I'd ask them if they'd like to bring in a group, and they said sure."

"You mean they'd show up . . ."

"To listen to the other guys."

"So it became a musicians' place."

"Yeah. It was totally a musicians' place. It was a fantastic experience, listening to music—all these people that were playing there were all serious musicians and so you wouldn't just listen to them play once in a while, you'd wanna hear people play every night, the same tunes, then they'd come back a few weeks later, and after a while it got to be so you were listening to the music as it developed, and as it changed. Extraordinary. There were a lot of painters there. Larry Rivers used to come down a lot. All the big painters. All the musicians that are famous today used to hang around."

Slug's was a place where creative people gathered, and was probably too far east and in any case too small to attract a really popular clientele. Its underground status was in a sense guaranteed by circumstance. But by the mid-sixties it became clear that underground culture was starting to attract a big popular audience. The underground press, papers like *The East Village Other, The Berkeley Barb,* and *The*

Los Angeles Free Press, were starting to define a large hip audience. By the end of the sixties, one of the radical underground press-syndication services alone served an audience of twenty million. Of course, the attraction of the underground press had a lot to do with its opposition to the Vietnam War, but its promotion of the underground culture, from drugs to music to poetry, was part of its program.

The underground was beginning to form its own alternative institutions, and among the most important, along with the underground press, was the Pacifica chain of radio stations. Started in Berkeley, it later established stations in Los Angeles and New York and, still later, in Houston. One of the early personalities on the Berkeley station, as "Johnnie Night Time," was John Leonard, who was to become the editor of *The New York Times Book Review.* WBAI, the Pacifica station in New York, had an audience in the millions during the sixties and was always number one or two among New York FM stations at any hour of the day or night. Bob Fass had a late-night show called *Radio Unnameable.* This innovating free-form program, which was a call-in show, was like a communications clearinghouse for what was coming to be called the counterculture, the switchboard for the underground community. Fass has a photograph from that period "of me walking my dog, and the dog is taking a shit, and it's five o'clock in the morning, and there's a crowd just gathering around to watch." As an index of popularity, that beats Bob Dylan, who once said that people at the Newport Festival would follow him into the men's room so they could watch him piss.

This growing popularity, however, became a problem for underground culture in ways not so obvious at first. Part of the mystique of the sixties was participation, and the youth generation was not simply becoming an audience for underground culture, it was joining up, in sync with Allen Ginsberg's *Evergreen Review* advertisement to "join the underground." I was delighted at the time. For me it was as if the world had suddenly come over to my sensibility and predispositions, and I kept thinking of a line by Wallace Stevens, on whom I was writing a book: "I am a native in this world,/And think in it as a native thinks." But what many were mainly joining was an unexamined life style, backed up with an instinctive but basically intelligent reluctance to get chewed up by a stupid war. The recognition that followed of other abuses endemic to society was all to the good.

It's an exaggeration, but one that has truth, to say that the Hippies who were then beginning to drift into the East Village were picking up on the hedonistic side of the artist's life, elaborating on Beat culture, without themselves having the intense drive for accomplishment characteristic of the Beats or of any serious artist. These people were not interested in the artist's life—they were living as if art were life, given over to pleasure and excitement without practical consequences. This may have been partly the result of a too-literal take on the problematic relation between performer and audience, between art and life itself, that was one of the innovations to come out of the art of the sixties. In a nontraditional country like America, where art has constantly to justify itself, if art is too closely identified with life, one of the inevitable reactions you're going to get is "All right, if art is life, then who needs art?" In fact this was the reaction embedded in such developments as the New Journalism, at the extreme of which you get Tom Wolfe saying that its realistic reportage was what Henry James and James Joyce were really trying to achieve in their great fictions.

But whatever else, the underground in the mid-sixties was fun. Wendy Serkin was a teen-ager from Far Rockaway at the time with granny glasses, Grecian sandals wound up the calf, and long hair parted in the middle down to her waist. She'll tell you she started going to the Village when she was thirteen. That's a long ride on the subway. Later in high school she had a Mercedes. "My father bought it for me. I was a Jewish American Princess." With red leather seats. She had a knack for meeting interesting people. She would meet them in the street, or in Washington Square. She hung out in the coffee houses, the Fat Black Pussycat, and the folk music places, the Folklore Center and Blind Lemon Jefferson's, in musicians' pads and rich apartments in the West Village. She met her first boyfriend at a weekend hootenanny in Washington Square, painter Larry Rivers's son, when she was still in junior high school. He would take her to Slug's. A girlfriend from Far Rockaway High got to know Bob Dylan. "Bob Dylan loved her ass, and one day, it was snowing and I'll never forget this, the two of them were standing on MacDougal Street, and I was like just gettin' into the city and oh there they were, and I went up to him and Berta and I said, 'Introduce me to your famous friend'—I think his first record had just come out. And he looked at me and he said, 'This is Berta.'" She talked Andy Warhol into inviting her to a Park Avenue party for the Rolling Stones at Faye Dunaway and fashion photographer Jerry Schatzberg's place. There she danced with Mick Jagger and the girlfriend she went with "actually scored Brian Jones and had a long affair with him." When Ed Sanders sat down next to her in the audience at a Fugs performance, she told him she could sing better than their female singer and ended up singing with the Fugs for a summer. "As soon as I walked onto the stage the second time, Ed Sanders like picked me up and, I don't know how the hell he did it, threw me over, and he had my legs like upside down in the air. And then they would all start going into this, like, gobble, gobble, gobble"—she bursts into laughter, shaking her very black hair, now frosted here and there with gray. "The turkey gobble dance. Which, you know, to me was like really nice. I didn't understand at the time what that meant. So we were all just having fun."

When Bob Fass first heard BAI on the radio, at a time when the furthest out radio got was wry iconoclast Jean Shepherd's night show, his reaction was typical of many listeners. "I couldn't believe it. Really, I just, I don't know what it was that I heard, it was so—impossible. Yeah. Brecht. Bertolt Brecht. And Gertrude Stein. And on the radio! A children's program on existentialism. Yeah, I became very devoted as a listener." But to put the impact of hearing BAI in perspective, you have to go back to Fass's experience at Midwood High in Brooklyn.

"I wanted to be an actor when I was in high school," says Fass, a handsome if somewhat burned-out-looking guy. "I read, I wrote poetry.... I thought all art in a way was underground. I wouldn't have put it that way, but it was outside the normal everyday concerns of almost everyone that I knew. I would go to the meetings of the literary magazine, *Patterns*, I would go to the Folk Music Club. Now folk music was probably the most subversive influence in my life." We, myself no less than Fass, were coming out of an incredible cultural innocence, and the fact that it seemed like sophistication at Mid-wood only makes it a more extreme innocence, in which Gertrude Stein on the radio could be shocking, and folk music, without any other radicalizing experience or even, in most cases, study, could be a subversive force. And this is New York we're talking about, not Peoria. Imagine the astonishment of a Roman bourgeois, or even a Parisian *lycée* student, at the information that all art is underground. Even at a later period, for Fass, "underground meant fucking in the afternoon, underground meant putting a book of poetry inside a brown wrapper, underground meant going to the Stanley Theater on Eighth Avenue where you could see Russian movies, underground meant" —his voice goes ironic—"knowing a Negro, dating a Negro. It certainly meant jazz."

But there was a renegade wisdom in this innocence too, in its perception of the meanness of the official culture. The popularization of this perception in the sixties, however, without disentangling it from the innocence that had initially prompted it, led to a kind of vulgarization, if not corruption. If the official culture was bad, then anything that violated it was good.

One day, for example, I decided to go over to Hudson's Army-Navy Store. My all-purpose black turtleneck sweater is worn through at the elbows, and about every two years I go over there to get another one because they're incredibly cheap. Mostly I decide to go over there at this moment to get a visitor out of the apartment, an officemate from a temporary summer half-time teaching job at one of the colleges in the city. This guy is a grad student at Columbia and lives on the Upper West Side but says he's heard all about the East Village. He's wearing one of those blue-and-white-striped nylon seer-sucking jackets that seem to be the summer uniform for men on the Columbia campus. I have the uncomfortable feeling he's slumming.

We walk down Twelfth Street over to Third Avenue and Hudson's, the cheap-clothes mecca for East Villagers. A labyrinth of interconnected basements and old storefronts, it represents the metamorphosis of the myriad army-surplus stores that sprang up after World War II. Hudson's has been discovered by a new freak clientele that digs its amazing clothing prices and invests its working-class styles with a sense of chic whose heritage can be found in the Punk sleaze currently sold in the Antique Boutique and Canal Jeans.

When we get to Hudson's the scene, as usual, is maddeningly chaotic. I can't get anybody to tell me where the sweaters are. Nobody who works there can ever seem to find anything anyway. The salesmen are fat cigar smokers out of the old Jewish Lower East Side who are totally skeptical of the mixture of hipniks, assorted ethnics, and Bowery types who comprise the clientele. Or they're thin glazed-eyed Puerto Ricans who look like they're mainly focused on their next needle. Everybody is yelling at everybody, and shoplifting is so rife that the lifters don't bother to be subtle about it and the salesmen try to discourage them by slapping at their hands to make them put things down, or even pulling things back out of their pockets. Judging by the amount of business they do, the place must be an unexpected gold mine for its owners. Some years later when Hudson's would get more organized and businesslike, and more expensive, fewer and fewer subterraneans would go there. The wave of hip consumers had passed and gone elsewhere. Probably the people who owned Hudson's, like any other American businessmen, were just trying to upgrade their operation. They didn't understand that no longer cheap and grungy meant no longer hip, or that the store had been the object of an alternate consumerism, complete with a counterchic no less fickle than establishment chic.

When I finally find my sweater I'm told the price is $10.95.

"What do you mean?" I respond. "It was eight dollars last year."

"That was eight ninety-five, Buster. Two years ago."

Incensed, I decide the hell with it, I'll try elbow patches. When we get outside, my acquaintance pulls a pair of red earmuffs out of his seersucking pocket, the price tag still attached.

"What's that?"

"I ripped it off," says my acquaintance smugly.

"But what are you gonna do with them? I haven't even seen a pair of earmuffs in ten years."

"Well, who gives a fuck? I did it just like that."

Suddenly I'm aware that the East Village is being invaded by straight people who want to be hip, and who impose on it their conception of what they think the underground is like, gathered from sources such as *Time* magazine. And little by little, the underground gets more and more like what *Time* wants us to think it's like, partly through intrusive publicity, and partly because of a lack of interior intellectual coherence or, at least, one that is effectively communicated.

"In less than two years," says a 1966 article in *EVO*, "New York has given birth to a new and radically different Bohemia." Its components are pot, underground films, the integration of young Blacks and Puerto Ricans, underground literary magazines, and "the passion for the frenetic, exultant, near-tribal dance catharsis of today.... Dancing has become an open war on self-consciousness and inhibition." This rosy picture is extended to the slum tenements of the quarter, "the old and sentimental architecture," which "most New Bohemians hold sacred." What!? My crumbling, filthy, roach-infested building with its rats, pissy halls, leaky plumbing, garbage-piled air shaft, and its tendency to catch fire at the drop of a match, whose only virtue is an apartment for thirty-three dollars a month? And I live in a *good* building. What never-never-land of intellectual wish fulfillment is this fellow coming from? What we have here is neither an effort of analysis nor an attempt at description, but simply the selling of the underground.

The sales pitch, whether in the mass media or in the underground media itself, begins paying off in an influx of envious straights and superhip kids, soon to be known as Hippies, neither of whom have any investment in the underground as a means of resistance. One day, midafternoon, I'm sitting in Stanley's dressed in a dark flannel suit salvaged from undergraduate days after an interview for a job Uptown. Some guy I vaguely know sits down next to me and invites me to a meeting nearby. He says it's going to be fun. I immediately think of the rather stilted Congress of Racial Equality meetings I've been going to and I'm not in the mood. But he says it's going to be more like a party, so I tag along. We go up to this big apartment in a building on a corner of Avenue B, as I remember.

The first thing I notice is that after we get in, the guy who opened the door closes it with about five, no exaggeration, different locks, *clunk, clunk, clunk, clunk, clunk.* The next thing I see is that the place is filled with mainly two types, hip-looking Black guys and prim and creamy blondes almost all of whom, it turns out, are from some very proper Catholic college up the Hudson. There's a lot of pot and hash being handed around, quite a few people obviously stoned. Here and there people in various groups are making out with various degrees of intensity. From one of these groups a real pretty blonde, nineteen or twenty, detaches herself, slithers over and more or less onto me, offering me a joint, which I take. The stuff is strong, and shortly we are very relaxed together. As we engage in a few tentative fondles, the guy she detached herself from comes over and I quickly straighten up but she doesn't move. The cat just stands there smiling over us, and then bends down and says something encouraging. I'm suddenly finding this a huge turn-on. I look around the room and it seems to me the action is increasing, that we are collectively about to go into higher gear, or is it just the pot?

At about this point somebody decides to lock about five more locks on the door, *clunk, thunk, clank, clink, clunk*. I'm a little self-conscious about my suit, but as the girl is taking off my tie, I have the impression I'm not going to have it on much longer. But something else is bothering me, I don't know what. Something doesn't feel right about this scene. Maybe it's the locks, maybe it's that my desire to get it on is outweighed by my desire to be able to get out once I get it off. I don't know what this is, what it's all about, who they are. Nobody seems to be in a mood to explain. If I'm here I must know what it's all about, and if I don't, what the hell am I doing here? I don't want anyone to start asking me that question, since I don't know the answer myself.

Just about then, one of the hippest- and toughest-looking guys there gets up, and, with a look of ambivalent disdain that I imagine reflects my own feelings, asks for out. I take the opportunity to split myself, much to the disappointment of the blonde and her, what, boyfriend? who try to persuade me to stay. From subsequent information I guess that I somehow found myself in the middle of something called the Karista love cult, or the Karista Free Love Society, a group under the sway of a guru whose politics seem to be what I can only describe as reactionary-pacifist. In an early *EVO,* Umbra poet Steve Cannon has a letter complaining about the politics of Karista's leader, and suggesting that other alternatives to him might be found within the cult itself.

"Karista was a very strange outfit," says Lorenzo Thomas. "Supposedly they owned an island in the Caribbean that had been given to the guru or what have you. But supposedly their notion was they were going to pack up and move to this island. And I remember going to a Karista party once at Christmas Eve. We were just party-hopping. Well, we went to this party and somebody said it's a Karista party and I said, 'Well, I don't really know if I want to get involved in their trip.' 'Come on, come on,' 'Sure, why not?' So we got to the party, and it turned out to be one of the tamest love cults I've ever seen—men and women and little toddlers were all running around nude, but not doing anything. There was a guy sitting in the corner naked with a walkie-talkie, right? And he's got a little naked kid running around the room with another walkie-talkie and he's talking to him. This was the love cult. I was expecting to see great wild orgies, you know, dope smoking. It was like anybody else's party, couples with little kids, except they just didn't have their clothes on. Maybe the walkie-talkie was the kid's Christmas present. It's interesting to think about the possibilities."

Karista was a small sideshow in the general unleashing of explosive erotic forces bottled up by the Silent Generation and uncorked by the pill, the influence of a sexually liberated and increasingly popular underground culture, the Dionysian effect of hypnotic, heavy-beat music, among other disruptions of the status quo, including the sensuous effects of acid, which was becoming the drug of preference among the hip and pseudohip. There were still problems of suppression. Ed Sanders, who, as erotic provocateur, besides being a Fug, was publishing a literary magazine called *Fuck You, A Magazine of the Arts,* making a film called *Mongolian Group Grope,* selling pubic hairs of famous poets, and running the Peace Eye book store on East Tenth near Avenue A, received more than one surprise visit from the cops and had many an artifact confiscated as a result. But it was a losing fight on the part of the authorities. I knew their game was up when I could buy Henry Miller over the counter, and before long you could buy soft porn on the newsstands and see it in the movie houses. In the fight to decriminalize porn, and along with it, art that the authorities considered pornographic, Barney Rosset and Grove Press should get major credit.

But the delights of eros did not come to us, even then when the world seemed new, without wrenching ambiguities. Fidelity, jealousy, and exploitation were not problems that were going to be disposed of by ignoring them, though we often did. We quickly learned that it was hard to explore a liberated sexuality without paying a bitter price in terms of humane relations. And I just as quickly decided I would rather pay the price. There was no way to put the cork back in my bottle, no matter what. I was just living the kind of erotic life I had always assumed I would lead, but now the world, and not just a special underground milieu, was ready to accommodate me. I found myself making it not only with other subterraneans and assorted art molls, but with Uptown girls and prep school products as well. Oddly, their totally promiscuous behavior began to irritate me from time to time. Their "liberation" was too facile. They had done nothing to earn it except come of age (which seemed to be about thirteen or fourteen at this point) at the right time, grow up in privileged families, and read the right slick magazines. At times I felt downright exploited. But, what the hell.

If the evolving erotic situation called into question, for men, the nature of their basic relationships, loyalties, and interpersonal ethics, for many women the ambiguities were even more profound. At the limit, their very relation to their bodies became problematic. On the one hand, they were now permitted a frank indulgence of sensual pleasure but, on the other, did this not simply lead to further sexual exploitation by men? If social pressure had formerly led to a numbing repression, was it any improvement if now social pressure simply led to an equally thoughtless promiscuity? If liberation resulted in freedom of all kinds of erotic expression, did it not also let loose a tide of porn that exploited women's bodies?

One of the key issues in the underground at the time was prostitution. With the emergence of a counterculture audience for the underground, subterraneans were discovering they were salable. Maybe not so coincidentally, as the underground discovered its new markets, the idea of selling was definitively distinguished from the old taboo of selling out. Hustling of all sorts became acceptable, even admirable. There's probably always a certain amount of whoring in the demimonde. Nude modeling for painters and photographers, fairly normal work for underground women, can easily slide into prostitution, and often does. But now women's liberation combined with sexual liberation to provide an ironic rationale for prostitution. Housewives were basically selling their bodies in marriage, the argument ran, but cheaply, so why shouldn't women professionalize and at least get advantageous terms? Or was that just the ultimate exploitation? For some middle-class women, apparently, there was an ultimate erotic excitement in prostitution. I knew one redhead, very attractive, working her way through Brooklyn College by turning tricks with the complicity of her husband. They both seemed to get off on it. They were obviously in love, and always seemed to be glowing with a palpable erotic energy. If it was doing them any harm, other than the normal risks of the trade, it wasn't obvious.

One young woman I was going out with had idly mentioned that a friend was trying to talk her into turning tricks, but I hadn't taken her seriously. She was a pretty, bright graduate of one of the better colleges. She would get married or she would find a job in publishing or advertising or something like that. One day we're lying in bed when she tells me she's got a modeling job that evening. She says it's her first modeling job and she's nervous about it, and tentatively suggests that I come along. At first I refuse, because I don't want to find myself in the middle of a painting class with nothing to do but look at the model like some pervert. But she says it's an individual session and she only wants me to come to the hotel. Hotel?

Anyway, I finally say okay, but when we get to the hotel, one of the better ones, she gets even more nervous and insists I come up to the room with her. I'm wearing my usual Downtown dirty jeans, beat-up leather jacket, two-and-a-half-day beard, and no signs of haircut. The door is opened by a dapper, affluent-looking, middle-aged man, and when he sees me standing there he almost closes it again but she reassures him, I can't remember, nor can I imagine, how. He doesn't look like an artist, but he doesn't look like a seedy lecher either. In fact he looks like a reasonable and reasonably interesting human being, who seems to be as nervous about the situation as my friend is. He couldn't be poor because he not only has a room, he has a suite. Finally he says he likes to do life studies and his equipment is in the other room. They retire to the other room and stay there for fifteen or twenty minutes, it seems to me. When they come out they both look noncommittal and we leave immediately. I never ask what went on in the room, and she never mentions it. If the guy did a life study, it was a quickie.

From there we retreat to the East Village and hit a bar she knows, and I don't, on Avenue A. It's not too crowded, and as we walk in she spots a guy she knows talking to the bartender. This guy is a well-known folk singer who is one of the main heirs of the Woody Guthrie tradition. She stops to say hello to this Brooklyn cowboy, then we go to the tables in the back, where we sit down with a girlfriend of hers who hangs out there. After chatting a while my friend goes back to the bar to talk to the cowboy and stays there about a half an hour, leaving me to talk with her boring friend. I'm suddenly getting sour on this girl, and I don't like her friend much either. I think it may be time to remove myself from the arena of her sexual explorations. I now recall that she likes to make love with the shade up and the guy in the apartment across the street watching. I go to the bar to tell her I'm leaving her in the hands of the cowboy for the rest of the evening.

I don't know what she's been telling him, but before I get the chance to communicate my sentiments, he starts coming on like the most obnoxious, arm around my friend, casting himself in the role of girl stealer and if I don't like it then fuck me. Before I know it I'm involved in a rather tense exchange of insults, further complicated by the arrival of the other girl, to whom he also starts coming on, like do something about it. At this point even my friend gets upset, but her efforts to head the cowboy off only make him more obnoxious. I'm real worried about getting into a fight. I don't like to get into fights, but you know how fights start. You don't plan it but suddenly someone reaches kindling point and wham! Besides, I've heard rumors that this guy carries a knife. That, and a quick glance behind me at the bartender, whose knuckles are whitening around the neck of a beer bottle, and I think, *Forget it.* I just walk out, and the two girls walk out behind me, probably the cowboy is too violent or too drunk to be fun, or whatever the problem is. And then there I am in a cab between the two girls, neither of whom I want to get next to, rebelling against the sexual revolution and heading toward the Upper East Side because my friend has decided to move into her girlfriend's place up there and get out of this seedy neighborhood. And guess who pays the fare?

In 1971 there was a public discussion among feminists and prostitutes about the prostitution issue, recorded by *The Village Voice,* which seemed to settle very little. "Susan Brownmiller got up. 'It's hard for me to talk,' she said, 'because I am very ambitious and I have a self-survival instinct.' With immense pain ... she spoke of her own experiences as a prostitute. Many years earlier, when she was studying acting and poor, her friends all 'turned some tricks.' 'I felt being a secretary was the most degrading possible job.... One john paid $150. I was a very bad prostitute. I cried.... It was the most horrible experience of my life!' " On the other hand, the prostitutes who showed up seemed to like being prostitutes. "What do these feminists have?" asked one. "Nothin' but a lot of sex hang-ups and money hassles. Prostitutes are really the most liberated ladies. Isn't selling your body ultimately controlling it?"

About a month later, a friend of mine, Elsa Rush, wrote a reply to an article, "What Price Whoring?," that Brownmiller had published in the *Voice* in the interim. "Here are some things one can sell or rent without being identified as exploited or degraded: (1) One's highly developed aesthetic sensibility, (2) one's erudition and articulateness, (3) the benefits available from the transference of a neurotic human's emotional connection to his/her mother onto oneself—the supply to be cut off instantly on non-payment of fee, (4) one's hemoglobin ... Ms. Brownmiller's desire for selective restraint of trade is discriminatory. If the origin of Ms. Brownmiller's revulsion at prostitution lies in the fact that she practiced it immorally ('a good crying act') it is an understandable revulsion ... but there are presumably honest

whores who give an unfraudulent service in exchange for their fee."
The interesting thing about this debate was not so much the valuation
of prostitution—which historically seems largely a matter of cultural
time and place—but the fact that selling oneself in general had suddenly become an issue.

As the Hippies began moving into the East Village, we began to
see the first of the teen-age runaway problem. Kids with no resources
turned up in the neighborhood, attracted by its reputation for the
liberated life. San Francisco, as it approached the 1967 "summer of
love," was subject to the same phenomenon, but maybe worse. These
kids, however street smart, were fundamentally defenseless, and they
were followed by predators of various kinds just as surely as the
wildebeests on the veld are followed by the lions, the jackals, and the
vultures. One of the more sinister developments was the evolution
of a local teeny-slave trade. Yuri Kapralov tells the story of one such
kid in his memoir of the East Village, *Once There Was a Village,* "a
beautiful blond from Wisconsin, Helen, seventeen."

Helen made the mistake of getting seduced by the wrong guy.
"She went to him because she thought he was the handsomest guy
she'd ever seen, and she wanted to fuck with him. Which is what
they did the first night. . . . Later that night, Jack gave her something
that knocked her out. . . . She woke up on a mattress in an empty
storefront. One of her legs was held by a pair of police handcuffs
attached to a motorcycle chain that was wrapped around a pipe and
had a lock on it. . . . People were reasonably decent to her; most of
them were Dominicans. They simply fucked her, one at a time, and
not more than seven in one night. The storefront was a distribution
point. While staying in the storefront, she saw three other girls come
and go. . . . One was twelve and she was crying most of the time. . . .
From the storefront, Helen was resold to a sadist who kept her in a
completely dark room on a short chain. . . . He was also feeding her
acid or perhaps a combination of acid and speed. She was losing her
mind."

Kapralov also talks of a brother and sister, twelve and thirteen,
who were sold for fifty dollars each to an "owner" who kept them
in a cellar on Eleventh Street with his three German shepherds and

fed them dog food. Helen and these kids were saved, more or less, by Kapralov's intervention, but he speaks of others "who were never heard from again. Ever."

In a 1968 article in *The Village Voice,* I described what had been happening to the East Village. Greenwich Village, "with its boutiques, its bead stores, its coffee houses, its hip shops, has been sending its finger down St. Mark's Place, across Avenue A, up Tenth Street, and, making a left at Avenue B, has poked itself right up the anus of the old East Side which, at that moment, suddenly became the East Village. Voila, a new market—Avenue B became the camp furniture mecca of New York. Book stores opened and closed. That was about when the Hippies moved in with their crash pads and their message of love. They added color, and it was fun for awhile. Tompkins Square was an astonishing scene. On a Sunday afternoon the Ukrainians, the men in their old-fashioned black suits, the women in babushkas, would congregate en masse on the west side of the park. In the center kids would be playing on Hoving's Hill, the mound of dirt that the residents insisted be left there after a recent reconstruction. In the playgrounds in the northeast corner some Negroes with conga drums would be playing terrific Afro music. In the southeast corner some Puerto Ricans with bongos would be playing terrific Latino music. Sitting on the benches or at the chess tables all through the park was the most complete interfusion of racial and national groups this side of Istanbul. . . . If you went around to Avenue A and Tenth at night you'd find these panhandlers, chicks sleeping on the sidewalk, poor stoned bastards with brains long since burned out on chemicals, and meantime there were these cats pulling up in Maseratis, Jaguars, and Bentleys, getting out to score one thing or another, and leaving their cars empty, with the motor idling. Can you imagine leaving a Jaguar with the motor idling in the middle of a New York slum? One time I even saw this scene out of a maroon chauffeur-driven Rolls-Royce, with a couple in furs and tails."

Tenth Street on A was the vicinity of Ed Sanders's second Peace Eye book store and the Psychedelicatessen, the world's first headshop. Sanders in the first Peace Eye on Tenth and others in '67 aided the kids pouring into the East Village. A guy called Groovy, who, according to Ed Sanders, "was just a sweet kid, you know, and he was sort of a maître d' for the scene, he would help people get housing. For a while, during the spring of love, the summer of love, which was like '67, I sort of turned my book store over to him. So he sort of turned my book store into like a, I called it a mattress meadow. And so I was on tour with the Fugs that spring and the landlord calls up and he's really hysterical and he says, 'Look you gotta get back here and get those people out of here,' because somebody was trying to open up a karate school in the courtyard. And I get back off tour and I go there and the windows are broken and boarded up and all the books are in the wastebasket outside. I mean, they needed the space, because they were drawing on the walls, and there were like eighteen or twenty mattresses, you could hardly walk around because of all the mattresses and the psychedelic candles and peacock feathers and candle wax all over the floor and the walls drawn on, no lights, the lights were out. And so, in order to keep the book store, the landlord was gonna throw me out, I just sort of terminated it, it was a crash pad. . . . There was a group of people who had wanted to use the book store for the community. See, you were supposed to give things to the community, so there were the Diggers, and the Up Against the Wall Mother Fuckers. I was trying to be a part of the community."

The Diggers and the Mother Fuckers were each important in the East Side scene for a time as community-oriented operations, though of the two the Diggers had by far the greater impact. The Mothers had a programmatic inclination to violence, though the only Mother Fucker I knew, now deceased, seemed quite gentle, which leads me to believe that the violence bit was highly ideological. He was, it is said, the son-in-law of the Marxist theoretician Herbert Marcuse. The Diggers, represented most prominently in the media by the late Emmett Grogan, started out as a San Francisco group. "One of the reasons the Diggers got together was because of this influx of young people that was coming into San Francisco. And nobody was taking responsibility for them," says actor Peter Coyote, perhaps recently best known for his featured role in *E.T.* He's a tall, lanky man with a face that starts in neutral and moves quickly into surprising riffs of expression. We're talking in his suite over breakfast at some luxe hotel just above Beverly Hills. "They were publishing all these media articles about the Haight-Ashbury, which was attracting young people to the city, and attracting tourists and revenue and all of this, but there were no provisions being made for the kids.... During the sixties the Digger movement co-evolved with the commune movement." I first met Coyote during the filming of the movie version of my novel *Out*, in which he starred. *Out* is about the sixties underground, and Coyote had said it resembled the story of his life.

"I was one of the executors of Emmett's estate," says Coyote. "He overdosed. They found him dead on April Fools' Day at the end of the line on the Coney Island subway. I spent a bunch of time in New York hanging out with Albert Grossman"—the agent who represented people like Bob Dylan and Janis Joplin—"and the Band and that crew. Grogan and I had an office in Albert Grossman's office, Albert made this office available to us, and had his secretaries answer the phone for us. We were kind of running around the streets of New York and putting stuff together and Albert was kind of fascinated and liked to run out with Emmett and I because we would take him to places where he'd never go. So Emmett and I were brokering a deal between Puerto Rican gangs and the police department to try to work something out. Anyway, Albert arranged for us to meet the cops in the presidential boardroom of CBS studios at seven o'clock at night. So that the detectives came up to the door and they were let in and sent up to the twenty-whatever story and there were Emmett and I, two street guys, dressed as we were always dressed, blue jeans, shirts, boots, I had long hair and a bunch of earrings, Emmett had an earring. So Albert liked those kind of games.

"Janis Joplin and I were running around together, and we stayed friends on and off for a long time, really. I think she liked Emmett and I because we never bought into the rock 'n' roll hype, we used to tell her the truth. I remember taking Janis around New York once to all these different blues clubs, and we walked in to hear Jimmy Witherspoon and he saw her come in and he sort of nodded as if to say, 'You know, you're on top now, but lemme show you something.' And he did a set that just peeled your skin off. We would do those kind of things just because somebody had to tell Janis the truth who wasn't making any money, you know. She was a good kid, she was a good singer, but she didn't really have the miles on her. I remember one time we walked past the Fillmore in New York and she was playing with Mavis Staples. Emmett said, 'Gee, do you think you're a better singer than Mavis Staples?' And she said, 'Oh, my God, no, Mavis is the best, blah blah blah blah blah," and Emmett said, 'Well, you got top billing.' So we had this kind of funky, druggy relationship. I had a key to her house for years and we would be pals or lovers or dope partners or whatever. And I used to spend a lot of time staying at the Chelsea Hotel after the band would leave, Emmett and I would kind of move from room to room. Either one of us would be Mr. Joplin for the day or make up some title and let Big Brother take the tab, you know. So we would stay for months in the Chelsea."

When Coyote and Grogan met, Coyote was one of the key performers in the radical theater group the San Francisco Mime Troupe. Under the influence of an obscure visionary named Billy Murdoch, Grogan "actually exerted enough energy and charisma to pull a whole bunch of us out of the Mime Troupe, and made us feel what was really going on was going on in the streets. We'd gone to New York in the summer of '67 or '8, and we won an Obie. And that sort of blew my mind, because here we were critiquing the middle class and they were giving us medals. And that really helped to make us see that anything that you paid for in America could not be radical. That when people bought a ticket at the door, they knew that they were going into a business. If they didn't like the content of the play, they were still reassured that there was nothing fundamentally antithetical to the values of business, because we were up there making a living.

"So one of the reasons that 'free' evolved was to take things out of the frame of reference of commerce. Free was the guiding force of the Diggers. The Diggers did everything for free. We fed people for free, we got the crash pads and the medical clinics for free. But free in a deeper sense also meant no identity. The Diggers were always anonymous. Unlike, say, Abbie Hoffman and Jerry Rubin, who we taught. The Diggers didn't get photographed, they didn't write books that, for instance, blew the hustles of poor people. We had big fights with Abbie Hoffman, because his book, *Free*, you know, showed every free hustle in New York City, and there were poor people living on the edge who needed those hustles, and then all of a sudden they were inundated by upper-middle-class kids from Connecticut. I like Abbie, very much, and I always have. I don't think he would disagree with me when I call him a media junkie in those days." Grogan, it has to be said, is scathing about Hoffman in his book *Ringolevio*, as one who ripped off the Digger vision. Whatever you say about Hoffman's activism, though, you have to credit him with the fact that he's still at it.

"To give Hoffman's perspective the benefit of the doubt," says Coyote, "he believed that the media was a way of transmitting information about cultural changes, and he became quite good at staging events that would announce to people what was going on. The Diggers were the first to do this, 'creating the condition you describe.' So if you wanna make a statement that Hippies are a media invention and they're over and we're celebrating the death of money in the Haight-Ashbury, you stage an event. You have a funeral or a coffin that says 'Hippie, Son of Media' on it, dollar signs all over it, and just by doing that event, no matter what the media says about it, your message will get across. The Diggers were very, very skillful about manipulating the media that way." Coyote, it should be noted, was well read in McLuhan, and in fact had gone out with his daughter at one point. He had also been taken under the wing for a while by the famous ad man Howard Gossage.

"The difference was that Abbie, and Jerry and Tom Hayden and all those guys, they attached their own persona to the change, so in effect, we always felt they were announcing themselves as the new leadership. In fact the Democratic convention of '68 was a canard. And we had a falling out about it, because they were inviting all these kids to Chicago to be extras in a piece of Police Theater that was going to present the Chicago Seven as a new radical leadership. But in fact there were no permits, and they knew it. There were no rock 'n' roll bands, and they knew it. It was as capricious and as manipulative a trick as anything Lyndon Johnson or Kennedy ever did, to get these kids out there to create this huge event, called radicalizing America.

"The Diggers, on the other hand, were saying, 'Fuck that. Send those kids back to their neighborhoods, teach 'em how to use the tax assessor's office, teach 'em how to use the library, teach how to go where they're not strangers, into their neighborhoods, to get landlords to turn on the heat, to fix the water, to use the municipal codes, to make their neighborhood better.' Anyway, so free meant, finally, not only not using money, it meant free identity, cut yourself loose from your job identity. Don't think of yourself as your job, don't think of yourself as your career. You basically took responsibility for an idea and did it. It was anti-ideological, you just did it, and you did it for free. You did it because it was your authentic impulse to do. The notion of life-acting, which was twenty-four-hour improvisational spontaneous self-creation, was being done on the streets, and it rendered theater, at that period, obsolete. The theater became a safe way of actualizing fantasies. We were doing them out there on the streets, in everyday life."

Grogan and Coyote wanted "access, to make things happen, to be kind of visionary puppet masters. Cracking the city meant figuring out how to get next to who you wanted to get next to, what you had to offer them, where you could get it. And it might just be people. It might be ideas, it might be dope, it might be women, it might be whatever it was, it was like being so in touch with whatever the possibilities of your reality were, it was like living in Poland, without money, you know. Money doesn't do you any good. But if you can get a pig you can get gasoline, if you can get gasoline you can use an apartment for a half a day, if you can use an apartment for a half a day you can get a woman."

"An American is a complex of occasion," wrote poet Charles Olson, last guru of Black Mountain, the pervasively influential and, in creative circles, most important experimental college we have had at least since World War II. In a country such as ours, with a tenuous attachment to tradition, it is possible that concepts like "free identity," and "twenty-four-hour improvisational spontaneous self-creation," are more than symptoms of a brief period of the underground, but stand against a culture in which the reality of self is constantly defined and redefined, and finally called into question, by the complex of exterior circumstance, by "reality."

Underground activities, however, did not go unnoticed by the authorities. Playwright Ronald Tavel ran into trouble because of a play about Indira Gandhi produced Off-Off-Broadway by the Play-House of the Ridiculous. The Indian government took offense, partly because it thought the play was supported by its enemy Pakistan. This was the result, Tavel thinks, of a credit on the playbill to an Indian-Pakistani restaurant for lending the production silverware and dishes. In December, 1966, he received a visit from the FBI. "They were very polite, it was three guys. They were very well dressed and they were very intelligent." They were also very frank and described the predicament of the government due to Indian pressure. "They said, 'This theater is not a legal theater, and according to the zoning laws neither are the fifty other Off-Off-Broadway theaters. They exist'— and this is the phrase they used—'at the pleasure of the city, and they can be closed overnight on a million technicalities. It's up to you to close the show or throw fifty theaters out of business, and thousands of people out of work.' We talked for many hours. It was a very frightening thing to happen. And I was alone. Nobody would stand behind me," says Tavel, his faun eyes expressing anguish.

Tavel was already under a lot of pressure, feuding with his theater company and generally under attack by the media for obscenity. Even the editor at Dutton who published one of his plays refused to shake his hand: "Look, I'm publishing this because I know I'll make money, I don't have to shake the hand that wrote it." Tavel was told by the FBI people not to mention the visit to anybody. They arranged for Sam Zolotow, who covered theater for *The New York Times*, to call him up and told Tavel what to say as his reason for withdrawing the play. Tavel withdrew the play over the objections of John Vaccaro and Charles Ludlam of the Play-House of the Ridiculous.

Though the cop in charge of the East Village, Captain Fink, was generally known as a good guy, and insisted that his officers live in the neighborhood for empathy, rather than somewhere out in the suburbs remote from slum problems, incidents, instigated God knows where, were not unusual. *The East Village Other,* run by Don Katzman, his twin brother, Allen, and Walter Bowart, with the assistance of John Wilcock, who wrote for it, had a circulation of one hundred thousand, according to Don Katzman. It was an obvious target. *EVO* was also visited by the FBI when the editors printed a phony wanted poster signed by J. Edgar Hoover. They were told that was a misdemeanor. Don Katzman wrote an ironic editorial about the incident saying they were sorry for taking J. Edgar's name in vain.

"When *The East Village Other* started becoming very well known we started getting hassled by the cops, the DA," says Don Katzman. "There was a park in back of where I used to live on East Fourteenth Street. Jason was about one year old, and I was pushing him in the stroller, minding my own business, when all of a sudden this guy in a suit, I mean he was dressed in very nice clothes, is walking towards me, stops, and pulls a gun. And he pulls the trigger. The gun doesn't go off. I guess it misfired or whatever. And the next thing I know is I take the stroller and push right into his ankles, wham, like that, it was the only thing I could think of, and I pushed it and I rammed it into his ankles and he dropped the gun. There was this cop, right across the street, was standing there. And everybody's screaming, 'Did you notice that?' And the police officer finally strolls over. He just strolls over. He doesn't even draw his gun, he strolls over, he sees the gun on the floor, right, he picks up the gun, grabs the guy, he says, 'I'm taking him down to the Sixth Precinct.' So I get his number. I take my son, I bring him back up to the apartment, I go down to the Sixth Precinct, and I report it. And what happens, they say, 'We have no such police officer. No such number, no report in either.'"

Another time, a bomb went off in the *EVO* building. On yet another occasion, "I was in a restaurant with my wife having breakfast. I'm sitting there, there was this Maoist group called the Mother Fuckers, four of them come over to me, and they say, 'Katzman, we're gonna beat the shit outta you, we didn't like what you said'—my brother had written something in the column. And I said, 'What're you talking about? I'm not Allen Katzman, I'm Don Katzman.' And they go, 'Oh, you're Allen's brother, right.' So they walk away. So I come out and they're still there, and they're cursing me, and I said, 'Take it up with my brother.'

"So I take my wife back to the apartment and I go back and tell my brother. So he's standing in front of the Fillmore East talking to its owner, Bill Graham. So I tell him what happened. And while I'm talking to him, with Bill, all of a sudden we're surrounded. They got these chains, they got these bicycle chains. And Bill looks, and he just freezes. Bill, I think, was in a concentration camp when he was a child, he's got that tattoo on his arm, and he sees this and he just freaks out and he freezes. So there's just me and my brother and here's about six guys with chains. So we split apart, and I said, 'Let's go get 'em.' It's about the only thing you could do. And we go forward and they come after us and there's yelling and screaming and people are running all over the place and meanwhile Spain Rodriguez, a tough guy, but nice, is upstairs and he's shouting down, 'What's happening?' 'Someone's attacking the Katzman boys.' Spain usually carries a hatchet. He jumps out of the window onto the marquee, he takes his ax, jumps down onto the pavement and they see this wild Gypsy, with his hair out to here, a huge guy with an ax, and they split, all over the place, and he chases one of the guys down the street. And they had this new cop on the beat, doesn't know Spain or anything, and the cop goes right out and tackles Spain. And Spain's yelling, 'You stupid bastard, that's the guy you're supposed to get,' and we go running down and tell the policeman, 'You got the wrong guy.'" Katzman laughs.

One night *EVO* was invaded by Food and Drug Administration agents, smashing down the door and carrying guns. Publisher Walter Bowart was due to testify for Ted Kennedy before a Senate committee on drugs, so after the FDA left he called Kennedy in the middle of the night. "He woke him up, and Kennedy said, 'I'll get back to you.' Well he never did get back to us but what we got was Goddard, who was the head of the FDA, phoned us to apologize."

None of this, however, prevented subterraneans from getting together to set up organizations that would be still more provocative. "We were in the back room of *The East Village Other* when it had moved to Second Avenue," says Don Katzman. "And we were forming the Yippies. The meeting we had was Walter Bowart, myself, my brother, Abbie Hoffman, and Jerry Rubin. So we were discussing what we were gonna call it. See, I wanted to form a third party, a third political party. But I wanted something that was viable. The arguments went back and forth, what they wanted to do, and it came out, well, you know what it came out. It was not really a viable political offensive. It was just something that was a joke. We were discussing what we were gonna call the new party, and Jerry Rubin and Abbie Hoffman came up with the idea of the Crazies. So then Jerry turned around and looked at me and says, 'Well, what do you think?' And I said, 'If you wanted to have a reason for the cops to take a good shot at you, call yourself the Crazies. You got a perfect reason for them to take out their guns and shoot you. If that's what you want, then go for it.' So Jerry said, 'I think you're right.' Abbie Hoffman was arguing for Crazies, but Jerry said, 'No, I think that Don is right. Let's not call ourselves the Crazies. We can't give 'em any more reasons for taking shots at us.' So finally they came up with the Youth International Party."

Subterraneans who were attracted to the exploration of violence, unlike the Mothers, seemed mostly interested in learning how to deal with it, perhaps in themselves as well as in others. The protest at the 1968 Chicago Democratic convention, criticized from the underground itself by Allen Ginsberg, Peter Coyote, and many others for defective, or even cynical, organization, was a test in controlling violence that the underground failed, though with the wholehearted help of Mayor Daley and the Chicago cops. But the symbol of primal violence in the sixties was the Hell's Angels, and intersections between the Angels and the underground are recounted by Tom Wolfe in his book about Ken Kesey, and by poet Michael McClure in his book about biker Freewheelin' Frank.

"We made friends with the Angels," says Peter Coyote, "because we were all in the streets together. And when Chocolate George was killed, we went to his funeral, and the Angels thought that took a lot of class for street guys to come up and be there. And one of the women, a woman named Phyllis, used to live with this guy, Hairy Henry, she's a friend today, she was this great little fourteen-year-old runaway with this incredible ability to empathize with people and get next to people. She became a nurse, worked in a psychiatric ward, and she was one of the brokers [between the Angels and the Diggers]. And so we became friends. And at that time the Angels, you know the president of the Hell's Angels now is a lawyer, at that time they were a party club, and they had not yet taken over the Methadrine trade, they were definitely rough guys but they were not sort of organized crime. And they were a very complex group. They were a blood brotherhood and you were definitely outside of it, and as a matter of fact at a certain point I had to get lost, because I'd hung around too much. They used to come to my ranch and party and people got nervous that I had too much information about them. And there just comes a time you either join or you don't, and I didn't want to join because I noticed that when they came around all the musicians got scared, and all the poets, and all the gentle people who were also my friends, were uncomfortable."

"How come you weren't scared of them?" I ask.

"I was scared. That's why I was there. Because (*a*), I like to face my fears, and (*b*), they were really interesting. Some of the most brilliant guys I've ever met were in the Hell's Angels. That holds true to today. Also some of the most sociopathic and psychopathic. And I thank God that the brilliant ones were there to take care of the psychopaths. And one of the things I learned is, you know, there are some people that it's not easy to be. You know, their inner life is such hell, and such madness, I'm glad I'm not them. My take on them was they tended to be the fascist underbelly of America, which was something that I was upset about. There's an element of white supremacy, and kind of an alliance with forces of repression that I was always uncomfortable with. The fact that the police would give them a shopping list of radicals, maybe in return for Sonny Barger's release, was always a very eminent and real possibility. But on a one-to-one basis, I was respected and honored and protected and taken care of and learned a great deal from guys who really tuned themselves on a life-and-death parameter. And their nervous systems were so sandpapered and so tuned, it really pushed and stretched you to be around them.

"Now ultimately, it got to be something of a drag, because they were sort of the only ones that could get cocky or get loose or get crazy, because if you did, and got in a beef with one of them, you'd be under a pile of fourteen people. And if your friends there happened to remember, and got you out before your jaws were wired up, you'd be okay. But the stakes were so much higher for anyone else to get in an argument with them than vice versa, that it finally got tiresome. In small numbers when they'd come out to my house and visit everybody had a good time, because they were there for ideas they didn't normally get and music and the kind of people and the kind of interest, and they didn't come with the force of numbers and the force of muscle to be intimidating. But you get thirty guys, forty guys, in front of a bonfire, stoned out of their fuckin' minds, with semiautomatic weapons and knives and endless bags of cherry bombs gettin' thrown under tables, it's pretty bizarre."

Coyote and Emmett Grogan went down to Los Angeles once with a sometime Hell's Angel named Sweet Willie Tumbleweed and another Digger. They used to stay with a producer named Benny Shapiro, who on one occasion picked up the phone and made five grand on an idea Coyote had just given him. Sweet William was "one of the early Diggers, he was an armed robber from New York, subsequently became a Hell's Angel, subsequently was shot in the head and paralyzed in half his body in a drug deal. Very gorgeous man, looked like a cross between John Cassavetes and Anthony Quinn. Very powerful, charismatic guy. Anyway, the four of us came down to work La-La Land, and hustle money and goods and access and check it out, you know. Fuck starlets, take dope. We were all sort of vain, flirtatious young guys, like, you know, 'You like these rushes, you can't have 'em.' We were very cocky and proud of the fact that we weren't for sale. And so that fact moved us through all these rooms. And as a matter of fact, Sweet Willie Tumbleweed was the guy who gave Dennis Hopper and Peter Fonda the idea about *Easy Rider,* sitting in Benny Shapiro's living room one day. They were talking about movies, and he said, 'Well, if I was gonna make a movie, I'd just do a movie about me and my friend, gettin' on our bikes and ridin' across the country.' And they said, 'Well, how would you make your living?' and he said, 'Well, you sell dope, you do this, you do that.' "

Despite the violence, if you knew your way around the East Village, you could actually live there quite peacefully, but that changed with the advent of "the summer of love." I've never trusted the American idea of love, a sentiment that veils many impulses more basic and often more base. The Hippies irritated the ethnic groups in the neighborhood and added to its long-standing heroin problem with major trade in speed and acid. Racial tensions were escalating, not only between the Hippies and the ethnics, but also the Puerto Ricans and Blacks were getting into turf fights, and the drug scene increased the tempo of muggings and burglaries. At one point my apartment was robbed three times in about two weeks. After the first burglary I was put in touch with a woman who ran one of the used-furniture shops in the area. The furniture was used because it was used in apartments in the neighborhood until it was stolen and converted into illegal substances by local dope fiends. This woman was known as the Junkie Queen of Avenue B, and sometimes you could buy back your stuff there, but in this case, no luck.

Just before the second robbery I'm out on the landing when some guy knocks loudly on the door of the hooker across the hall, so loudly I guess the people opposite her think it's for them, because someone opens that door. I thought it was a vacant apartment, but what I glimpse in there blows me away. It's filled with television sets, bicycles, furniture, radios, tires, parts of motorcycles, stacks of records, appliances, enough to furnish half the apartments on the block, which it probably once did. After the third robbery I go call on my neighbor over there and he's very apologetic, he didn't know some of the stuff came from my place, and I actually manage to get a few items back. And free too. My then father-in-law, quoting Robert Frost, observes that "good fences make good neighbors."

None of these thieves are ever caught, so far as I know. But one effort to do so nearly results in my own termination. One day I'm in the apartment working on my first novel when about ten patrol cars pull up to the building, sirens screaming, and all these cops swarm out. I don't know what's happening but I figure the building's about to blow up or something, and I race out of the apartment to find out what the hell is going on. So I'm tearing down the stairs when two cops come around a landing tearing up the stairs revolvers out and, startled by me as much as I am by them, they jerk their revolvers up and there I am unable to stop with two revolvers aimed at my chest by two panicky galloping cops. I don't know how I do it, but time slows down, my hands shoot up, and I actually manage to remain suspended in midair over the steps long enough for the cops to look me over and for one of them to say, "That's not him," lowering their guns as they race past me.

More serious crime was also imposing itself on the underground life style. "The murder ratio went up really bad on Avenue A," says Ed Sanders. "We saw a woman chopped up and died right in front of us. And then the guy across the street who had the sewing machine store, I mean a kid just walked in and hove in his head with a brick, the kid killed him, that's all, some young boy about twelve, thirteen. I remember having a book party for somebody in my book store and I went out to get liquor, and there'd just been a murder near my book store, and I had to step over a piece of what appeared to be human liver, it was a piece of something, in order to get the additional cheap white wine for my book party."

The OD situation was getting pretty bad. A woman my sister and I knew from way back had moved into the neighborhood from Harlem with the guy she was living with and her multitude of kids accumulated from various husbands and lovers. She was in business in a so-called antique store that had moved into the space where the Annex used to be. "Leo was on junk and she was on speed," says Gloria. "And she just got the wrong needle and OD'd. She picked up the wrong needle. And he panicked and ran and left the kids. He did some time for that, I think. At that point she had no teeth. She used to be really beautiful."

Then there were the riots. It was riot time in the U.S.A. but the normal-style riots were race riots. We had our own special kind of riots. Because it was such an ethnically mixed area, we had races rioting against one another, especially Blacks versus Puerto Ricans. And then we had races rioting against Hippies. Yuri Kapralov remembers the "first, biggest, and best three-day riot on Avenue C." It's started by teen-agers. "At the intersection—by now knee deep in broken glass, with bottles flying, TPF's and kids battling it out with sticks, guns, and garbage can covers, cars burning, a man lying in a gutter beaten half to death ..." The TPF, or Tactical Patrol Force, adopts the tactic of beating up any kid they happen to find and as a result, "many brothers and fathers, even some women, come out in the streets with sticks, hammers, chains, whatever they can get hold of, and it's a whole new ball game. A huge new garbage barricade is built across Avenue C."

But I mark the beginning of the end of the East Village as a habitable Bohemian quarter from the 1967 riot over music and the tripping Hippie chick at the new bandshell in Tompkins Square. Other concerts had been held there, including some by the Fugs, and they had always been peaceful. But this time anger on the part of the locals against the encroaching and alien Hippies boiled over. "A hip-rock group came on and started playing," says the account in my novella *The Death of the Novel.* "Right away the Puerto Ricans in the crowd clutched their heads and started yelling bloody murder. Wha kina noise's this? They call this music? Pretty soon a few bottles hit the stage. Local conga drums struck up a loud counterpoint. The kids pulled up several oil drums and started pounding on them with sticks to drown out the musicians. Firecrackers were going off all over the place. The kids were climbing up onto the stage.... Huge crowds of kids were racing unpredictably from one side of the park to the other like flocks of nervous pigeons.... Suddenly there was a tall blond on the hill in the middle of the park in the center of a milling crowd. My impression was that she was wearing something white and flowing. I say my impression because the next minute she was nude to the waist, clutching a rag of whatever it was she was wearing to her breasts, and then that too was ripped away.... Part of the skirt came off, and then the rest was torn away. Through all this the girl was silent, staring wide-eyed at the crowd.... Suddenly she was lifted up into the air in her panties and carried that way at a run across the park toward Avenue B at the head of a streaming mob. Kids tore past me on bikes saying, Hully jeez, Hully jeez.... A cop car was in the crowd, trying to make its way through to the center. Everybody surged around it rocking it back and forth, banging on the windows. A kid shouldered past me shouting, These chicks come round here to play their games man, this our turf."

The October 19, 1967, issue of *The Village Voice* features two stories. One concerns the disposal of the corpse of Che Guevara by Bolivian soldiers in the small town near which he was killed. The other is a story about the murder of Groovy, along with rich-girl-turned-Hippie Linda Fitzpatrick, in a basement on Avenue B across Twelfth Street from where I was living. Together the two stories mark the end of a phase, on the one hand of romantic revolution, on the other of innocent rebellion. Linda and Groovy "died near a pile of their clothing, not merely rubbed out, but smashed faceless." It "happens all the time," writes Richard Goldstein in the *Voice*. "A man and his woman are hauled or lured down to the boiler room, where amid rags and ratsmell she is banged senseless, and both are stomped dead. . . . Fear is all over the East Village. . . . It is a slum; Groovy's death seems to have awakened that realization. . . . Flower power began and ended as a cruel joke. The last laugh belongs to the mediamen, who chose to report a charade as a movement. In doing so, they created one. By the thousands, the real victims of flower hype poured into the slums of both coasts. Lifelook filled its pages with technicolor testimonials to the young drop-outs living the love ethic their leaders were wary of." Now, and especially beginning with the Linda-Groovy murders, those same mediamen began to use the Hippie phenomenon to discredit rebellion of any kind. The subterraneans had gotten the knack of manipulating the media, but there was a real question of who had the power to manipulate whom.

But there was no going back. There had been a revolution of sorts—no doubt, in Paul Goodman's terms, an "incomplete revolution"—but things had changed enough, for better and worse, to require substantial reorientation, a reorientation that is itself incomplete today. At about that time I got a call from high-powered publishing figure Lynn Nesbit, who was to become my first literary agent, about the manuscript of my first novel, *Up*. "I like it," she said. "I was really surprised." A lot less surprised than I was. I was stunned. This wasn't supposed to happen. High-powered literary agents were not supposed to like my book. I was supposed to struggle for years to get it published. I was supposed to encounter nothing but hostile indifference from the literary establishment. Sooner or later the book was supposed to be discovered by a prestigious underground press, like Allan Swallow or New Directions. It was supposed to be ignored by the media as too, quote, experimental. It was supposed to sell a grand total of five hundred copies. The first year. But the next year it was also to sell five hundred copies. And the next year and the next year. It was supposed to accumulate a growing underground reputation, particularly among younger writers and critics. Finally, after many years and other books obscurely published, it was supposed to be rediscovered and published by a discerning editor like Malcolm Cowley, after which I was supposed to get a job at a good university as writer-in-tweed-and-elbow-patches.

I figured I must be doing something wrong.

5

THE
STORE

An average afternoon at Max's Kansas City. The regulars are starting to come in, going right to their spots either at the curving bar or
at the tables. The regulars are there every day, every night, some
arrive at eight in the evening and leave at four in the morning. Coming in from a day of bright sunlight you have a little trouble adjusting
your vision. On one such day at cocktail hour, writer Fielding Dawson walks in and almost trips over an elephant reclining on the floor.
Laughter and wisecracks from the bar. "Seeing elephants again,
Fielding?" Dawson continues over to his place at the bar near the
register. It's lying there, about the size of a large cow, a baby elephant, there on its side waving its trunk. People talk about the horse
coming in, and the chimpanzees, but an elephant in a bar, its pon-

derous reality, beggars hallucination. "Buy that elephant a drink," yells painter Neil Williams.

Mickey Ruskin, proprietor of Max's, has a following of creative people who have been going to his places all over the Village for years since the Tenth Street Coffee Shop, and who tend to refer to whichever place it is at the moment simply as "Mickey's." And Mickey, mimicked by the inner circle of regulars, calls whatever place it is "the Store." The trademark of Mickey's places is that he allows artists of all kinds free rein. Or even reign.

Early afternoon at the Store is conducive to all sorts of playfulness. Things are slow. Kids and dogs come in. Classical music from WQXR is playing on the speaker system. The clientele changes gradually from lunch through cocktail hour. The lunch crowd of insurance company executives dwindles and later some come back for after-work drinks. Cocktail hour is when the mix that makes Max's max begins. The jukebox replaces QXR. The straights lay their bucks on the bar next to the regulars like Dawson and Williams. The insurance execs mingle with the freaks coming in for their meatballs and chicken wings, the free hors d'oeuvres that probably keep some of them alive. Ted Joans has no patience with the toothpicks provided, he brings his own fork. Carolee Schneemann carries home "dog bones," packages from the help in the kitchen "for the dog," and "in them would be crushed bits of shrimp smushed into a bit of steak and wilted lettuce and potato skins with slight lipstick imprint." The dinner crowd starts at seven, some straight people and a few freaks who come early, and by eleven o'clock it's all freaks, Hippies, artists, musicians, and an assortment of celebrities and characters ranging from senators to drag queens. The jukebox slams it out and doesn't stop till four in the morning when the bar closes, but the action often keeps right on going anyway, with the regulars joining the waitresses and bartenders for drinks.

The rhythm accelerates toward the middle of the night, but in the relative calm of the afternoon, writer Donald Phelps sits at the bar reading and writing. The afternoon is an endless, soothing sentence. The only clock in the joint has no hands, it just changes colors. Only regulars can read it, and it's a great icebreaker for pickups, all you have to know is whether it's day or night. Though some of the regulars often don't. For Phelps, the relaxation is pure and unchallenged, you experience a kind of "cradling," a "burgeoning tenderness," which Phelps encourages with beer, followed by an immense coconut-covered chocolate ice cream "snowball," followed by gin. Willem de Kooning comes in and leaves a brown paper bag with the cashier for the absent Mickey Ruskin. When Mickey picks it up hours later it turns out to be a de Kooning, a contribution to a benefit auction of artwork to help Mickey pay for back taxes on Max's.

The place fills up, the regulars, whom Mickey considers more friends than customers, drift in from the outside day. For the regulars Max's is an ongoing party, one 8-year-long night with everything happening at once. The bar is a club. At certain times Jerry Houk, one of the bartenders, will know, say, forty-five out of fifty people at the bar. A regular comes over to cash a check. Mickey okays it. Someone tells him the check is probably going to bounce since the guy's last three checks have bounced. "I know it," says Mickey, "but this time he told me it's going to bounce." Fielding Dawson, at the bar, is talking to Roy Lichtenstein about Pollock. Sculptor John Chamberlain, painter Neil Williams, and poet Robert Creeley are sitting in a booth together. The novelist Ken Gangemi happens in and finds himself in a conversation with the son of novelist Kenneth Fearing that leads him to his first chance at getting a literary agent. Larry Poons is talking to another painter about his motorcycle. Actor Bobby Darin is talking to Phelps about art collecting. Warren Beatty and Faye Dunaway come in past put-down looks from regulars at the bar and sit in a booth looking haunted. Carol Bergé comes in with her editor, Bob Amussen, and introduces him to Dawson who, luckily, is in the Store that day "a little longer than I should have been," and that's how two of Fielding's books get published.

Mickey, at the bottleneck between the bar and the main room of the restaurant, grows increasingly alert as the dinner crowd starts to come in, his quick glance computing every detail. He has a way of exerting control without movement, by imposing his presence, what he calls "controlling the room." With his stringy black hair falling over his face, his overintense eyes and seedy old clothes, Mickey looks like someone the management might want to keep out, except he is the management. "He walked around like he was in a trance," looking like "one of the waiters that was about to be fired," says Carolee Schneemann. "It was very difficult to talk to him for more than thirty seconds at a time. His eyes were always roving for something that was either gonna go wrong, or something he should be watching," remembers journalist Dave Behrens, who says a lot of newspapermen used to hang out there. Behrens has a feature writer's wry eye. "He reminded me of a hockey goalie watching for flying pucks."

Mickey sits down at your table without saying hello and starts talking in a low conspiratorial mumble, then gets up and leaves in midsentence. The Store is really running well all by itself and Mickey looks characteristically depressed, maybe, one of his friends suggests, because things have moved beyond his control. Fielding Dawson, who considers Mickey a kind of genius at what he does, told me recently, "He did like the power aspect, there's no question about it, but it's a cold power." Though aware of Mickey's positive qualities, he also points out "that he could be a very cold person, he was a natural castrater, I mean the piranha fish opened my eyes right away." Mickey kept a tank of piranhas behind the bar, and every night they would be fed goldfish with people standing around cheering. "He really enjoyed that."

Behrens knew Mickey from student days at Cornell, as I did, but Dave was his fraternity brother. In Max's, Mickey would always give him the fraternity password, with a cynical smile. At Cornell, Mickey had been very shy, "one of the loneliest people I ever met," says Behrens. Mickey used to tell me how he wanted very badly to get into a fraternity and almost couldn't. He was tongue-tied and impossible with women and thought of himself as a loser. But he wanted to be "not like everybody else," says Behrens, "which I suppose ran through all of Mickey's life. In the sense of wanting to be special." Mickey had the temperament of an outsider from the beginning. After he graduated from law school and started practicing law with his father, he had what Behrens says Mickey referred to as "his nervous breakdown, and he said he just decided he couldn't practice law anymore." It was during that period that he got into the Tenth Street Coffee Shop.

Mickey started Max's as a bar-restaurant at Park Avenue South near East Seventeenth Street off Union Square only because he had made an agreement with his former partner in the Ninth Circle not to open another place in the Village. The grand opening party was in January, 1966. Union Square was as close to the boundaries of the Village as Mickey could get. But Union Square was a significant step in the direction of Uptown for an essentially Downtown scene, a move toward the posh Upper East Side with its museums, galleries, and wealth, and away from the Village and its hip and defiant creative grunge, away from even the old Cedar Street Tavern, five or six blocks Downtown. The new location immediately implied a new mix. And Max's was a mélange at every level, where different styles and attitudes kept interacting to produce new syntheses. Though there was a lot of drug dealing in Max's, it wasn't basically a drug bar. There are stories about people smoking weed there when that was still risqué and some people coming in on acid trips and drug dealers and the help on heroin and freaks poking themselves with amphetamine in the back room and of course wherever you find fashion people you find speed. But it was a place where people who never touched drugs might meet drug people over, say, a glass of champagne. At one table there would be a bunch of concept soldiers in support of whatever art movement, next to a table with Hell's Angels, next to some models, next to a politician and his entourage, next to some male hustlers. The fact that artists and other subterraneans could always get a table, while people who were just there to gawk at the freaks had to wait, ensured Mickey the loyalty of the demimonde. And it also made Max's much more attractive to the Uptown crowd.

Max's was the result of a lot of factors that came together at the same time. It was the change in the gallery scene, from Abstract Expressionism to Pop, Op, Minimal, Conceptual, and Color Field painting, at the same time pop music tastes were changing out of folk music, jazz, and blues into a new kind of rock 'n' roll, when fashion was going through important changes in exhibiting the body, when there was a strong underground film scene, when Off- and Off-Off-

Broadway theater was exciting, when the antiwar movement was gaining momentum and the civil rights movement was important. There couldn't have been a better time to open a very large bar where all these elements were welcome, the more so since the Cedar, down University Place, had been closed for a while and had moved. And Max's was attractive. It wasn't a dirty, funky boho bar, it was modern in design with a warm, inviting sense of space. It was even elegant, with red velvet booths, tan walls with distinguished art on them, and a light level brighter than most bars, a kind of Uptown bar Downtown.

Like New York, Max's Kansas City was a city with five boroughs, not one bar but five bars in one, each room having its distinct tone, rhythms, and clientele. The geography of Max's dictated the action. There was the arabesque-shaped bar on the left as you came in, leading into the middle room, which was the most anonymous area, often filled with a miscellany of photographers and models, nobodies and celebrities. The red alcove off the bar in the front room was where the artists hung out—John Chamberlain, Robert Smithson; Larry Zox, Poons, and Rivers; Clement Greenberg's crew, others. The back room was the home of the Warhol bunch and assorted rock musicians. And upstairs was the music scene, the first rock disco, the beginnings of Glitter and Punk, the room that helped launch the careers of various rock and country musicians: Bruce Springsteen, Alice Cooper, Waylon Jennings, Willie Nelson, Billy Joel, Bob Marley and the Wailers, among others.

Mickey was a master, as maître d', at composing the world of Max's, composing, according to sculptor Carl André, like an Impressionist, a Monet. The composition was based on where to put people, how, for example, to make an empty room look full and later at the door, when there were no empty rooms, whom to keep out, whom to let in, whom to seat near whom. Still later, when there were crowds outside all the way around the corner waiting for admission, Mickey's basic principle was simple: "I found very quickly, from the first coffee shop I had, if I followed my instincts and didn't let in the people I didn't like and only let in people I liked, I could make a living, learn, and really have fun." Mickey, at the door, denies entrance to one of

the straightest individuals you can imagine. Why? "I didn't like him."
The bartender makes a little motion to Mickey and he goes over to
the door. "Had there been a mention in *The New York Times*," says
Carolee Schneemann, "Mickey would suddenly be confronted with
these middle-aged couples who were decently dressed, and he'd hold
the door and smile at them in a vague way and say, 'Did you come
for dinner?' and they said, 'Yes.' Mickey would say, 'Oh, I'm really
sorry but you know my cook has left tonight and there's no food,'
and he would close the door. Then there'd be a nice-looking group
of gay guys, the waiter would give a little signal and Mickey would
scurry over to the door, he'd open and say, 'Tonight is couples only,
I'm sorry, but you can come back next week.' Every time he'd have
a story, like bikers would come in, he'd hold the door and say something like it was only tennis players." At the same time some scruffy
undesirable nobody would be allowed in without question.

Dorothy Dean, a small, frail-looking Black woman from Radcliffe
and Harvard who was one of the bouncers Mickey had working the
door—he preferred women or smallish men there as less likely to
attract hassles—says Mickey told her that Max's "should be a place
where old, he used the word 'old,' in particular artists, could feel
comfortable. He said be very careful about not refusing admittance
to somebody who looks old and shabby, because it could have been
somebody who started out as a painter. The most dreaded category
of people, people he did not want in there, were what he called the
OB's, other boroughs—he didn't want family types from New Jersey,
Queens, and weekend tourists. Those were the people to be excluded.
There was a series of excuses. 'Do you have a reservation?' Now this
is ridiculous, there were no reservations. And if somebody says that
they did have a reservation, then you'd get this phony piece of paper,
and you'd ask for the name—'I'm sorry, your name is not here.' That
kind of thing."

Max's, which made a million dollars for Mickey and then lost it for
him, was less his business than his living room. Mickey's places were
his way of being at the party he was too shy to go to. The fraternal
atmosphere was in a way a continuation of the old Italian bar scene
in Greenwich Village where the Bohemians used to hang out, familial

and tribal as well as commercial. In fact, for the regulars, Max's was as close to a fifties fraternity as you would want to get in the sixties, only it was hip and girls were allowed—though it is said that wives hated the place. There were risks to Mickey's blackball system of course: refusing admission to Jack Lemmon, or seating William van-den Heuvel in the Siberia of upstairs with the tourists. With a kind of reverse snobbism, Mickey liked to brag about whom he didn't know, just as he liked to brag about all the things he didn't know were going on in the Store, indicating that there was so much going on, so many celebrities coming in, that nobody could keep track, which in fact was true. "By the way, Mickey," drops model Benedetta Barzini, "I'd like you to meet Andrei Voznesensky." "Do you know who that was you just made me put out so you could close?" asks a bartender. "Robert Rauschenberg." "One time this kid comes in with a Black chick," says Mickey, "and I give him a little table in a corner somewhere, and somebody comes over and says, 'That's Brian Jones.' I wasn't even sure who Brian Jones was." Bobby Kennedy is hustled out by Secret Service agents who whiff some pot. Writer Michael Brownstein says the scene had less to do with who was saying what than who was noticing whom. It had more to do, he thinks, with posing and art as celebrity than art. Part of the Max's scene was a quality Studio 54 would later pick up on that was alien to an artists' bar, so in a way what you liked about it was what you didn't like about it. *I must be doing something wrong.*

As you walk through the store you notice the art: the big Chamberlain sculpture near the door that immediately announces something different is going on in here, the Judd, Armand, Stella, Williams, Warhol, Zox, Flavin. Max's is not only a bar-restaurant, it's also a gallery, with painting and sculpture from the customers who exchange them for credit in the Store, pieces that Mickey chooses by instinct at the artists' lofts, just as he chooses people at the door, according to what painters are personally interesting to him. Who knows what aesthetic quality is anymore in painting anyway, the whole idea has been called into question since the advent of Pop Art and the reification of Brillo boxes. At La Mama, according to Ross Wetzsteon, Ellen Stewart never reads scripts but picks playwrights for her theater on the basis of her impression of the writer. Mickey is a new kind of collector who is not so much a patron as a pal. Besides, as poets reading are becoming more interesting to many than reading poetry, thanks to the reading circuit, so painters are becoming more interesting than paintings in an art world where the creative act is tending to displace the object created. The line descending from Action Painting's emphasis on the gesture of composition is in the hands of theoretical literalists minimizing the value of the work in favor of its context in the world. So a restaurant, according to Carl André, can itself resemble a painting. Conceptual artists are at this point in the evolution of artistic theory, doing away with the artifact altogether in favor of art. Justification for such attitudes as Mickey's are in the air. Luckily, Mickey knows a lot of interesting painters.

The painters literally help create Max's. For example, you can follow a red line in the air from the plate glass window up front, down the bar, and all the way into the back room where it makes a little red spot on the wall, not far from the red Flavin fluorescent light sculpture that stains the back left corner with its slightly lurid hue. The red line gets more intense as the atmosphere gets smokier and it picks up the particles in the air. This is the result of the free play encouraged in Max's among artists and other segments of the bar's population. One day singer Bobby Neuwirth and sculptor Frosty Meyers meet a guy there whose business is selling portable lasers. "We got shit-faced drunk, and he sold us a bunch of demos," says Meyers, whose demeanor retains something crisply boyish.

"He would, like, take the demos he was using," adds Neuwirth, in whom you can detect remnants of goldenboy youth, "and he would scratch them with a key or something so they weren't perfect, and he'd sell them to us."

"Every time he came to Max's we would wine him and dine him and introduce him to pretty girls," says Meyers.

Frosty drills a hole through the window of his studio, which is a couple of blocks up Park Avenue South from Max's, aims the laser through the hole, and puts it on a timer so it goes on at eight o'clock at night and off at four-thirty in the morning after everybody piles out of the bar. It draws a red line diagonally across the street, goes through Max's front window, then hits a little mirror and goes on down the bar into the back room. "This was in the days of Minimal

Art," comments Neuwirth, referring to the laser's resemblance to a Minimal Art piece.

"Also," says Meyers, "it worked nice when it was snowing because all the little flakes would light up."

Max's was like Alice's Restaurant, where you can do anything you want as long as you're an artist and a friend of Mickey's. In fact, Alice was a friend of Mickey's and the two were involved for a while in a hip country scene in the Berkshires where Alice's Restaurant was located. You had the feeling that anything could happen in Max's because of the synergy of its mix. It was a place where the attitudes of Abbie Hoffman and Jerry Rubin met the media knowhow of Madison Avenue. At a certain moment you might have seen Mel Brooks, making a movie up the street called *The Producers,* walk into the bar, sit down with some strangers, reduce them to hysterics in ten minutes, get up, and say, "It's been a pleasure working your table," and go on to the next table down the line. "It was no cover, no minimum for the greatest show in town," says record impresario Danny Fields. If something wasn't happening in one room you could try the next. Late at night you might hit the transvestite scene that started at 2 A.M., and then later the bartenders getting off work from other bars, and you could have breakfast there till 3. "I ate my meals there, I got my intellectual stimulation there, I got drunk there, I got laid there," says Frosty Meyers. "It was like having this incredible living room, or studio for life, where I could really study. That's where I grew up."

Hanging out at Max's was for some people like going to a very worldly college, with a lot of the social and intellectual education people are supposed to get on campuses. It even had its own jocks —the famous softball team, which Mickey flew all over the country and as far as Los Angeles on one knockdown, drag-out drunken occasion to play a series with the Café Figaro's team after Tom Ziegler had moved his place to the west coast. Fielding Dawson, the team's pitcher, tried to get Jane Fonda to join the women's team in Max's one day, but she declined, giving him a rose as pinch hitter. Some people got their mail and phone calls in Max's, and it even served as a bank. When Max's closed there were several bar tabs of eight thousand to twenty-four thousand dollars. You could change money there.

Bobby Neuwirth remembers coming back from Europe and paying his bar bill in francs. When Dave Behrens had a bad auto accident, he took a cab from the hospital directly to Max's to get some cash. Mickey had his own Max's credit cards for selected regulars. Being able to charge things at Max's gave you the feeling you'd never be hungry again, according to Behrens. But Mickey would get furious because some people would sign for their bills so you couldn't read their signatures. If you gave the waitress a good tip she wasn't too fussy about legibility. Max's was where the artists could cash their checks. Good or bad. A painter could go there with a check of many thousands from a sale and get some cash on it till it cleared.

Simply as a restaurant, Max's had good food, and good service too. The prices were low, it was comfortable, and it had a good wine list for those who wanted it. And always, there was a feeling of protection for the freaks, a sense of freedom. When some outrageously drunk regular went over and unfastened Germaine Greer's bra she just laughed, nobody got uptight. It wasn't like a bar where if you got a little too loud or you did the wrong thing a bouncer would come over. "We lived there," says Frosty Meyers. "It was our bar. We owned that bar. We could do anything in that place."

Max's was a permanent party and the artists, to whom Mickey felt closest, were chronologically the first to come when the place opened in 1966. Then the fashion photographers who had their studios in the neighborhood started coming in. The first one was Jimmy Moore, at that point the hottest photographer around. "I'll never forget one day this group of what looked like thirteen-year-olds walked in," says Mickey, "and I'm ready to go over and clock them for age when someone says, 'I want you to meet Jimmy Moore.' " And after Moore came Jerry Schatzberg with Faye Dunaway, Jerry Czember, Jerry Salvati, Chris von Wangenheim, a whole bunch of them with their models. It was through the photographers and fashion people—designers like Diane von Furstenberg, and Betsey Johnson of Paraphernalia—that the Max's crowd first made a connection with the world beyond Bohemia. Then the musicians started coming in with Danny Fields and that was the beginning of the big mix. Finally Andy Warhol came in and made the back room his casting studio, according to Mickey.

Mickey preserved the privacy of the well-known types who came in. There might be crowds of people outside waiting to eat with the downstairs half empty, but he shunted them upstairs to touristville so the downstairs people were unharassed. At such times Max's was a little like a private club for celebrities, without being so private that you couldn't meet a lot of new faces. But nobody was pressured. Some people ordered champagne cocktails and filet mignon while those less flush could spend hours there just going to the coffee machine and taking free coffee. It resembled a European café scene where you could sit and talk all night over coffee or a single beer. Part of the Max's formula was in providing a place where the successful but hip could meet the hip but unsuccessful, and though the place was full of celebrities it was never a celebrity ghetto. Mickey as host was sometimes referred to as a Downtown Sherman Billingsley, but it always felt like a Village place.

Another kind of synergy going on at Max's was that of generations. The sixties was a period of transition, and it involved a kind of conversion experience that can be traced in the career of Mickey himself. Mickey, who started out as a nice Jewish boy from New Jersey with a law degree, ended up as the rabbi, as Carl André called him, of the demimonde. The break-out generation of the sixties broke out of a very straight background. Many were belatedly liberated by kids themselves recently hooked by a freer atmosphere. "When I came to work at Max's," says a waitress, "Mickey would be practically shocked if he thought you smoked pot. He didn't drink any liquor, he didn't take any drugs, and if you did he'd think you were a little odd, a Hippie. Club soda, maybe." And he wasn't much into screwing waitresses either. "In eight years of Max's I fucked three waitresses," says Mickey, "and naturally one out of the three I fucked I caught stealing." But Max's was a place where, among other loosening-uppers, you could encounter the attitudes of the next generation, experiment with their habits, including drugs, dance to their music, turn on to their casual sexuality, and not only turn on to them but go to bed with them.

"You just took that step and you couldn't turn back," says Joe LoGiudice, who owned an evanescent art gallery. "You stepped into some kind of unknown." With a lot of the hip people in Max's you'd discover that this dude who was sitting in front of you, maybe smacked out of his mind and in LoGiudice's phrase, "coming out of gangbusters" or someplace, had recently been a kid hanging out in front of the drugstore who went to the local prom. And suddenly he was in this space where anything could happen. "And that's where art is made, in that little space beyond mediocrity where anything can happen, and Max's helped create that little space, and that was the kind of energy that got released there, it didn't really matter what you were talking about, you'd walk out feeling that anything is possible, if I just keep doing it, it'll happen." For some people it happened and for some people it didn't, but when you walked into Max's it was as if everybody had sort of agreed that they were off on some other planet, and because of that, "you get a whole different ball game," according to LoGiudice. The comparison that comes up is the kind of space Paris used to provide Americans in the twenties.

"This whole thing was pretty shocking to me," says artist Susan Kleinberg, who came to New York and Max's from Arizona and after quitting Yale Art School. People could do anything. "Jesus, I'd just never seen people look like that, talk like that, it was a little bit surprising, all the drugs, you didn't quite know what it was or what you were into." There was nothing like that in Arizona or Pomona College. "It was like a free structure, that was what was so amazing, you could just go there and you'd almost always run into someone you knew." Or didn't. It wasn't like a bar where you stayed in your own space and didn't interact with anybody else, the choreography was more like that of a party. "There was a common assumption that you were all in something together, a kind of acceptance." Says Carolee Schneemann, "I was one of the people who felt like a princess of Max's. Now I've found out there were hundreds of us, but since most of my aesthetic and intimate life was conducted there I was never aware of how many other women were having the same sort of dance."

Max's started at the time when acid was coming east from California in a big way, when the first Be-in in Central Park took place, when Hippies were becoming a rage, and when the East Village started coming west to cross-fertilize with the sophisticates, the curious, and the opportunists from Uptown. "Being one of the first Hippies is like being a god," says one of the first Hippies, "it gives you power, because you're standing for something culturally." And Uptown people were intrigued by it all because of the sense that something was going on here they weren't privy to but that it was essential to co-opt before somebody else did. That's the attitude of the culture business, according to Bobby Neuwirth. How close to it can we get without having to take acid ourselves? "Well, the closest you can get is to go to a relatively safe gathering place with these weird kinds of people where they're not going to bite your lips and eyelids off," says Neuwirth. And they find Betsey Johnson there, who's already designing miniskirts, and Edie Sedgwick "taking Bendel skirts and cutting them off so they're midthigh, then Seventh Avenue sees it and says, 'We'll make miniskirts next season,' " says Neuwirth, Edie's longtime boyfriend. Edie and Bobby, incredibly, were Mickey's idea of the perfect all-American couple.

One of the essential ingredients of Max's was the sexual revolution. When the sex bomb hit, the scene there became something unbelievable to someone like me who had grown up in the fifties. Some people claim they were getting laid three times a night out of Max's. They would just go off to somebody's apartment and then come back. Some of the inner circle would use Mickey's office upstairs. Some people would use the phone booths. Some would use the bathroom floors. Even the arabesque bar was not unknown as a place for hardcore sex. In an amazing reversal of manners, women would try to pick me up. And not only women. I remember an odd campy dance Andy Warhol pulled on me, smiling, before he'd let me get past him one night, my unique experience of gay pursuit till James Baldwin started chasing me around the revolving door at the entrance to the Dial Press building. It's difficult to describe the erotic intoxication that took hold in those years. It was like Wilhelm Reich a-go-go, especially concerning his ideas about free adolescent sexuality, the ones that shocked even me when I read them as an adolescent. Of course, the sex bomb had more to do with the chemical intervention of the pill than any kind of inherent sociocultural evolution, much less intellectual development, but we weren't complaining. Bohemia was suddenly flooded with Uptown "teenyboppers" and "Bronx bagel babies" who couldn't wait to come Downtown and get it on with some artist or, especially, musician.

There were some lovely Romeo and Juliet stories to come out of middle-class confusions about liberated sexuality, and not only in Greenwich Village. Jill Littlewood, who is frank about saying she is the model for the young heroine of Scott Spencer's novel *Endless Love*—"It's clearly about my family.... Jade Butterfield ... is clearly me"—was a pioneer Juliet with parental blessings. She received her sexual initiation at twelve hanging around the radical Student Peace Union in Chicago, where she was "essentially the mascot." The two young lovers met at the Student Peace Union when she was thirteen and he was seventeen. She split from her previous lover and they "just fucked like crazy for four years or three years or however long it was." Her parents bought her a double bed. "We weren't getting any sleep making love on my little bed in my little room so they bought us a double bed which took up virtually my whole room." Finally she had to ask for a moratorium. "Partly I was just run ragged, I was so emotionally ragged, and I was trying to go to high school, and I never got any sleep."

Yet, "in any real sense," says Littlewood, a good-looking auburn-haired woman with an open Midwestern face, the book is "not about me at all.... There's no character that's ever developed that is anything like me.... I don't have a character, I was just this person that he fills up with fantasy." For one thing, the book doesn't catch the quality of sexual intensity that was involved. "It would go on for days, and we would never leave the room, and there was some way in which, you know, we kept pushing boundaries, I mean, out of I don't know what, it wasn't lust anymore." Eventually, the Italian director Franco Zeffirelli made a movie of the book, "because he'd done *Romeo and Juliet* and he saw this as another vehicle for that story." Brooke Shields is Jade Butterfield. "It's the most ridiculous movie you ever saw in your life."

Even if the film had been less ridiculous, she would still have found herself in the absurd situation of having had her intimate experience replicated, packaged, and sold. This was not what Mallarmé meant when he said that the world exists to end up in a good book. In life, the story ends with Littlewood revolting against her urgently permissive mother and trying "to become Miss Peck and Peck. At that point I said, 'I'm gonna do well in high school.'" At sixteen, she bought herself a hundred-dollar briefcase, "and I literally just walked around downtown in this little secretary suit. . . . That was my rebellion." While her parents "were getting kinkier and kinkier, I was getting straighter and straighter." This phase didn't last, however, and Littlewood is now an artist, living in Los Angeles with a husband who is both a doctor and a highly successful screenwriter.

The secret love affair of American Romeos and Juliets is not with one another but with themselves. It is an impulse for those growing up with the imperative of individualism to become individuals precisely because they feel they aren't. As Littlewood herself realizes, their motive "is that whatever there is, rebel against it. . . . I mean, it's that whole ethos, which is so American, of self-differentiation, and that is finally the ultimate thing that we're supposed to do, to differentiate. And to do that we have to rebel, and so if it's drugging and whatever you rebel against that, if it's not then you rebel against that." The American need to be special within a mass culture leads easily to seeking identity through a public stance rather than simply accepting your own singularity.

During the sixties, half of America joined the underground, mostly the younger half. The Hipsters and Beats, however inadvertently, spawned hordes of Hippies who inaugurated the "youth culture." As much as it represented a genuine movement of personal, and even political, liberation, the youth culture became a means of merchandising the underground and vitiating it as a form of resistance. Thanks to the underground, Romeo and Juliet grew up with more liberal ideas about personal life style, which modified middle-class values to produce a looser, more adaptable "Hipoisie." The underground had its impact on, and much of it was simultaneously co-opted by, the establishment. But as with sex, there was a long moment of genuine rebellion before the whole counterculture was digested by the consumer society, and that moment was what made Max's.

Max's provided creative people with a style they were unaccustomed to, and changed the way they were able to deal with society. It transformed them from aliens to citizens of the middle class. It upgraded artists socially and they started dressing better and felt more comfortable talking, and talking business, to Uptown people. Some creative people didn't know whether they were buying in or selling out or whether there was a difference anymore. There was an incredible amount of culture business going on in the Store, creative people selling paintings and making movie deals and meeting people from other walks of life eager to use art as a fast ticket to social prestige.

"When collectors would come to town to see my work," says Frosty Meyers, "I'd take them to the gallery, then I'd take them to Max's. And this was the most entertaining thing in New York at the time, there's no doubt about that, and I'd show them my art on the wall next to the other artists', and introduce them to other artists whose art they might go see the next day. But it was a place where you could do business and command some kind of respect." Max's was where the transition took place from artist as outsider to artist as insider, from Jackson Pollock to Andy Warhol.

Always behind the crowd noise is the jukebox, maybe the best and certainly the hippest jukebox in town, so good I come in sometimes just to listen to it. The jukebox is programmed by Mickey, with the help of friends like Danny Fields, one of those instrumental in bringing the new rock music to a popular audience in the sixties. "He hands me a record one night and says, 'Put it on the box,' and it was something called 'Break On Through,'" says Mickey. "Then two weeks later he hands me another record and says, 'Put this one on,' and it's 'Light My Fire.' Apparently he'd been bringing the Doors themselves in regularly, I mean I had no idea who the hell they were." In other phases the box is dominated by Mickey's taste in country and western.

You sit down at a table for dinner and open the menu. Your waitress might be Debbie Harry, later of Blondie, or, for a short period, Emmylou Harris—she doesn't last long, they say the cooks hassle her for singing in the kitchen. The cooks can be difficult. One, a crazy Cuban sometime drug dealer and jailbird who is especially abusive and vulgar, yells at the waitresses to kiss his dick, and that's if he likes them. Mickey isn't easy on them either. He's capable of firing them right off the floor. "It was a very rigorous, terror-filled kind of job," says poet Mei-mei Brussenbrugge. "Mickey would tell you you did something wrong or not, depending on what his mood was, and I think fire people or not." But it's a glamorous job that brings them into contact with interesting, often famous people. It's said that no girl who ever applied for a job as a waitress at Max's wasn't "looking." Looking to be discovered, looking for a job in her real profession, looking for a man. Or just looking. So that if there are no other girls around, which is however very unusual, there are always waitresses to put the make on. Or busboys. There are always a few cute busboys too. "Not every one of my waitresses was beautiful," says Mickey, "but almost every one of my waitresses was interesting. The bartenders are another scene, the bartenders with rare exceptions have to be straight and a little macho." Says Robert Creeley of the waitresses, "I always loved the tone of those women, not just that they were hip and sexy, but they were very bright people, almost without exception."

This is the era of miniskirts, and some of the waitresses are so beautiful they drive the guys right up the wall. "The idea that outside a whorehouse the help has to be sexually appealing to the clientele is an innovation on the restaurant scene in 1966," says a guy who likes to pick up tricks. "Money wasn't it, but there was no question that these girls were potentially available in the right circumstances. Or busboys. The gay world was a very important part of this whole scene." Max's is a precursor of the whole Studio 54 trip, with the sexy help, the straights and gays together and nobody cares. But the waitresses are not simply decoration, they become actresses, artists, media people, fashion designers, and, sometimes, even wives. Some of them even put Max's on their professional résumés. And the ones that are discovered in Max's for film are not so much the ones found in the back room by Andy Warhol, like Viva and Ingrid Superstar and Ultra Violet, they're discovered by Hollywood people. During the first year of Max's, according to Bobby Neuwirth, a significant proportion of the waitresses are discovered this way. And then it gets to be a real interesting place for beautiful girls to come and work at. So for at least three or four years the most beautiful women in New York work as waitresses in Max's. It's like Schwab's on the east coast.

"Steak, Lobster and Chick Peas," went the logo for Max's, invented, like the name of the place itself, by poet Joel Oppenheimer. The story is that Mickey asked Oppenheimer to think up a name for the place and Oppenheimer immediately came up with "Max's Kansas City" because Kansas City, like the new place near Union Square, was farther away from anything than any other place he could think of. The story of the logo is significant. Steak and lobster was a menu innovation in those days, but "Chick Peas" was something Oppenheimer just threw into the logo, maybe because it sounded good, and since it was in the logo Mickey had to serve the free dried chick peas, imported from Egypt, that became one of the trademarks of Max's. The story shows how Mickey was always willing to trust the creative instincts of his artist friends, which is one of the reasons Max's was such an inventive establishment instead of just another bar. In fact Mickey didn't much like Oppenheimer's name for the place at first, but some of his painter friends talked him into it. And artists Neil Williams and Frosty Meyers were very influential in the design of the Store. Max's was conceived on a napkin in a sketch by Williams.

By the time Max's reaches its normal crazed pace toward late evening, it's a kaleidoscope of simultaneous scenes. Five hundred different trips are going on in five hundred different heads in the five spaces that define the choreography of Max's. From the Flavin-stained "Bucket o' Blood," as some call the corner of the back room tinted by Flavin's light sculpture, to the sexual sizzle of the world's greatest pickup scene in the front, a tempo threatens to break loose that no *chef d'orchestre* can hope to control, not even Mickey. Five times as much is happening ten times as fast as it does in the world outside, to the beat of the bass booming out of the jukebox with the sixties rock message that life can be a permanent state of liberation, joy, and rut. As the waitresses above all know, darting among the tables and dodging or encouraging advances, you have to be quick to survive in Max's. But even the quickest can't keep up with the surges in mood, the interactings of the actors, the groupings and regroupings, the encounters, the matings, the constant tragedies, comedies, tragi-comedies, soap operas, and various outrages always going on at the same time. It's like a tank of tropical fish where suddenly some chance pattern forms among the exotic specimens, lasts a minute, dissipates, some colorful example holds your attention for a brief space, then disappears into the swarm. Huntington Hartford steps from his limo outside and comes in, very visible with his mane of gray hair, walks slowly down the length of the bar looking from side to side, walks like that all the way into the back room, comes back through and without sitting down, without even talking, goes out the front door. "He's looking for chicks," someone says.

The key to Max's is the chemistry among the types who patronize it. One night Bobby Neuwirth is out in Forest Hills for a concert by Janis Joplin and a lot of people are there, Geraldine Page and Rip Torn and Emmett Grogan with Tuesday Weld, itself an interesting combination. The concert is rained out so they go to Max's. "Because that's where you went, you went to Max's," says Neuwirth. "At that time in New York there was one place to go, not like now when there are twenty different places. In the course of an evening, every-body who went someplace would probably cross through Max's be-fore four A.M." And when you get a group like that together the energy spreads, it's not like everybody running over to see who's who, it just gears up the whole tone of the bar, the thing winds itself up somehow. Anyway, environmental sculptor Robert Smithson is there at Max's, and Robert Smithson has had a crush on Tuesday Weld for years and years.

"I saw Smithson there and it just clicked, I remember he'd been raving about one of her movies, he'd been to see it ten times. And I thought, tonight's the night. So I introduced him to Tuesday Weld. And here's Robert Smithson, who's operating on a conceptual level that prevents him from having a meaningful discussion with most people on the planet, being introduced to an actress who in most people's eyes is two levels above thumb sucking, and the two of them hit it right off. They sat down and had a discussion that was just special. They were talking about art, they were talking about films, they were talking about the differences between art and films, you know Smithson's art was done with bulldozers and airplanes and photography and concepts and writings, and they were talking about how that related to films. Tuesday Weld was a very erudite young lady and knew whereof she spoke, and Smithson turned out to have an incredible knowledge of Tuesday Weld's career. It was like one of the great milkshakes." It's the kind of thing that happens in Max's where the most famous person who comes in can end up at a table with a street singer and a Lower East Side poet and a dress manufacturer, like street person Tommy O'Donnell sitting down to talk about the Brooklyn Dodgers with Cary Grant, or Sargent Shriver coming in late one night with Germaine Greer and getting introduced to a bunch of drag queens.

The exchange at Max's was not always as sweet as the Weld-Smithson milkshake. Among the painters, for example, things could be tough. At that point in the culture business, art was where it was happening. Artists were influencing theater, they were influencing design, clothes, films, writing, and they were very aware of their importance. It got to the point where the sculptor Marisol was voted one of the ten best-dressed women in the United States along with Jackie Kennedy. The stakes were high, and maybe they weren't the right stakes, but for a young artist to be at Max's, where there were plenty of collectors hanging out as well as painters, to be seen at a table with Larry Rivers or de Kooning was a good move. The collectors started thinking, *That must be a young artist de Kooning is interested in.* Former gallery owner Paul Bianchini says that when an artist did something interesting in New York, the news traveled very fast by word of mouth among the painters. Consequently, all the artists in his gallery had been recommended by other artists.

So some young artist comes over to sit at, say, Carl André's table, knowing that André—in 1985 accused of throwing his wife out a thirty-fourth-floor window—has a reputation for being strict about who sits with him, and you can imagine how much guts it takes and how much is at stake. And there might be eight people at the table and André says, "You can't sit here." Says Joe LoGiudice, "It sounds petty, but under the pressure of the times, the availability of fast fame even for some mediocre talents, that kind of putdown was a major setback." When Bianchini takes on the painter Robert Ryman, Ryman, according to Bianchini, makes only one demand. "Paul, you know, I know you don't have any money, but I'd like to get a little bit of money. I would like to have enough money to go once a week and have dinner at Max's Kansas City." By the late sixties and early seventies, too much money is involved, too many reputations are too big. Pop pieces start breaking the hundred-thousand-dollar mark in the late sixties, according to Bianchini. Painters start sitting at separate tables because there are factions, it starts breaking up into cliques according to various schools and theories, and the exchange of ideas stops.

"Smithson and Serra were quite a team," says artist Joseph Kosuth. We're talking in his New York loft, an enormous block-through space, a white cockatoo roaming on the white-tiled eating area raised above the black floor, large white bulldog, a black and white cat. Kosuth himself habitually dresses in black. Kosuth is a Conceptualist who now thinks the idea of "dematerializing" his work, partly to defeat its commercialization because there was nothing to sell, was a mistake. "Besides the fact of all the real estate I'd own now." His work is now rematerialized. "You would sit at their table, and would just be absolutely, you know, wiped out, like fastest-guns-in-the-West art conversations, you know, real pricks, real killers. Carl André, Smithson, and Serra. I used to give them a fight, but on the other hand I thought a lot of it was macho posturing, and not really that productive. But of course if there were, you know, attractive young ladies around, our masculinity was on the line so we would have our art battles. Other things at other tables were more interesting, and also, I couldn't convert those guys, so why waste my time?" Pop artists and Minimalists and Conceptualists and late Abstract Expressionists and Color Field artists were all down on one another.

The problem of the artist's relation to success was still a contentious factor for some, though the adversary posture was quickly losing its force to the success drive. At a party given by curator Henry Geldzahler behind the Museum of Natural History, Frosty Meyers started screaming at Larry Poons that he had sold out, a scene that ended in a fist fight with Geldzahler trying to separate them. On another occasion things went as far as Dan Christensen and Michael Steiner of critic Clement Greenberg's clique going down to a gallery and literally kicking a Chamberlain sculpture to pieces. On the other hand some artists were beginning to suspect they all had the common horizon, for better or worse, of mass culture.

The painting scene with its macho tone in the front room was a carryover from the Abstract Expressionist era at the old Cedar Tavern. "To get to the Warhol section you had to walk through the Smithson section, which was like all the dark dirty vibes. It was like walking through heavy metal to get to strawberry shortcake," says art critic Peter Schjeldahl. "It was certainly a turning of the tables on the macho hero, which was just asking for it, I mean it just really had its chin out, and Warhol decked it out but good. Warhol reduced it to blithering idiocy."

Warhol had his own scene in the back room that represented a sharp break with the past and its values. Down with "painterly" qualities in art, with the aesthetic purity of artists. Down with the "tyranny of jazz," in Danny Fields's phrase, as the standard for pop music, and up with extramusical values like noise, volume, performance, dance, politics, sex. No more neat, well-made narrative in film and fiction. Out with sentimental notions about sex. Warhol's serial photo silk screens of Marilyn Monroe are about as sentimental as Fords coming off the assembly line, each one a different color but each one the same as every other. In the sense of his mechanical reproduction of multiples, Warhol is as American as Henry Ford, or as Thomas Edison in his drive toward replication through recording processes. What happens to the idea of originality with the advent of mass production, or to the idea of the unique artifact? As with the computer, there is only the abstract program and the "hard" print-outs it can reproduce infinitely. It is perhaps because of such factors that Paul Bianchini insists that Pop Art represented America's first real break with European tradition, and, one might speculate, a final and irreversible one, as opposed to Abstract Expressionism, which can be seen as an extension of European ideas. The consequent ambiguity between art and reality is illustrated by an anecdote told by Bianchini. His gallery had an "American Supermarket" exhibition in which he had some

Campbell's soup cans signed by Andy Warhol, and after it was over, he stored the cans at an artist's studio for the summer. When he came back the artist apologized to him, saying, "Gee I'm terribly sorry, but I got rather broke this summer and I ate all the cans."

The feelings between the front room and the back are not marked by mutual admiration. A few people bridge the two scenes, but not many. Some of the painters in the front don't consider Warhol a serious artist, though most agree he's some kind of genius. Carolee Schneemann refers to his voyeurism, self-abstraction, "the vacuum that attracts," his vampiristic invention of art as commodity that was absolutely correct for the cultural moment, an art that was superficially available but that lacked the sacred quality of art that satisfies underlying human needs. Peter Schjeldahl, on the other hand, admires the fact that Warhol's art "was what it was": It had "no anguish, no doubt, no apology, no existentialism, no expressionism, nothing except what it was." We're talking in the Art Café on Second Avenue, Schjeldahl laying it out with his acerbic voice. The sixties, says Schjeldahl, "went too fast for absolutely anybody, except somebody who would live only on the surface. That's why Warhol could keep his feet. Anybody who went into any depth in any degree at all in anything, you know, lost fingers and toes. The assumptions of things changed so fast, and so many unfamiliar realities were making themselves felt."

Warhol deflated the mystifications connected with high culture, but at the same time he devastated the adversary position of avant-garde art in relation to the middle class, the position that in America had generated the avant-garde's vitality, if not its reason for being. As Schjeldahl says, "he was the prophet of the embrace, of the integration of the avant-garde and the middle class." There's also the point of view that, as a young artist who was part of his entourage says, "everyone took Andy seriously as an artist because he sold," a remark in itself indicative of the new criterion he promoted.

In fact, the adversarial ideas about art that Warhol demystified were themselves ideas that the middle class accepted. They represent a projection of the middle class's guilt about its values, which Warhol knew how to relieve and simultaneously justify. Warhol let the middle class know that it was culturally contemptible while he assured it that, don't worry, there's nothing about art that you don't understand. There is an element of vindictive contempt in Warhol's activities, in view of which it is fascinating to consider Schjeldahl's observation that Warhol is one of the few American artists who has ever come out of the lower working class. "Warhol went from the bottom of the heap to the top without ever passing the middle, so it's like he was completely free of the middle-class perspective." With regard to his spiteful tendencies, you might consider Warhol's penchant for put-on, or his OXIDATION series, pieces that were created by means of Warhol's or an assistant's pissing on a copper emulsion, and that were received with critical acclaim. "The negation, the contempt, the nihilism of that gesture are not admitted in recent critical discourse," writes art critic Daryl Chin. Or you might think of his exploitation of those feckless children, and especially daughters, of the rich, like Edie Sedgwick, who were attracted to him. Or you might consider John Wilcock's description of what happened to apartments wealthy people opened to Warhol as film locations.

The Warhol bunch "would go up to West End Avenue somewhere and ring the bell of this smart, big apartment, and a woman would come to the door and Paul Morrissey would step forward and say very charmingly, 'I think Mrs. So-and-so told you about us, I'm with Andy Warhol, and I think you said you might let us film here,' and she'd say, 'Oh yes, yes, come in,' right, thereby opening her life to the dervishes. Life would never be the same afterwards, the place would be ravaged as if locusts had gone through it, you know, every conceivable drug would disappear from the medicine cabinet at some point during the filming, things would be broken, things would disappear in this chaos. But first of all, I suppose, the hostess would have been absolutely infuriated and stuff, and for the rest of her life would be so proud that Warhol's crowd had once wrecked her apartment. It was like a sort of a typhoon invading somewhere."

One regular describes the difference between the front room and the back at Max's as that between a relationship and a blow job—the front clings to old habits, the back is much more impersonal. The back room, in its feeling of cool, its pansexuality, its *nouveau* commercialism, its mystification of the superficial, its sense of staginess about the emotions, spreads the seed of the future: Pop, Punk, New Wave. You had music and art coming together through Warhol, as well as his famous movie scene. The Velvet Underground and its accompanying show, the Exploding Plastic Inevitable, including Lou Reed, John Cale, Nico, Gerard Malanga, was the real precursor of Punk, along with MC 5 and the Stooges, out of which the Sex Pistols were fabricated. When Malanga first saw Jim Morrison doing a performance trip in leather his immediate reaction was "They're stealing my act." Dorothy Dean claims that the three transvestites who used to hang around the back room, Jackie Curtis, Candy Darling, and Holly Woodlawn, are immortalized in Reed's hit "A Walk on the Wild Side."

It's cheap for Warhol, who always has a lot of money from his early Mad Ave. advertising career, to take fifteen or twenty people to Max's and he is hardly known for his largess. He's filming something, say, and then afterward he takes the whole crew to Max's. In addition, a lot of musicians start to hang out in the back room after their gigs. You might see Janis Joplin, loud and outrageous, Joan Baez, Neil Young, or Jim Morrison and Nico nodding out on each other's shoulders under the red glow of the Flavin, or Lou Reed, Mick Jagger, and Iggy Pop camping it up around one table. The dealers would be around. One night a guy gets arrested upstairs with a pound of hash. Others are bigger time, one a dealer to the stars, including Joplin, who often cuts a sorry figure, drunk, on junk, lonely and troubled. She likes to talk to Dorothy Dean, and when they sit drinking together people tend to leave them alone. Dean says Joplin liked young boys. One of them confided to Dean, "I can't keep it up. She's too demanding sexually."

Warhol sweeps in, five or six people in his entourage, with a lot of waving and yelling back and forth to the tables, to take possession of the big round table in the back room, the center of attention—especially since the room is small—called by Malanga "the Captain's Table." Warhol, who hardly ever talks, holds silent court among the faithful in a grouping that one photographer with an eye for composition thinks of as the *Last Supper*. Around the table sit Malanga, art critic and poet René Ricard, maître d' Eric Emerson, Nico, and any one of a number of Warhol "superstar" discoveries.

Mickey lets the back room do its own thing. He goes out of his way not to go in there because if he does he knows he's usually going to have to stop something. Anything from a striptease to drugs under the table to the frequent "chick-pea wars" conducted with the dried chick peas in the bowls on the tables. "We'd fire them across the enemy table if we didn't like somebody, or even if we liked somebody to get their attention," says Malanga. The striptease is frequently performed by Andrea Feldman, who pops out her tits, takes off her blouse, and jumps on top of the table singing and proclaiming, "I'm the greatest." Sometimes the stripper is Eric Emerson, whose act is more elegant. Feldman not much later jumped out a window and Emerson also was doomed to a short life. "If I liked somebody," says Mickey, "as far as I was concerned, they had an absolute right to do whatever they wanted."

There's a certain amount of back-and-forth between the back room and upstairs. The musicians who hang in the back room can be found upstairs, sometimes performing. The night Mimi Fariña is performing, Jagger and Van Morrison are in the audience. Joan Baez joins her sister, Mimi, and they invite "the Englishmen" to come up onstage. So Jagger gets up on his table and they shine a light on him and he says in a very loud voice that he doesn't like to perform in a nightclub atmosphere. By this time Sandy Bull is also onstage so he and Baez and Fariña and a couple of other people sing, but during the entire set, instead of putting the lights on the stage, they keep them on Mick. Finally he leaves. Upstairs is the hottest place in New York for music. For a while it's the first and only rock disco in town. The upstairs is used at first for the overcrowding on weekends as a place to put the tourists. Then there's a major fire and when Max's reopens the gross drops in half. So somebody brings around Sam Hood, who used to run the music scene in the Gaslight. Mickey shows Sam how small the room is but apparently, according to Mickey, Sam is in a desperate situation personally. So Hood gets it together, and till the Bottom Line opens, Max's is the major room in the city.

At that point things begin to happen, like John Hammond, Sr., calls up and says, "I want to bring somebody down who I think has some talent, I'd like your opinion." Tuesday night is tryout night. Mickey brings a few people up who are quite impressed with the guy and it becomes obvious they have something. The guy is Bruce Springsteen. A lot of musicians get started like that up there, or get going there. Billy Joel starts there and eventually buys out of his contract because Max's has options for five grand. Garland Jeffreys. Alice Cooper has a rough week without any publicity from his record company. The New York Dolls. Mickey remembers their calling him over one night and saying, "Hey, Mickey, we're forming a group." And he laughs, he doesn't know who these kids are really, they're just a bunch of Hippies to him. "The only group that ever paid to play that room on Tuesday night," says Mickey, "was a group called Aerosmith, because Sam couldn't stand them. I think to this day that Leber-Krebs, the managers, expected the Dolls to be their big group and not Aerosmith and it turned out just the opposite. I can remember listening to Willie Nelson there when there were seven of us sitting in the room. I can remember listening to Charlie Rich, who really broke out from New York with 'Behind Closed Doors,' with eight or ten people in the room." The only country star who really draws enough in those days for Max's to break even is Waylon Jennings.

A lot of music business gets done in the Store but sometimes it's hard because it gets so crowded and noisy. There's a maximum occupancy sign up front that's completely beside the point. Getting a table at Max's is not like getting a table at Elaine's Uptown, where you have to know the right people. At Max's sometimes you have to elbow your way to the right people and fight for your table as well. The big joke is always the guy who comes in and says, "I want a table, I'm a personal friend of Max's." Whoever Max is, if there ever was one, must be Joel Oppenheimer's secret, though some people think of Max Finstein, who went off with Oppenheimer's wife, then started one of the first communes and has since died.

On a crowded night the bathroom is an insanity. "It was the dirtiest, most lowlife, ugliest place in the world," says painter Jim Jacobs, "but you'd walk in the bathroom and people would be having a business meeting. There'd be two lawyers and a rock 'n' roll guy and they'd be having a business meeting there because that was the only quiet place." Nobody can ever make a phone call in Max's, forget it. There are two booths across from the bathroom. Someone walks in, sits down in one of the booths for two or three hours, and that becomes his office. He just pretends to be on the phone while holding the receiver down because his calls are coming in. People know from four to six, say, that's his office number. "Nobody would ever answer the phone in the phone booths unless it was somebody who was sitting there," says Jacobs. "Because you knew what it was, everybody knew."

One night Dominick Izzo, who runs the discotheque upstairs, is sitting downstairs at the bar with Frosty Meyers after the disco has closed at 2 A.M. Dominick is a sculptor who used to run the Waverly Gallery, but with his large bulk and deep voice he comes on more like a Mafia street torpedo. Meyers goes to the phone booth to make a call and he comes back and says someone's sitting in the phone booth and won't get out. So Dominick walks back and asks the guy, hey, do us a favor, we want to use the phone. "Because the phones are always jammed," says Dominick. "Everybody's callin' their connections, their bookmakers, or whoever the fuck they were callin'. So the guy gives me the finger. So I wait a while, I didn't say nothin' because Mickey didn't like violence. I don't blame him, I don't like it myself. So finally I go to the phone booth door, I says, 'Listen, I work here, come on, get outta there.' The guy is sittin' there and he was steamin'. He was steamin'. I says, 'Get outta the phone booth, get outta the fuckin' phone booth.' He says, 'Whadda you think, you're a tough guy?' I says, 'Yeah. Get outta the fuckin' phone booth or I'm gonna drag you out, one or the other.' He says, 'Oh yeah?' He gets up and he yanks the door open, I back off a little. He says, 'Hey, you! Commere!' I say, 'Who you tellin' commere?' And in slow motion, he starts to knee me in the balls. But it was in slow motion. I hit 'im a fuckin' crack an' I knock 'im across Max's floor, I mean the guy really slid across the floor, right? So everybody jumped in, some little fuckin' rat grabs my arms. So I walk away from it, I go in the back room and here's Mickey. Mickey comes back with the long face and the nose. He says, 'You know who you hit?' I says, 'Wait a minute, you know who tried to knee me in the balls?' He says, 'That was Rip Torn,' " the distinguished actor. Then the next night Torn comes in with a bottle of champagne for Dominick and apologizes. But after four drinks he's trying to start a fight again. "I say, 'Hey, Rip, forget about it, it's all over.' " He does that for two nights, he brings a bottle of champagne, then after that they become friends.

There is a rhythm to the evening. "A lot of the guys would get to the bar, let's say, about nine o'clock," says bartender Jerry Houk. "They'd talk about their work or somebody else's work. By twelve o'clock it had gone into bull shit. There were always the ones who would get drunk and have these serious conversations about art, and then one of the other ones who'd be drunk next to them saying, 'Hey, why don't you shut the fuck up? Who wants to listen to this shit anyway?' You know. The alcohol would get to them. By one they were looking to get laid." Things get more heated as the evening gears up toward some unknown climax. "Upstairs was fun at night when it got late because it was so wild," says Mei-mei Brussenbrugge. "It was just really crowded, people were always ordering, like, champagne for half the room, you know, just so much drama going on." Max's is a collective imagination, a heightened sense of personality, attention, expectation. Mini-plots develop, like episodes out of a freak *Duffy's Tavern*. People come into Max's and they become characters in a drama, their doings become stories, sometimes stories that change their lives. A painter comes in with his wife, she meets Jimi Hendrix there, walks out of the bar with Hendrix, and leaves her husband. For keeps. "I got over it," says the painter. "But Hendrix got over it faster than I did." For many it all merges into one unbelievable fairytale.

It starts slow. Relaxed male camaraderie and practical jokes. Mickey gets a counterfeit hundred-dollar bill, so regular Bob Povlich buys it from him for twenty dollars. Then he goes over to the cash register when Mickey isn't there and gets five twenties in change. He tells Mickey and Mickey just laughs. "One time following a fire in the place, I came in after an exceptionally long drinking afternoon," says writer Donald Phelps. "I felt a sense of abandon and a pervasive feeling of freedom. This is something of which I have no memory at all but I was informed afterward that I attempted to walk off with the cash register. It was sort of nice to hear because it suggested I'd been incorporated into Max's general tapestry of legend. One version of it was that I started to sing a song from *Up in Central Park* that goes, 'The fireman's bride, the fireman's bride, won't sit home by the fireside.' The only construction I can put on it is I was picking up a cash register as a ready prop for a fireman's bride, or that I was involving myself in allegorical depths that I seldom venture into in my sober hours."

The man working at the door spots a group walking down the street toward the bar so he steps outside and asks, "Can I help you?" and one of them slams him in the mouth. Just like that. They walk on in and sit in a corner. "And I'm standing there," says Mickey, "and somebody says, 'That's Peter O'Toole.' So I'm standing there like a shmuck. And suddenly I realize, what the fuck difference does it make who this is, this guy has just whacked my man with absolutely no reason." Mickey walks over to the table and says, "I'm sorry, I'm not serving you." One of the women with them asks, "Why?" and Mickey says, "Because Mr. O'Toole just whacked my employee for no reason at all." And they get up and leave.

At midnight Mickey likes to feed goldfish to the piranhas in the tank behind the bar. "Christ, people would line up at the goddamn bar and they couldn't wait to watch the piranhas get the goldfish," says Jerry Houk. "Finally, some of us get tired of it." Somebody, drunk and after closing, takes a quart of Beefeater and pours it in the tank and gets rid of the piranhas. This time Mickey is really pissed.

"I can remember one night with the Hell's Angels," says Mickey. "Some huge guy was there with a bunch of others and I could see immediately that this was one I wasn't going to handle by myself, so I called the cops. He was just very drunk, he was hitting on chicks, and he was just bothering people. And there were a group of them, and Hell's Angels, when they get together, you can't separate them and if you go after one you're going to have to go after all of them. . . . So four cars show up, the cops, I tell them the situation outside, and they say, 'Well, what do you want us to do?' And they were kinda leery to come in too. So I said, 'Well, why don't you guys wait out here, and I'll see if I can talk 'em out.' So I walk up to this one big guy who's really making the trouble and I say, 'I think you had enough to drink, and I'm cutting you off and I'd like you to leave.' And the guy looks down at me, and he goes, 'You and who else?' So I said, 'Me and the eight cops standing outside.' And the guy, all of a sudden, changes his tone entirely and said, 'You're violating my civil liberties, we're gonna talk to our lawyers about this.' And they left."

The tempo increases. Robert Creeley, one of America's best poets, is sitting in the front room with Dorothy Dean, whom Mickey considers the smartest woman he knows. Mickey introduces Dorothy to Bob because he thinks it should be an interesting meeting, and Dorothy immediately starts insulting him. "Bob is drunk out of his skull, and Dorothy is also smashed. And Bob is being a perfect gentleman even in his drunken stupor," according to Gerard Malanga. "I was trying to be kind of confidently curious," says Creeley, "which was like pouring oil on fire, it was just incredible. She got more and more glorious in her really harsh and kind of wildly obscene tongue." She is very bright, Creeley emphasizes, and had been given an extremely sophisticated education at Radcliffe. "And Bob said something that totally irritated Dorothy," says Malanga, "and Dorothy just hauled off and smashed him in the face." Later Creeley writes a poem about it and eventually they become good friends. "Bob ended up saying to me, 'Can I crash on your floor?' " says Malanga. "So we got home, and I had a bed loft, and I'm lifting Bob"—who is about three times the size of Malanga—"up to the loft and he almost falls on top of me and we almost ended up going out the bedroom window together. And then in the morning Bob said, 'I'm going to see Charles at New York Hospital,' " meaning Charles Olson, Creeley's great friend and poetry cohort. And that's when Malanga realizes why Bob is in such a state. Olson dies a week later. Fifteen years later, just recently, I would have to give the news of Dorothy Dean's death to Creeley.

Nobody knows all the things going on in Max's, there's too much going on, and it's going too fast. Jim Morrison is sitting at a round table and he has to piss but he's very lazy and drunk and he doesn't want to get up. There's an empty wine bottle on the table and he holds it under the table, pisses in it, and then puts the cork back. "And we're getting up to leave and he says to the waitress, who's all agog at the idea of serving Jim Morrison, 'I couldn't finish this bottle of wine, why don't you take it home?'" She thanks him profusely. "I don't know what became of it," says Danny Fields. "It looked like wine." At another table a chimp with shades appears to be reading the wine list. At another table a buxom woman says she's hot; her boyfriend says, "Take your shirt off, nobody'll notice." She takes her shirt off and sits topless for half an hour, forty-five minutes. Nobody notices. And it's real crowded. The waitress comes and takes her order and doesn't notice: "Yeah, whadda you want?" Up at the bar a famous Scandinavian movie star is hiking her skirt and exposing herself and nobody notices that much either except the guy sitting next to her, who notices a lot. "I'm working her over. But meanwhile I'm trying to make believe it's not happening. The bartender had no idea what's going on. There was something nice about it, you know what I mean?"

A rather straitlaced British woman comes over to a booth and asks a guy she knows if she and her friends can sit down. So they sit down and the British woman looks at the guy's lady companion and says, "Why don't you introduce us to the lady?" The guy says, "I don't even know her name. She just pulled up in a car outside and opened her trench coat." The British woman says, "What do you mean?" and the other woman pulls open her trench coat, under which she's wearing nothing, and says, "This is what he means." Everybody continues eating and drinking, trying to be polite, but finally the guy says, "All right, keep the booth," and takes her outside. A little later he's screwing her in the car in a parking lot, the car shaking and the windows fogged, when he notices somebody looking in. He reaches for a baseball bat or something but she says, "It's all right, let him watch."

Upstairs on the dance floor a famous American movie actress is picking up maître d' Eric Emerson with her famous French movie maker husband. "His big kick was watching Eric Emerson fuck her," says Mickey. Eric Emerson will go home with anyone of any sex. By all accounts, according to Mickey, he's the only guy on record who actually screws more than he talks about it. Emerson was terrifically handsome, according to Dorothy Dean, and also absolutely obnoxious. "Mickey for some reason I have never figured out absolutely adored this kid," she says. One night when she can't sleep, Dean goes out to a soul food restaurant in the Village named the Pink Teacup and Emerson is there with someone else she knows. She tries to ignore him but he invites her over to their table. "He says, 'I want you to read something to Joe for me, cause I can't do it myself.' I said, 'What do you mean?' He says, 'I don't know how to read.' " So they get to talking and after a while she asks him why he's always so obnoxious. "He said the truth of the matter was he was terrified of people." Emerson is found in the street one night supposedly run over by a truck, but they say he OD'd on heroin and was thrown under the truck afterward. Mickey is so upset by his death that he throws a big wake for him at Max's with free liquor for everyone. Lou Reed, who has the reputation of being crazy and nasty, is also real upset, according to Dean, and writes a song about it.

"Boy, it looked good, boy, in the early sixties it looked real good," says Peter Schjeldahl. "There was a definite kind of expansionist thing with poetry, I mean Ginsberg, and also in the Russians, Yevtushenko, it was like kind of a worldwide sense of poetry as being a generational thing. And Frank O'Hara seemed to show how to be terribly erudite and terribly sophisticated and at the same time have the common touch. But then the roof fell in, in a lot of ways. Poetry went in the toilet, mainly because its generational role was completely taken over by pop music, by Dylan and the Beatles. Pop music, poverty, and drugs just absolutely burned the heart out of it, in the sense of social irrelevance, the depression of being so poor, and the complete delusions brought on by drugs. Everybody took too many drugs, no, I think they were terribly destructive. Especially amphetamine," which was the big drug at the time. "It's a drug that tells you you're doing something when you're not. And you can spend your whole life thinking you're doing something and not doing it, while your personality is disintegrating and your stomach lining is developing gaping holes."

There's all this stuff going on that Mickey doesn't know about, he likes to boast. People getting sucked in the phone booths, fucked on the bathroom floor. "I'd like to have a nickel for everyone who got fucked in my phone booths," says Mickey. An artist is fucking a woman in a phone booth while a second artist is blocking the booth from a third artist who happens to be the woman's husband. In the front room Povlich invites painter Dick Haas, a newcomer to whom he's showing the town, over to the bar where they find a girl engaged in fellatio with all comers. "Jesus Christ, Povlich," Haas says, "you certainly know how to entertain." "I turned around one night," says a painter, "and this girl was down on her haunches and she was giving this guy a blow job. Then she turned around and went to the next guy. And she went up the bar and if a guy didn't want it, another guy was ready to take his place." But she's discreet. The place is, as usual, jammed, and not many people can see what's happening. When they finally catch her and throw her out she complains, "Not one of those guys was able to get it up." A girl from New Jersey.

Dorothy Dean is working the door of the disco upstairs when Robert Rauschenberg comes out, blood absolutely streaming down his face. "Consensus had it his dog had attacked him. He always brought his dog with him. He'd gone up there with his dog and also a boyfriend, and there'd been some kind of an argument, and the lover had broken a bottle and slashed his face with it." Suddenly, downstairs, one of the stagy "cowboy fights" erupts between John Chamberlain and Neil Williams, knocking one another over tables like in a Western. They're old friends, according to photographer Richard Davis, "and they love one another." Somebody walks over to Warhol and dumps a beer on his head. Some girl strolls in casually with a boa constrictor wrapped around her throat. Upstairs Dominick starts dancing with someone and then realizes it's Monica Vitti. "Performing those days," says Carolee Schneemann, "we'd come in, ten or eleven of us, almost naked, with greasepaint and glue and the performance would be sticking to us. I remember being wheeled in there once in a grocery cart that was a prop left over from a BAM performance that we did. And that was just fine, to have me naked in the grocery cart being wheeled up the aisle. That meant that Mickey would have a little extra delight in that evening, and," she laughs, "I'd get a few extra dog bones."

Mickey eighty-sixes a customer and tells him to get out of the place the fastest way possible. He does. He's an acid freak and he's so high you can practically see him levitating. He seems to get higher and higher. Finally he gets up and floats like a bouncing balloon toward the plate glass window at the front of the Store and with one last, unhesitating leap before anyone can stop him he crashes through the window, his molecules somehow passing through those of the smashing glass because he ends up, standing on the sidewalk amid the smithereens, without a single scratch on him. But apparently puzzled by the debris, he surveys the ruins of the window and, in the silence of the awed bar before he brushes himself off and gets into a cab, is heard to say, "Jesus, that wasn't supposed to happen."

CHINESE
CHANCE

W hat happened had already happened before it seemed to happen in locations like Max's. It had happened over years in East Village apartments and cheap lofts with hard work and often in anxiety and loneliness. Max's was the party where you went when you were done to relax, blow off steam, and trade thoughts that had come up in the course of your work. At the party something else happened: What was happening in the East Village alternative culture was bought and sold as the youth culture, to the point where the old myth of artistic purity was shattered and American creative artists lost their innocence forever. *That wasn't supposed to happen.*

The Store was a place where freaks mingled with businessmen, where Uptown met Downtown, where the middle class joined the underground and vice versa. It was a time when avant-garde artists were making fortunes and innovative writers were being snapped up by the publishing industry. It was an atmosphere in which a generation discovered the avant-garde could be a vehicle for making it. In Max's you could see the underground simultaneously celebrating its success and ensuring its failure as a cultural alternative. Max's was a symbol of the culture explosion known as "The Sixties" at the moment it reached critical mass and detonated, radically influencing the mainstream at the same time it blew itself apart and left in its wake a half-bred Hipoisie. The thin membrane insulating the life of art from the life of commerce was broken, releasing a shock of energy that disoriented everyone. Many artists liked it and wanted more. But when the store appeared to be sold out and it looked like nothing was happening anymore, it was in fact still happening, though from the viewpoint of a consumer you never know what's happening until it comes to market.

When Sukenick found himself sitting at a bar table with Norman Mailer, Dwight Macdonald, and Robert Lowell after the 1967 antiwar protest at the Justice Department, he felt uneasy, if fascinated. *I must be doing something wrong.* The mere fact of inclusion, however incidentally, among a group of eminent writers, disturbed his sense of himself. Though he knew by now that his real self was a creation that had to be constantly reinvented to keep up with his sense of the world, he was also aware of his often irresistible impulse to imitate those around him. He was supposed to be an outsider, a subterranean, but here he was forced to mirror himself in the glass of celebrity. Mailer, it appeared, was busy trying to bait Lowell on the topic of his pacifism, but was doing so in an imitation English stage accent that Sukenick thought was a joke until Mailer's persistence in this mimickry forced him to think again. Sukenick was amazed to discover that everyone else at the table seemed to take Mailer not only seriously, but indeed with the cautious attention that one might normally award a time bomb audibly ticking.

It dawned on Sukenick only much later when he read Mailer's book *Armies of the Night,* about the 1967 Justice Department and Pentagon demonstrations, that Mailer, by his own third-person account of himself, is no mere mimic but is a multiphrenic with a handy miscellany of personalities. Mimickry by itself was an impulse that Sukenick could well understand and sometimes justifiably indulge, as here that of the book in question, since such imitation, properly executed, brings along with it an intuitive comprehension of the ideas, attitudes, and modes of feeling that produced the style of expression at hand. Now, striving to comprehend through mimickry Mailer's dualities, if not pluralities, Sukenick intuited that the persona Mailer assumed at the table had a certain utility in helping a Brooklyn Jew spar with a man of Lowell's aristocratic breeding, a speculation bolstered by the fact that *Armies of the Night* is based on Mailer's assumption of the persona of another Boston aristocrat, namely that of Henry Adams of *The Education of Henry Adams,* the appropriation of whose style is acknowledged by Mailer only through sly allusion in the name of a hotel.

But the matter of moment here was Sukenick's troubled status as a subterranean. At the time of this episode Sukenick was still an innocent, that is to say he was still caught up in the schizy dualities that have dominated the culture at least from Henry Adams down through their interplay in Mailer. Adams called them the Virgin and the Dynamo, creativity and power; Mailer, mystery and technology, Christ and the corporation. For Sukenick in that small moment they resolved into underground and establishment, purity and sell-out, but all came down to the same schizy split. Americans professed to believe, oddly, that power is nasty and sterile and that passivity is creative and virtuous. You could argue that this merely provides a way of exercising power without taking responsibility for it. Mailer, crazy and shrewd, reveled in the contradictions of American culture, personifying one side of a duality and then the other, instead of synthesizing them. Adams, allowing each side its place, was drawn to the Dynamo as much as he loved the mystery, and in the end for him they came down to the same mysterious energy. It is an energy whose power is sometimes passive, sometimes masterful, of mysterious source and invisible agency, notwithstanding, Sukenick thought, the confidence placed by Mailer and the Beats and the succeeding McLuhan generation in visibility, publicity, and even celebrity. They say that publicity is power, but Sukenick tended to believe that, except in special conditions, publicity is an ephemeral and negative power, conceding more to the public opinion it is meant to sway than influencing it. Whether Sukenick preferred his own invisibility to the visibility of Mailer is something that you will have to ask Sukenick.

I, however, have different ideas on making it than those of Sukenick twenty years ago, and they are echoed by novelist Steve Katz as we talk in a Village café on La Guardia Place called Bruno Bakery. "Someone keeps tossing the coin and it falls on one side or the other. I mean look at Philip Glass. When I met him he was living on Twenty-third Street in this kind of slanted apartment in a condemned building. But Phil always had a talent for cultivating the right people. I don't know if I was one of them or not. But the first concert I saw of his was in some little basement somewhere and it was actually Paul Zukofsky, the great violinist, playing a piece of his, walking around the room. It was very beautiful. I mean, now the sucker is writing the score for the next Olympics, you know, when the guy runs in with the torch."

"A lot of people say his music has changed," I remark.

"It's slicker. He made that decision himself. He wanted to cultivate the popular audience. Like Laurie Anderson, he wanted to appeal to a broad audience."

"Remember he did a whiskey ad?"

"Cutty Sark. Yeah, he got a lot of flak for that from people in the art world. I think that it's a great thing. Paid the tuition of his kids for a year, anyway."

Some people have a talent for cultivating the right people, some people have a talent for a particular art, some people have both. Whatever the case, the quality of the work is not necessarily the key to money and celebrity, which have more to do with the toss of the coin. When Jean Stein vanden Heuvel invited Steve Katz to a party after his first novel appeared, he had no idea who she was or that her scene was one of the centers of the radical-chic literary establishment. Katz, a blue-eyed street Buddha from Washington Heights, was playing handball that day near the party, so he said, "Well, listen, I'll come up after handball," and he did. "So I went up to this party and

I walked in and there they all were. The French maid opened the door, Jean came over and she introduced me to Norman and Arthur and, you know. And I was standing there with my handball gear and my sweat shirt on. But I didn't know how to handle that. I think if people knew how to handle it, they could do it—if people had those ambitions, they could do it."

"Well what would you have done?"

"I don't know, if I knew what I would have done I would have done it, and right now I wouldn't have to be talking to you, because I would never have been in the underground."

There are, however, some talents that can't be digested by the establishment, and perhaps Katz is one of them. There are also those who refuse to be. Ross Wetzsteon points out that though Sam Shepard is considered our best playwright even by the establishment, he's never agreed to a Broadway production. But this may indicate a more complicated adversary situation than the traditional one between an avant-garde and the middle class since, in fact, Shepard has become something of a star in Hollywood films. For theatrical people, Wetzsteon says, Off-Broadway is no longer a ladder to Hollywood, but rather there is a kind of shuttle between the two worlds that allows actors to do different kinds of things for different kinds of audiences. This situation does not challenge the legitimacy of the more sophisticated audience. On the other hand, there is no longer the shock of betrayal that was part of the impact of Seymour Krim's article "Making It!" in which he sardonically advises going all out for money and fame. But serious confusion remains. Says Katz, "Selling out is doing something for someone else, rather than for yourself or your own vision, and that's become very confused now, because people have figured out that their own vision is what'll make them money, like 'My vision is a million dollars.' "

While there is nothing wrong with making money on your art, confusion derives basically from the fact that though art is salable, it is not merely merchandise, and the artist's worth cannot be measured by the money he or she makes. It used to be taken for granted that worldly success is not necessarily the same as artistic success. A creative artist can make a million dollars and be considered—or feel like—a failure. In effect, money is not enough to pay artists for what they do. Even celebrity, the ultimate status in electronic America, seems in the arts somewhat sleazy. A writer on a talk show is a little like an organ grinder's monkey—if he knows enough tricks, he might come off looking good. Celebrity is a form of esteem based on media attention, as distinguished from fame, which is based on accomplishment but which may gain very little attention, at least in the mass media. This is a distinction derided, typically, by Norman Podhoretz. Nevertheless, a figure such as Samuel Beckett is famous, but he is not a celebrity.

A cultural underground sustains the distinction between artistic achievement and worldly success, even when envious of the rewards of that kind of success. The underground audience of peers and hip critics may not be disinterested, but it probably provides the most authentic consensus today for artistic success as such in a culture increasingly dominated by commercial factors. This is in part because an underground calls status quo values into question rather than reinforcing them, thus asserting an independence of judgment. An underground is neither necessarily a physical place nor a particular life style, but precisely this mutinous attitude. It is an attitude conspired in by dissidents inside the establishment and those at its fringes, without participating in the dependent duet with the middle class called alienation. A true subterranean feels no remorse about his divorce from the middle class, which was not a matter of alienation but enthusiastic choice. Since the upheavals of "The Sixties" it is the middle class—for example, in the Yuppie phenomenon—that has shown signs of seeing itself as problematic and alienated. Yuppies seem to regard themselves as outsiders on the inside. Underground art is defined by a kind of consciousness for which social values are, to begin with, problematic, always to be questioned. Subterraneans have learned by now to be at home with that mentality. The underground is a form of resistance to conventional wisdom, constantly testing the status quo that mainstream art basically accepts in its acquiescence to conventional forms of discourse, even when it expresses dissenting opinion. Not that subterraneans are endowed with an inherent moral superiority. On the contrary, subterraneans at bottom don't give a damn about the ordinary goals or even conventional decencies of society, which they will often ignore in pursuit of excitement, joy, knowledge, or seemingly inexplicable self-destructive adventures of the psyche conducive to, among other things, releasing the imagination.

One consequence of such an attitude, however, is a distancing from the mainstream, encouraging along with other influences a critical perspective on middle-class values. It is from this vantage point of difference, rather than alienation, that an underground serves as part of the conscience of a culture, and a culture may be measured by the degree to which it can accommodate such a critical force. This is true beyond questions of institutionalized moralities and righteous politics. Cultural undergrounds are notoriously unreliable in terms of ideologies and politics, but the other side of the coin is that they can free themselves of political cant and ideological rectitudes to make their judgments as they will. When an underground loses that kind of independence it is no longer an underground. It has lost its adversarial freedom, its ability to mount a critique of the culture. In individual cases, such loss of perspective is part of the reason American artists are often addled by success. I've seen more than one friend suddenly come on like a great artist when his work starts making money, as if money certified genius and those with the power to dispense it necessarily had cachet. I've also seen such artists put down by former friends for excessive ambition or even for selling out. But worldly success is aesthetically neutral, even when the means to it are ethically noxious. Life is not art, and the work may get more beautiful as the artist's life gets more repellent, as well as the other way around.

In any case, worldly attention is fickle. French-born novelist, jock, and ex-paratrooper Raymond Federman speaks in his heavily accented "Franglish" of "the pace at which we function in our society. Suddenly, you and I are supposedly part of a movement which some people have called Postmodern or whatever they call it, and this movement is now being pushed aside because the next one is already present, they call it the Minimalist or the Neorealist or whatever they call them, and so that nothing gets finished, nothing gets to the end of its possibilities. You can see it in the last forty years of painting in America, it has put out these marvelous works in painting, and yet no one knows what happened to it, the next movement is always there, the next wave is on. The same thing in the theater. So that no one is able to sit down and evaluate it, to give it a value, was that good or bad? Pscht!—it's out of the way. Basically, the economy, we are part of this grinding machine that has to grind new products out. I always wonder about these new improved products they sell me, it means that for several years I was using a deficient product, I kept brushing my teeth with this Colgate, that's why my teeth are falling out, it was not improved, but now it's improved, but I know that next year they're gonna improve it even better, you see."

The economic grind was part of the reason that there was an exodus of subterraneans from the East Village at the beginning of the seventies. New York was getting more expensive. The question was what would make money, or where could you get along with less of it? Those few who had made it had it made, those who hadn't had to start thinking about a way to live that made it possible to get home at night without getting mugged or raped on the way, to open the door without finding the place burglarized again, to send kids to decent schools, to earn money without putting in long hours at mind-granulating low-pay jobs. Thus plain demographics had a lot to do with the crumbling of a coherent creative community. Subterraneans started moving at a rapid rate to Vermont and Maine, the west coast, or hospitable college campuses all over the country. But there were more profound reasons too that have consequences for us today, in the faltering of a cultural movement and its apparent fall into an interlude of incoherence and loss of direction. In fact an underground in a commercial culture will always exist, if only because subterraneans continue their work, which does not depend on financial reward. But an underground may disintegrate as a movement, or its relation to the mainstream may change to the point where it becomes for a time unrecognizable, even to itself. In such circumstances the underground will submerge and become invisible to media view. This gives subterraneans a chance, as individuals, to reassess their situations, and to confront the problems that in the rush of a dynamic movement have developed to the point of impasse.

What does a vanguard cultural movement do with a middle class that democratically claims a willingness to entertain—and be entertained by—any movements that come along, and assimilate them into itself without discrimination? In Europe the avant-garde sustained resistance to bourgeois ideology in successive generations for more than a century despite followers of critic Renato Poggioli, who like to cite his contention that such movements are individually doomed to co-optation by the permissiveness of the class they oppose, but not his insistence that the avant-garde in general will endure. In the United States the middle class does not pretend to an ideology, instead it pretends to be merely a situation incidental to capitalist economics. In such circumstances it is true that an adversary movement will get nowhere with a thrust whose rationale is mainly that it is against the middle class. The response of the middle class will be "Good, we're against it too," just as presidents now campaign against Washington. Ross Wetzsteon contends that the failure of the Off-Off-Broadway movement was due partly to its self-definition as being merely *against*.

A "counterculture" both opposes and complements the mainstream. The complementary attitude of a counterculture toward its indiscriminate acceptance by the middle class is its implicit yearning for acceptance and reward from the middle class. At the same time, the counterculture communicates the hidden message that it knows best what is good for the middle class. This is not implausible, since a counterculture is itself a self-critical projection of the middle class, though there is no reason why that should necessarily invalidate it. However, the sign of a genuine adversary movement is its power to provoke antagonism. During the sixties and seventies the middle class and the counterculture fell into a complicitous pseudopopulism, which in any case is the main phony mode of American politics. The major message of pseudopopulism seems to be that what is good for the middle class is good for the people, while the needs of actual people, middle class or otherwise, are ignored in the name of populism. The only way out of this impasse is to develop a positive program and maintain it in the face of both failure and, especially, success in middle-class terms. There is no intrinsic reason why "success" should corrode a well-considered and credible adversary program any more than "failure." Less. Henceforth, to be a rebel, you must know what you would do if you were on top of the heap as well as on the bottom. I do not agree with the basic contention, in Charles Newman's interesting potpourri of intellectual one-liners, *The Post-Modern Aura,* that an adversarial stance toward a middle-class culture itself out of control is impossible because there is no coherent target. If that culture is out of control it seems to be consistently so to the profit of the upper-/upper-middle-class segment of the economy.

Painter and critic Martin Washburn, who persistently maintains his own artistic pursuits outside the establishment, and who looks a bit like Gulley Jimson in the movie of *The Horse's Mouth,* traces the dilemma of an American oppositional culture in the evolution of the painting scene out of Abstract Expressionism. "I think that an enormous kind of fissure opened, or issue was broached, with Abstract Expressionism. Something really radical happened in terms of consciousness. To me it was like opening a piñata. The things inside are still wrapped, you don't know what they are, but it's filled with things. However, the main fact of it was shock. Now I think it was on the strength of that shock that Abstract Expressionism made its aesthetic statement. Well, the next problem is, what do you do once the piñata has been broken open—in other words, what's in there? Now the Abstract Expressionists not only didn't approach this problem, they acted like there was no problem. . . . I would say the Laurentian world emerged and was made visible in the American context in painting.

"De Kooning and all those guys, they're very smart guys, they talked to each other, they had a language for what they were doing. They deliberately made it unpublic. The problem is taking responsibility, really. They wanted to, by not naming things, by not letting things jell, make it so that they would kind of be pervasive everywhere, so they were like something you could never flush out of the system, so to speak." But the problem is, if you don't name it you can't change it, which made things very difficult for the succeeding generation to find something to take off from. The painters, by their refusal to articulate what they were doing, allowed their work to be isolated by the language of others, according to Washburn, kept it from developing, muted its implications, and made it palatable to middle-class culture.

Part of the problem was that "the Abstract Expressionists made their paintings out of their own vulnerability. A perfect parallel in a popular form is Marilyn Monroe," which may be why de Kooning found her so scary and seductive as an image for his paintings. The vulnerability came from the fact that part of their idea was that the painter should not completely understand what he was doing as he did it, that the process should create something unpremeditated, that artistic creation should be an act of communication that must be completed by the audience. So, with Pollock, his greatness is problematically linked with his weakness.

But in the historical context, the Abstract Expressionists also tried to freeze the moment of breakthrough where they didn't quite understand what they were doing, and thus never had to take responsibility for it, says Washburn. This then became a shrewd way of gaining acceptance by middle-class culture, which doesn't want its artists to act responsibly or to work out the implications of their discoveries—it prefers them as drunks, clowns, or crazies, addicts of any kind, and as infantilized as possible. The painters, however, were consequently left in a vulnerable position. "They weren't even able to protect themselves against their own court jesters. So I was at some party in the fifties where Greenberg turned to de Kooning and said, 'You're finished.' Now, see, the Cubists, anybody who tried to talk about what Cubism was, they would have killed the guy. Because Picasso could use words like, you know, he was one of the great critics of the century." What followed then, to abbreviate history, was the typically American schizoid swing, nothing having been thought through, to the opposite pole in Pop Art, rather than an evolution out of what had been accomplished by the Abstract Expressionists.

Its specific historical accuracy aside, and not denying the fact that at least since Abstract Expressionism, American artists are hardly lacking in theoristical justifications for their work sometimes even in the absence of a respectable body of work to justify, this analysis can claim at least a metaphorical truth to the cultural process. It has its analogues in literature, the theater, you name it. The Great American

Lout is a prime image of the hero, the Hairy Ape, Brando in *Streetcar,*
not only in works of art, but for our creative artists as well. Unthinking and inarticulate, he is a creature of unerring instinct, the instinct
provided by the middle-class intellectuals committed to the masochistic pseudopopulist idea that blind instinct is somehow superior to the
open-eyed and considered thought in which intellectuals are supposed to excel. In any case, instinct certainly provides an excuse for
not thinking, and for the projection of the guilt and assumption of
the rage that the middle class generates in connection with those it
exploits. This, in turn, is a convenient way of evading the source of
those feelings in class behavior with therefore no possibility of doing
something about it, and of getting the feelings themselves off in self-
defeating adolescent rebelliousness, frequently victimizing women.
"Ste*llah*!" I mean, imagine Martin Luther King as the intellectual's
vision of the populist hero and figure out how far he would have
gotten.

The necessary complement to pseudopopulism is pseudoelitism.
Paranoia about pseudoelitism is most often stirred up by culture merchants against cultural productions that are hard to understand and,
worse, hard to sell. Bearing in mind that a mere enclave of kindred
souls does not constitute an elite, the idea of a real elite, in a country
dominated by a homogenized mass market and that, moreover, does
all it can to deny the very fact of a class structure requisite for an
elite, is something of a joke. We no longer have an independent
intellectual elite, nor a power elite that dominates taste. The only
elite that could possibly be a factor in the cultural arena is the corporate elite that increasingly controls the mass market. Elitism is simply a red herring to prevent us from thinking about whether the
various kinds of creative arts we in fact have are adequately accessi-
ble, provide sufficient options to the public, and enrich the audiences
to which they are directed, however small or large. In the case of the
mass audience, the answer to these questions is obviously no.

By the beginning of the seventies, ambivalence about the anti-
intellectual streak in American culture had been compounded by newer
conflicts. The sixties, with an avant-garde vitality it is now fashionable
to demean, minimize, or forget, had redefined much in American cul-

ture, including middle-class aesthetic standards, but at the same time eroded the mystique by which artists had resisted the pressures of the marketplace. Recently I asked Seymour Krim what he thought now of younger artists' attitudes about making it, which he himself helped to create. "They all want to make it very quickly," he told me. "That sense of commitment is just old-fashioned to a lot of people in the young generation. They refuse to be suckers for what to them is a bogus spiritual commitment." It seems that the underground has caromed off the cult of failure—Bohemia's self-defeating reaction to middle-class ambition—back to the good old American cult of success. As Krim says in a recent article that can be taken as an update of his "Making It!": "The bullying standards of electronic show business ... have completely broken down the last resistance in even the once aggressively pure arts," creating a situation "in which one personality symbol, or idea emblem, succeeds another, with lobotomized unconcern as to continuity or worth beyond arousing an audience hard-on for some calculated end." And in which an apocryphal Hollywood reaction to Elvis Presley's death—"good career move"—makes a lunatic kind of sense.

On the Lower East Side, says younger painter Chip Spear, "galleries are popping up almost weekly. People twenty-two, twenty-three years old, these kids will open a gallery. It's almost as if the dealers are becoming more the stars than the artists"—that is, those who sell outshine those who produce. In many cases the dealers are also artists. They are inspired by presumably vanguard painters only a year or two older, like Keith Haring, Jean Michel Basquiat, and Kenny Scharf, who are already making enormous sums on their paintings, which have "a perfect showcase in the reclaimed lofts or gentrified houses in which so many upper-middle class urbanites now live," according to *The New York Times Magazine*. Basquiat's dealer was selling his paintings so fast that Basquiat "did not always feel the paintings were finished."

The situation in the graphic arts raises the question of whether the avant-garde will continue to be part of an underground in any sense. Clearly someone like Basquiat, if he is an avant-gardist, is no more alienated, not to mention adversarial, with regard to the status quo than a Yuppie entrepreneur trying to crack the supermarket chains with a new commodity. But, in fact, a vanguard is not necessarily adversarial. An avant-garde leads the pack, it does not necessarily oppose it. Furthermore, during our period of technological dynamism and political quiescence, the urgencies of knowledge, of stylistic breakthrough to new discoveries, seem to outweigh those of social mutiny, damping the revolutionary impulse of the avant-garde. Clement Greenberg's analysis of the avant-garde in his famous essay "Avant-Garde and Kitsch" is hardly correct about the avant-garde in all its phases, but it has a *de facto* veracity given the way things have evolved in the United States. In 1939 Greenberg claimed that the avant-garde, rather than revolutionary, has traditionally been attached to the ruling elite because it needs the elite's money. If it is the case today that the avant-garde follows the money, as it seems to be, then the underground can provide an adversarial alternative.

The avant-garde is merely the activist side of an underground, whose activism may or may not be misguided. Furthermore, culture is no longer the preserve of the rich and the powerful—a cultural elite in that sense no longer exists. Informed taste is as likely to be found, for example, on any college campus as it is in the boardrooms and salons of the wealthy. We no longer live in a cultural boobocracy of total ignorance. There is an increasing public for formerly elitist arts, and government grant programs now share cultural power with rich benefactors. Those with money to invest in the inflated art market are by no means those with the most acute cultural intelligence. Howard S. Becker, analyzing the gallery system in *Art Worlds,* notes that potential buyers are at a disadvantage partly because "the art world has become increasingly esoteric and professionalized." Buyers may help set trends but they lack cultural authority, and may add to the fluxy instability of the art mart. To the extent that aesthetic endeavor caters to this pseudoelite, it can only begin to succeed as art by incorporating a certain amount of cynicism: Sontag's Camp, Warhol's Pop, salon graffiti.

The fact that authentic art is less and less the exclusive domain of a power elite is in itself threatening to the authority structure of the status quo. The underground seems to endure, as both a Bohemia of

248

pleasure and an enclave of resistance. That tenacity, and its capacity to include diverse solitaries or groups and a variety of vanguards, the unlikelihood of its staking itself completely on the success of yet another one-shot "movement," makes it in the long view a means of creating, preserving, and spreading genuine culture for any audience that might evolve despite the corporate elite's control of distribution. A particular avant-garde, in success, may merge with the mainstream, but the underground, independent, exploratory, and inventive, remains as the critical and even prophetic component of the culture. This may be strikingly true under regimes that succeed in presenting themselves smugly as virtual Utopias, since in a culture already disrupted by discontent and upheaval, there is no lack of critical voices.

Krim, Mailer, Podhoretz, and Warhol have done a good job—maybe too good—of demystifying the cult of failure, but it was a cult that in any case had dubious sources. It derived in part from an attitude of tweedy elitism left over from the old genteel tradition, which held that valid artistic success could initially be recognized only by the happy few. This conservative genteel pose was improbably reinforced by the residual revolutionary mystique pervading Bohemia, inherited from the failed radical movements of the thirties, which assumed an antagonism between the best creative artists and middle-class culture. Add to these the hostility to success in bourgeois terms inherent in an essentially European avant-garde tradition, at a time when creative artists were becoming self-consciously American, and you get a combination that was increasingly irrelevant to the American situation at the beginning of the seventies.

The democratization in the arts that had been evolving through the sixties, crudely summarized by Warhol's dictum that "anybody can do anything," opened the door of opportunity to a great deal of slop but also to many genuine talents who might have been excluded. Punk rocker Jello Biafra had no musical training when he started singing and still hasn't any. At the beginning "it was more of a dream than anything else. We had no instruments, we had no command of instruments, we just had ideas dripping out of our ears." But sometimes technical crudeness helps because you can't be slick. There is always plenty of opportunity for slop, but it is more important that this trend allowed people to do something of creative significance without long years of expensive training or an almost crushing toll of personal sacrifice. Technique became less essential while at the same time all kinds of programs in the creative arts became more numerous and available. The old split in American culture between an Anglophile gentility and a native populism, reopened by the Beats, tended to give support to this trend of democratization. Finally, the counterculture was moving into an anti-ideological mode that brought it into conflict not only with New Left radicals, but also with the supposedly counterestablishment intellectuals—ideologues who nevertheless had themselves declared the end of ideology. Its diminution of ideology allowed the counterculture to become the scandalous darling of the establishment media—as in Ed Sanders's 1967 appearance on the cover of *Life*—increasing its availability to a broad constituency. This odd alignment of forces should itself have been sufficient to indicate that a new situation was at hand, one that has generally been described by the overly simple label of co-optation. In effect, the possibility of participation in the mainstream was being forced on the underground. Under these circumstances, many expatriates from the demimonde, including myself, began to grope around for modes of retrenchment and preservation of an adversary culture.

One night I find myself in a Denny's in Laguna Beach, California, at 2 A.M., contemplating plastic and wondering, like the Graduate, if that's what it's all about. I had just spent an evening around the pool with some wealthy conservatives who were neither corrupt nor Philistine, and who presented a persuasive example of a productive plutocracy. Was it wiser, finally, to align your values with the still impressive efficiency of the American production machine, or was it possible to oppose to it more humanely creative values as a participant rather than as an isolated drop-out? Shortly, two answers would be suggested, one in a personification of an older and more complicated Bohemian tradition than anything I had so far known, another in a figure who represented a novel contemporary solution.

I suppose I had begun with the belief, shared by much of my creative generation, that to be the kind of writer I wanted to be in this culture you had to live marginally, that residence in a poor neighborhood was essential and living more or less hand-to-mouth in defiance of the tenets of middle-class society was part of the package. Maybe it was something I had to do simply to find out that there was life beyond the middle class and to prove to myself, in face of class propaganda, that you did not necessarily cease to exist but in fact could intensify your life by escaping class limitations. My model was not the Beats at all but Henry Miller. The Beats, as far as I was concerned, were just Henry Miller on wheels. Just as Anaïs Nin had sent a book to Djuna Barnes, whose work had helped crystallize Nin's style, without getting a response, I had sent one to Miller, with similar results.

Miller, it seemed to me, had articulated something so essential about American life that you could live out your years in America as an alien unless, in one form or another, it became part of your psyche. This is what I would call the conversion experience, that epiphany of self-recognition that is a discovery of a real self beyond the claims of official existence, and at the same time a ticket, though not in Miller, to participation as a singular individual in a shared public life that subverts the claims of our homogenized mass-market culture. Completely secular, it nevertheless retains the form of religious conversion. You see the light, you understand your relation to the social realm. It is our substitute for the sense of one's place imposed by a more traditional culture. The infidelity, the disloyalty, the theme of frank betrayal that runs through Miller's books I took as a reflection that Americans, coming from elsewhere, always had to commit an original act of betrayal against their native cultural heritage in order to bond themselves to a new kind of life. For Miller and other Bohemians, the treason is against the middle class and leads to dropout, but its object is no less a new life. There is no going back to the world of our fathers, no matter how nostalgic you get about roots. This is a phenomenon that is detailed with an unselfconscious and perhaps even unconscious pathos in Podhoretz's *Making It,* as young Norman is weaned away from his Yiddish background, first by his Wasp schoolteacher, and then by higher education, and finally by an attitude of pragmatic careerism.

I'm sitting around the pool with Anaïs Nin at her home in the

Silver Lake district of Los Angeles. She's read my work and she's telling me I'm a new Henry Miller. A couple of months later she's telling me she's changed her mind, she now dislikes what she considers a crude sexuality in my books. "What about Henry?" I ask. What about her own *Journals,* I wonder, the visit to the whorehouse with Henry, the endless affairs recorded, yet so evasively that the uninitiate might never realize they were affairs? What about her current situation, in which her husband in New York may or may not be aware of her cohabitation in Los Angeles? Nin, Miller's companion in Paris, had lived the life of an arch-Bohemian whose erotic side was to be documented only in posthumously published extracts from her unexpurgated Paris diary in 1986. But it had been a life of complex contradictions. For one thing, being an Upper Bohemian, she had never been at the mercy of that life. On the contrary, she had often been in a position to act as a kind of muse, sympathetic protectress and even patroness of the arts. Her husband is both a film maker and a banker. Her Los Angeles home is a beautiful Lloyd Wright house in the hills bordering the city. In America she represents a tradition of European Bohemianism far more than the Europhile, but quintessentially American, Miller.

Nin emanates an air of delicate evasion, almost Japanese. She seems to do things out of complications and swift contradictions that are hard to pin down, for which the term "self-serving" would be too simple. At first she wants me to write something about fiction, then it turns out it should be particularly about her fiction. When I finally accede, what I write is largely about fiction in general and very little about her own, which does not please her. Yet when I start writing I realize she's correct in thinking I seem to have something to say on the subject, and the result is a series of essays about writing that eventually turns into my book *In Form.* Her delicacy seems to come along with an artfully manipulative strength. Though she must be seventy at the time, I notice, sitting there at pool edge, that she has the legs of a teen-ager and a perfect face, no wrinkles, masklike, certainly lifted, an artifact, emblem of a woman who has insisted on creating her life rather than allowing it to mold her.

Nin, when I knew her in California, did not seem marked by a convulsive, Miller-like conversion, but rather by a steady commitment to the creative life and to cultivating it wherever she might find it, both in herself and in others. She seemed, like the French, able to countenance the multiple contradictions of a complex society in a manner you would not want to call hypocritical, but rather something like creatively evasive. You can never resolve the self-contradictions of civilization, and sincerity doesn't help, may even, in its claim to finally get everything out on the table, comprise the profoundest hypocrisy. Perhaps, in a European view, civilization is knowing how to live with contradictions and make something of them. In any case, Nin was capable of containing much contradiction, and this allowed her, I believe, to base the oppositional function of the arts on their claim to cultural centrality. I don't think it would ever have occurred to her that the interaction of the creative, even underground, sensibility with the middle-class commercial culture could be in any way illegitimate. Her example suggested the possibility of an active cultural politics that might be an extension of creativity by other means, and that the Sukenick of twenty years before would have considered impure.

During the period when I'm still a new Henry Miller, Nin throws a large party that she says is in my honor. Though I have the eerie feeling she's told at least several other people the same thing, and maybe even, if true, because of that, Nin takes the opportunity to initiate some creative personal connections. At one point she brings over a somewhat South American Indian type, dressed like a professor, stocky, with a face that seems split into halves and eyes that seem to go off in different directions. He looks like someone who's been holding himself together under enormous strain. An acquaintance of mine once described Carlos Castaneda's appearance in an article as that of "a Cuban waiter," a description that apparently infuriated Castaneda. To this, and an incident in which his wife somewhat innocently crossed Castaneda, my acquaintance attributed one of the most spectacular series of misfortunes I've ever heard of this side of Job. Among other things, he developed a strange skin disease that nobody could diagnose, he had to leave his job, his wife started messing with other men and left him. To peg Castaneda as banal, a run-of-the-mill fake, is, I believe, an error, if not one that deserves affliction with a hex.

The first question I ask Castaneda when I meet him at the party is whether the books he's been writing are not really fictions. I ask this out of my own sense as a novelist that they are works of imagination. While his answer is obviously no, today, from this distance in time I don't think I'm far from wrong and would even go further in proposing that Castaneda's life is itself a work of imagination of which the books are merely records. As I subsequently get to know him I begin to suspect that Castaneda is capable not only of inventing himself but also of deinventing himself. I discover that he often makes a point of frustrating expectations, of creating discontinuities in his public image. He's notoriously hard to locate. He claims he's going to be in one place and mysteriously turns up in another. You expect to meet him here and you find him there. I go to meet him for a lunch appointment and am assured by his colleagues he's in Mexico —when one of them meets him in an elevator a few hours later he thinks he's having a hallucination. Castaneda announces he has to see me right away and abruptly leaves his office, then never makes contact with me. Now and then there are rumors he's dead. The best way to meet him is by accident, though this guarantees nothing. When I run across him in a Los Angeles coffee shop he looks me straight in the eye and says, "I can't talk now, I'm in Mexico."

Castaneda's books are not novels, but they do belong in the realm of the imagination. As such, the question of whether they are truthful or fake diminishes alongside other issues. We like to think of everything as true or false, which fends off realms of experience that make us feel uneasy. But art, which exercises the imagination on experience, cannot be judged as true or false. It applies, among other faculties, the power of feeling to the world. Feeling is neglected not only as a response in our culture but as a way of knowing and an efficacious force. For Castaneda's Don Juan, "the world is a feeling," so you can say that the power of a sorcerer is the power of feeling he can, through the imagination, bring to bear on our sense of the world. As sorcerer, Don Juan breaks down the schizy separation of imagination from life that tends to vitiate both. This lost connection is maintained in our empiricist civilization only in the arts, where it is allowed to survive as in a zoo.

The sorcerer applies the full force of the imagination to experience and in making this manifest, Castaneda creates a dialogue between the rational and the nonrational, between the modern and the so-called primitive, between the literal and the metaphorical. In the books Don Juan is Prospero. The world of the sorcerer is a stage and Don Juan is the skillful stage manager. That he uses fear, trickery, deceit, hypnotism, and drugs in performing his role is not only beside the point, but is part of the normal repertoire of the shaman by all accounts. If Castaneda uses some of these same stratagems in exercising his imaginative power on the public through his books, he is legitimately operating within the area outlined explicitly by their teachings. Castaneda is a mass-market shaman. As such, he is not so far distant from an effective novelist, except that he is exercising his imaginative spell directly on the world rather than through an intermediate fable. As Don Juan's whole effort is to "interrupt the normal flow of interpretation," so Castaneda's is to make us see the world as a nest of possibilities rather than as an immutable given. It is just this sense of reality as responsive to humane vision that energizes the artistic imagination in general and dominates the alternative sensibility of a Bohemia. And it may be in part because Castaneda's work encodes and preserves the energy of that vision that it became so popular with a waning counterculture. His success suggests that an adversarial vision can function in the mass market and in fact probably always has.

One day in Laguna Beach I received a letter from something called the Coordinating Council of Literary Magazines, an organization that I believe until that moment I had never heard of. It invited me to come to Boston, expenses paid, to participate in some kind of board or panel. It sounded like a bore and I would have decided not to go except that I was getting claustrophobic in Laguna. It was a decision I would come to regret as boards, panels, meetings, statements, planks, and long organizational phone calls began encroaching on my creative life like sand invading an oasis. In point of actual experience, boards, panels, and planks turned out to be as wooden as they sound, but the obvious fact soon dawned that out of them you could build a structure. And at the beginning of the seventies there was a damnable logic in the necessity of structures.

The various confrontations with power and violence that brought the flower power of the Woodstock Nation down to the realities of American life—the march on the Pentagon described by Mailer, the Chicago Democratic convention, the Altamont riot, and even the Manson murders—had destroyed some subterraneans, like folk singer Phil Ochs, who couldn't come to grips with the changed scene. Ochs committed suicide in 1976. "He felt he had been a shaper of society and couldn't figure out how to keep doing that," said his brother. The situation moved others, like Jerry Rubin, to frank sell-out. While some were driven further underground or became, like Abbie Hoffman and Timothy Leary, actual fugitives, one of the courses that had been opened to subterraneans moving into the sixties was that of creating their own alternative institutions. Black Mountain College, the commune movement, listener-sponsored Pacifica radio including WBAI, *The Village Voice*, and the later underground press organs such as *The East Village Other* were some of the more important alternative institutions that had been highly effective. However, many of them had either failed, were failing, or, in success, were becoming increasingly mainstream. Communes like the one Jill Littlewood's mother started in the Carmel Valley ran into the problems of city folks trying to live in the country, and presented a tableau of houses patched together with various materials, chronically half finished. The most enduring communes tended toward an authoritarian structure. The Pacifica stations fragmented into political splinter groups that turned off their audiences. The underground press was the object of a largely successful campaign of government repression, documented by Geoffrey Rips's book, *Un-American Activities,* sponsored by the PEN club, and some of the papers just ran out of steam. *The Village Voice,* which was sold so the owners could cash in on it, and then was grabbed successively by Clay Felker of *New York* magazine and media mogul Rupert Murdoch, is now run by ex–*New York Times* people and, according to some old *Voice* hands, has at best a conventionalized and passionless adversary relation with the establishment, especially the cultural establishment.

In addition, it was becoming apparent that the sixties opening to unconventional art was an atypical deviation, given our fundamentally commercial culture. With the special exception of the graphic arts, we were moving into the era of cultural conservatism and the tyranny of the bottom line. The year after Nixon was elected I was hired by Roger Corman to write a radical peace film. While I was working on it there were denials in the newspapers that the new administration was cracking down on "campus" movies. One gossip column cited the film I was working on. But every time I sent a version of the script in, it came back with the message from the studio that it was too radical. It was pretty clear it wouldn't be produced if it was too radical. At the time Corman, a thrifty man, had commissioned a hundred scripts, he told me, and had filmed ninety-nine of them, the exception being a story about Robert E. Lee, which he didn't want to produce during the civil rights movement. The film I was working on didn't get produced either.

In the age of conglomerates, the appealing American image of artist as lonesome cowboy had all the practicality of a horse on a highway. There were those who still liked that scene—the wandering minstrel on the poetry circuit with the indulgent university as patron, the iconoclastic outsider with the working wife. But good cowboy boots were pushing $150 a pair, and nobody asked the Lone Ranger how he afforded his silver bullets. Even the small presses, once directed to the happy few regardless of profit, were rapidly assuming a small-business mentality. It looked like bye-bye, Miss American Pie, as the song says.

While the commercial world withdrew cooperation, the nonprofit sector threatened co-optation. In the sixties the old story of the committed genius holding out against a corrupt society had become a myth for suckers. Much of the avant-garde decided it wanted in. Now. Uneasiness was swept aside by many examples of creative people who were successful in both commercial and avant-gardist terms. Since we wanted in, we no longer had our myth of the outsider to sustain us, either when the bottom fell out of the market or when, more confusingly, some of us were granted our middle-class fantasies of success, or even moderate support. Suddenly the avant-garde was being supported by government grants. The dependent whine of the supposed maverick feeling shortchanged by the dole became a familiar sound. To introduce a new antiestablishment nonprofit publishing company I was given a page of *The New York Times Book Review* to write an article about it. Rebellious writers, formerly inclined to spit in the face of academe, were being hired by creative-writing programs, and those who weren't wanted to be. Caught between the institutions designed to make money and those designed to give it away, artists, one way or another, were being turned into beggars. It was becoming apparent that the only way to deal with a world of institutions, public and private, was to be based in institutions of your own.

For creative artists, work in organizations, institutions, and bureaucracies is dreary and corrosive, and this is doubly true of artists who are temperamentally subterraneans or just plain outsiders. But as there are crucial times in political life when urgency dictates that you go out into the streets, so there are crises in the arts when you go into the motel meeting rooms. At the start of the seventies the squeeze was on from both profit and nonprofit institutions in the culture to neutralize creative life. From secret government suppression, as of the underground presses, to exclusion or co-optation, as of the literary arts, the situation left few options between surrender and organization. And, since the opportunity to organize was at hand, if you didn't do it, you knew somebody else would, maybe even some ghoul who actually enjoyed doing it, someone with culture commissar potential, or culture czar, as the case may be. In a country of organizations, it's hard to avoid them if you want to exert any amount of economic or political control over your creative life, rather than leaving it to people who have no idea about—or perhaps have contempt for—what you're doing. And maybe the most important payoff of the effort of organization is the network of associations it produces, with its consequent broadening of cultural vision.

By the early to middle seventies, Allen Ginsberg had established a writing program at the Buddhist Naropa Institute in Boulder, Colorado; Peter Coyote had become head of the Literature Program of the California Arts Council and then a participant in a similar program for the National Endowment for the Arts; co-founder of *Partisan*

Review William Phillips, iconoclastic novelist Ishmael Reed, and myself, among others such as Charles Newman, Charles Simic, and Russell Banks, were heavily involved in the Coordinating Council of Literary Magazines, which funded literary magazines on a national scale, and I had also helped found a writer-controlled publishing company, the Fiction Collective, and a book review magazine, *American Book Review*. At about the same time, after fifteen years or so of avoiding it, I found steady employment at the University of Colorado, where my task was to put together a creative-writing program. As I got more and more involved with the Coordinating Council of Literary Magazines, *American Book Review*, the University of Colorado, and the Fiction Collective, my friends started asking me, "Why do you do it?" meaning my administration of CCLMABRCUFC. I wondered myself, since the power involved was minimal and, like most power, seedy, and I know I'm not an altruist. Now that I've shed enough of these organizations to have time to think, I think I did it for a surprising reason—to align my real self with a participatory public self I could believe in. Given a business culture that does not now so much ignore artists as it remains ignorant of what an artist is, this was a way of endowing myself with social reality. Yet odd and sometimes disturbing things happen when artists stop being outsiders and especially when they hook up with institutions.

At a certain point in the history of the Jack Kerouac School of Disembodied Poetics—the creative-writing program started by Allen Ginsberg in Boulder, Colorado—Ginsberg and Gregory Corso were given to wearing suits and ties on public occasions. This was perhaps an effort to escape the stale Beatnik image, but was perhaps also a gesture in the direction of the Naropa Institute, the Kerouac School's parent organization, and of the Buddhist community, whose adherents favored suits and ties. It was not so surprising that Ginsberg, who is super-organized, would end up founding his own organization, but it's still significant that Ginsberg, everyone's image of the anarchic Bohemian, has taken an institutional path. Along with him he has pulled into the school's summer workshops his wide net of creative acquaintances, who come though for the most part they are not Buddhists like Ginsberg. But in at least one case the conflict be-

tween the creative element and institutional Buddhism was an instructive disaster.

"Once the door was broken down, the furniture pushed aside, Loring was the first one in; luckily the first two guys wore glasses, cause
Merwin came out with a broken beer bottle and went straight for
their eyes. Loring got some really bad cuts.... The next guy in, after
Loring, was this very macho guy that prides himself on his karate
knowledge.... So he went charging in.... Barnstone got cut as if
the beer bottle went around the eye.... When he saw the blood
dripping out of Loring's eye, he [Merwin] realized that he had to ...
go downstairs."

"I said [says Merwin] as I understood it, one couldn't be forced to
celebrate.... He [Trungpa] got angry and threw his glass of sake in
my face.... He wanted us to join in the dance and celebration and
take our clothes off.... He asked, 'Why *not*? What was our *secret*?'
... He said that if we wouldn't undress, we'd be stripped, and he
ordered his guards to do the job.... Dennis White and Bill King
tried to stop it.... Trungpa stood up and punched Bill King in the
face, called him a son-of-a-bitch, and told him not to interfere....
Merwin wasn't buying any of it. He was screaming: 'Hitler, bastard,
Nazi, cop!' Then they went to strip Dana ... and she fought back!
... Then Dana was standing there, perfectly pretty girl, no scars,
everyone's wondering, does she have scars or something?"

The foregoing is from *The Party*, an investigative report directed
by Ed Sanders on the stripping of eminent poet W. S. Merwin and
his girlfriend at a Tibetan Buddhist seminary headed by Chogyam
Trungpa, Rinpoche, Allen Ginsberg's guru, in 1975, an affair that
came to be known as "Buddhagate." The seminary group had been
in a mountain retreat for nearly three months and was having a Halloween party, a wild one, to which Trungpa wanted Merwin and his
woman to come. They had chosen not to. The resulting confrontation
caused bitter splits among writers all across the country and was most
intense in Boulder, where Naropa and Trungpa were based. There
the scene was paranoid hysteria, people screaming at one another,
some even claiming that shots had been fired at them. No one could
stay out of the feuding, including myself. The harshest conflict was

among writers who were old friends and acquaintances, and it should be pointed out that *The Party* was written in a seminar under the auspices of Naropa itself. Many writers were, I think, justifiably appalled that Ginsberg refused to condemn Trungpa for his behavior. But there is another side to the story, one that perhaps even Merwin would not deny.

Lynn Gingrass was running Karma Dzong, the Buddhist community of Boulder, and was an administrator at Naropa, though he has since cut ties with Buddhism, and by force of circumstance had spent a lot of time with Merwin the summer preceding the seminary. Merwin was not really qualified for the seminary in terms of Buddhist training, but managed to get invited by ingratiating himself with Trungpa, according to Gingrass. "And at the risk of getting mythological, it was like he had this Promethean obsession. You just knew that Merwin felt that there were secrets that were going to be taught at seminary. . . . Everybody began to realize that Bill Merwin was there to get the goodies and run. And then came the Halloween party, and as I understand it, it was a very drunken party, and at some point, as everybody knows, Rinpoche commanded that everybody take off their clothes. It was a costume party, so there was literally a kind of unmasking, which I'm sure as you know has many spiritual metaphors as well. . . . [But] it's one thing to talk about unmasking and dropping all your defenses and all of that . . . I think there's another side of it that's strictly sort of authoritarian crap. They strip prisoners also. I think there are really two sides to all that. . . . Merwin really wanted secret teachings, and made no bones about wanting to integrate them into his poetry, but never made any claim about wanting to actually implement them in ways other than to his own personal ends."

If you add to all of this the fact that Trungpa also thought of himself as a poet, and was obviously interested in Merwin because of his reputation as a poet, you begin to suspect that there was a mutual effort going on to exploit one another's secrets. "What was our *secret?*" Merwin reports Trungpa demanding as he ordered them to strip. But Trungpa's secrets are the property of an institution to which you have to commit yourself in order to learn them, while Merwin's secret is that of the creative talent which by nature can be neither public nor controllable, even by the artist himself, and may well be unknown even to him. This kind of secret can never be anything but at odds with institutional demands, and it is no wonder that Merwin refused to commit himself to Buddhist claims. I'm sure everyone who gets into such situations intuitively recognizes what is involved when an artist is committed to an institution. It is no accident that "committed to an institution" can be read in two ways. The spontaneous element of creativity is so antithetical to the operation of most institutions that institutional participation in itself threatens to cure artists of their talent. The middle-class imagination must assume that creative talent, anomalous as it is in a business culture, derives from some scar, some defect to be cured, otherwise what's the mystery, what is there to hide? "Everyone's wondering, does she have scars or something?" This accounts for the currency of the "wound and the bow" explanation of artistic genius, the artist's talent, his bow, as compensation for some otherwise debilitating flaw.

Another way to see it is that creative talent derives from an imaginative power to heal the psychic wounds of civilization that all people bear to a greater or lesser degree. The secret of this power is that it is by definition pure potential till the instant of its rediscovery in a particular circumstance. I once asked W. S. Merwin to write something about writing and he declined on the grounds that he didn't want to spoil the mysteries. The mystery is simply that which is not yet known and must be arrived at intuitively. For a poet to operate in an institutional context that must depend on common knowledge can be in itself a stripping, a divesture of potency, a humiliation that does not require physical stripping. It is the sort of humiliation you dutifully inflict on yourself to function usefully in the world, while knowing better or, to put it another way, while knowing there is something better. There will always be a basic conflict between art and the organization, but that doesn't mean the two are always mutually exclusive. A Buddhist once played me a tape of an argument between Trungpa and William Burroughs over whether Burroughs could take his typewriter on a Buddhist retreat. That time the writer won.

Raymond Federman escaped the Holocaust in France as a child

when, starving, he overcame a sense of transgression and jumped from the boxcar he was supposed to be on, to eat some potatoes in a boxcar on the next track, which happened to be heading in the opposite direction, away from the camps. He understands that it is sometimes necessary to do what you are not supposed to do, even when it is a question of the fundamental conflict between quality and equality that simultaneously disrupts and energizes our democratic society. Federman has served on such arts grant organizations as CCLM and the New York State Council on the Arts, which are supposed to reflect the composition of their constituencies. "There was something in this so-called democratic system," he says, "there was something fishy. We have to keep in mind geography, we have to keep in mind ethnic groups, we have to keep in mind this and that, and so the criteria were wrong according to my feeling. By necessity, ethically, those of us at the beginning who invented or maintained CCLM had to allow different groups to come in, it was our responsibility.... They were serious, those discussions we had at board meetings about being fair, giving the money fairly, not unfairly and because of quality. These were very important discussions, and the notion of fairness, which is very American, was what opened the door.... Personally, I am against all that. I could become an authoritarian figure."

"Well, you could've but you didn't," I remark. But all of us in CCLM had to deal with a democratic ambivalence over the inequity, if not iniquity, of talent in a supposedly egalitarian society. The very idea of grants for talent is considered by some as inimical to the anarchic freedom of the creative act. Suzanne Zavrian, who now runs the New York Small Press Book Fair, and was for a long time managing editor of Pocket Books, used to run the half-million-dollar Ford Foundation distribution project for CCLM when I was its chairman. The dependence of writers on grants, she says, "is one of the things that has done more for promoting bad literature than it has for helping anybody. It drained an enormous amount of vitality. You no longer had the tension of, there we are outside of a culture looking at that culture. I always had a vision of the ordinary person driving down a road and looking in a rear-view mirror, and what they saw was the past. And the artist wasn't looking in the rear-view mirror, the artist was looking through the windshield ahead, which is why the artist could spot things that were happening now, is someplace psyched into what's about to happen. And I think that functions when you've got a tension where you literally have the artist as outsider. And the minute that they are co-opted into the mainstream, that whole distinction gets blurred and they no longer can see."

But maybe the most legitimate reason for the underground's remaining outside society was that it had to. Maybe it doesn't have to anymore. Maybe instead of its romance with the outsider and the subversive, the underground is strong enough to make a stand for its point of view within the mainstream of the culture. Maybe subterraneans are moving once again from mere resistance to outright attack. According to Zavrian, in any case, there are some younger elements of an adversary culture that are now commercially successful.

"They're in the mainstream and they're taking the mainstream and they're holding it up and they're saying, 'Look at what this garbage is.' Instead of being outside and attacking you're attacking from inside, and maybe that is one of the answers. If you listen carefully to them, what have you got? You've got every banality and every cliché juxtaposed and you just recoil in horror from the whole society, and that's what a lot of these kids are doing. And what they're doing actually is being rebels within the culture itself and being successful at it commercially. And that's a whole new twist." An older twist is exemplified by Zavrian's own career. She has consistently been involved in both the underground and commercial worlds. "My whole life I have functioned in two worlds. Always, with one foot in each of them. And I've always found it remarkably comfortable. I use each one for the other. It works fine, and I've never found it a problem at all because I've been always involved in the commercial world but outside of it, totally uncommitted to it, and it's a comfortable way of making a living."

Zavrian, who, like Nin, might be indistinguishable from the middle class in superficial style, has nevertheless pursued a lifelong commitment to underground adversary values with relentless energy. On the other hand, in contrast with the situation before the sixties, you do not have to look far to find individuals who are underground in life style, but whose basic commitment is making it in the middle class. Furthermore we can no longer pretend that the underground is positioned outside society. We now have to realize that no one is outside society. Even the most marginal minorities are conditioned by the social discourse, dropping out of which is not an option. You cannot drop out of that discourse, you can only change it. Even outsiders must acknowledge they are inside in that sense. The Postmodern individual and especially the writer, according to critic of the avant-garde Charles Russell in his recent *Poets, Prophets & Revolutionaries,* "now experience and articulate themselves self-consciously from *within* the social context from which, nevertheless, they may still feel alienated and of which they may still be critical. . . . There can be no simple opposition to culture, no transcendent perspective or language, no secure singular self-definition, for all find their meaning only within a social framework."

The tragic outsider and the genius in the garret waiting like Cinderella to be "discovered" are vicarious projections of a sentimental Mittydom. Not that such unfortunate destinies do not exist; sometimes they are unavoidable, but they must not be sought after as paradigms. It's the comfortable citizen, harried or bored, who yearns for the artist as shooting star, spectacular and self-destructive. Artists already tend to balance on a psychic edge between sanity and the unknown; why impose the burden of helplessness too? If you like that trip, you take it. The drop-out must now be replaced by the hold-out, working stubbornly in the wasteland of the mass market, ruthless in his effort to define and dominate his appropriate territory. He (or she) is not on the make. Money is insufficient reward and celebrity is an insult. He may be a loner or not. The hold-out may prowl with a pack on the impoverished margins of the culture or he may emerge from within the heart of the establishment, where you will know him only when he makes his move. He may find refuge in the tenements of the city or the underground of the psyche. He uses whatever he can use, cultural guerrilla tactics or lobbying and applied grantsmanship, to call into question the values of the status quo. An adversary culture must now acknowledge a more complex situation than it has faced heretofore, requiring more sophistication and less indulgence in image and flashy gestures of style. No more Lone Rangers, silver bullets, or white horses. The hold-out looks just like you, and could be you.

The Punk and New Wave movements, despite a genuine rebellious impulse, still depend very consciously on image. The first time I went to the Mudd Club, Allen Ginsberg, who always seems to be everywhere and who was there, introduced me to some people, including Steve Maas, its owner. The Mudd Club, which opened in 1978 way downtown to one side of Tribeca, the artists' quarter that was then still cheap enough for artists to live in, took over the tradition of the artists' bar, which had produced no exceptional examples since Mickey Ruskin went bankrupt and sold Max's toward the mid-seventies. Maas's style, cryptic and nonverbal, clued you to some of the changes that had gone down during the Me Decade. The underground now had a Punk edge, and was more a sociological than an artistic phenomenon. You might say that the kind of kids, not particularly interested in art, who had joined the underground in the sixties were now taking it over to the extent of determining its style. Of course music interested them, but like Maas, they were not very verbal. They favored image and exhibition, and if they had a particular art form it was performance, which suddenly started getting big.

Performance artist Leonora Champagne talks about "Euro-trash," which is an American as well as a European offshoot of Punk, and whose big scene was the RedBar over in the East Village. Champagne, a smallish woman, speaks with a loud, clear voice. "All these totally drugged-out wealthy European kids. People don't talk to each other, even the men have small mirrors, they're looking at themselves to see if their makeup's right or if their hair's in place, and it's all about image and look." The Punks themselves, in their inventive ugliness—some call it body art—are expressive and energetic, at least, if not necessarily with a kind of energy the middle class digs. "I remember going to this concert at the Palladium where the kids went wild. I feel like it was a real Nazi event almost, it was frightening, because of the way they used lights the way Albert Speer had used lights, to make those columns of light, there was this projection of an eagle, and the kind of energy was very dark and intense, and the kids were standing on the chairs with their arms like this"—she raises her arm over her head—"like cheering it on, and it resembled a Nazi youth rally as far as I could tell. As much as I found it frightening I found it fascinating, and I had an argument with some Columbia professors after that, who were saying Punk is a totally negative movement, it's not like the sixties when kids were politically involved. The thing is that Punk comes from a whole generation that essentially is disenfranchised, they have no jobs, they're the kids who are messengers or B.A.'s doing lowest-level indexing. They're trying to find a sort of fuck-you identity—it's not that they're necessarily politically reactionary, it has to do more with 'I'll deface myself rather than be faceless.' "

Speaking of "Decadent Jew," a number done by a group called the Nuns, Jello Biafra, leader of the Punk rock Dead Kennedys, says, "I don't think any of the Nuns were really right wing, it was just something to do. And a fair number of the people in the Nuns were Jewish." All that counted, he says, was to shock the middle class. The Punk costume was intended to make a statement of "a combination of shock, alienation, plus to prove to other people who went out of their way to make their own so-called Punk rock clothing in 1977, 'Hey, I do this differently, I'm somebody too.' " Biafra tries to make his music "as extreme as possible. I've just never really liked sappy-sounding things, and never liked artists and music and anything else that lied to me." Biafra is now being harassed by obscenity charges, but if you look behind the hostility involved in the act—Jello will hate me for this—the Dead Kennedy lyrics express a moralistic liberal point of view. The extremity is the emotional dimension of the Punk attitude.

"What we did," says Biafra, who ran for mayor of San Francisco in 1979 and came in fourth, "I left the stage, I would cut through the crowd, go back to the people at the tables, knock over their tables, pour their drinks on them, chase them with lit cigarettes, throw ashtrays in their face and whatnot. In other words it was very one-on-one primal confrontational shock. A lot of people who came in, it was like 'Hey, get a drink, suck it out of a straw, and let's sit at our table and have a nice time.' And so the purpose of the Dead Kenne-

dys was to prevent anybody from having a nice time." He would also
tear his clothes off on stage, and ended one show with nothing on
but two belts, argyle socks, and wingtip shoes. Biafra was a west
coast musician, but did come to New York where the big scenes were
CBGB's and Max's. CBGB's picked up on the Ramones, the New
York Glitter scene, including the New York Dolls, and the tail end
of the Velvet Underground, much of all this having happened at Max's.

"Then it was time to play at the great Max's Kansas City, wow,
all these people got started here." On the west coast the audiences
were about eighteen to twenty-two, but it was an older crowd in
New York and "the audience was more sedate." Biafra, who even
now is not that much older than his west coast audience was, moves
with a kind of caged energy. The Kennedys decided to emphasize the
confrontational aspect of their show. "What it turned into was tables,
chairs, and beer pitchers flying in both directions." Somebody hit Biafra
over the head with a chair. "It was very improvised, of course, but it
had to be done right. It was like, walking offstage and sitting down
afterwards, 'Oh my God, we just trashed Max's.' It was an attempt
to take Alice Cooper's knack for really graphic, ugly horror, and Iggy
Pop's making it personal, in other words not illustrating the horror
so much as becoming it, making the horror too close to home. Instead
of horror movie stuff, we would turn it more into like death squads,
being jumped by rednecks, having abusive parents, making it a situation that could actually happen to somebody, and try to act it out.
Or some of the other lyrics are more just straight biting social satire.

"An average suburban person in a more conservative family could
play Blondie for their parents and they'd like it," continues Biafra,
"but if you played the Ramones for your parents and they took one
look at the packaging of the record, they wouldn't want anything to
do with it. In other words, Punk was the threatening edge of this
new so-called movement, and New Wave was the commercially acceptable edge." In the case of Detroit White Panther John Sinclair
and his group MC 5, the tone was distinctly blue collar. Sinclair used
to come to Max's and guzzle steak and booze, and when asked about
this high living in view of the revolution is said to have replied, "I'm
the revolution." He was sent up for years on possession of one joint.

"The Detroit angle was more gut rage or in Sinclair's case directly confrontational—'Let's just go fuck 'em up,'" continues Biafra. "Another unusual thing about the Detroit people was almost all of them came from lower-middle-class or working-class families." As for Iggy Pop of the Stooges, "he put it down on tape while other people like that shot George Wallace and Robert Kennedy. Apparently the Stooges' guitarist collected Nazi memorabilia." Biafra is active in a movement of musicians against fascism to counteract the Punk right.

The Kennedys were a consciously underground scene, and represented a more sophisticated generational attitude than that of the old cult of failure. "By the time we got started, the first time we played was about two or three months after it really hit people that 'Look, this really is gonna stay an underground, thinking person's movement, and you either stick with it and keep with it or you get out, cause there's no way you're ever gonna be a great big rock 'n' roll star or successful media figure this way, because the straight media is not gonna touch you.'" The compromises that would be needed to go mass market would mean "wrecking our music, for number one, mellowing it out, changing the lyrics, changing the name of the band and allowing myself to be used as a talking head, just a puppet of a cartoon, allowing myself to be turned into a zoo animal in order for somebody else to make money selling records of ours."

Any underground artist who wants to penetrate the mass market is either going to have to tailor his act or put up with the kind of merchandising reported in a recent *New York Times* article about people like Laurie Anderson, Philip Glass, and Eric Bogosian "crossing over into the commercial mainstream." Much of the marketing strategy for a new film by Anderson, says the article, "is convincing the public that the cutting edge does not hurt." The consequence is that not all, but most work directed to the mass market is going to be innocuous. The alternative course, taken by Biafra, is to cultivate your own market. Having your own audience of like-minded sympathizers as a base is one of the best defenses against being killed by mass-market success, should the occasion ever arise.

The kind of New Wave scene you got at an art-crowd place like the Mudd Club was at the same time lighter and more decadent than that of Punk proper. "The experience of the modern world is that of shock," says Champagne, "and in order to handle shock you have to respond very rapidly, your reflexes have to be quick, but they don't go deep, and your experience is different from the experience of people who have more time and less stimuli. The kind of drug culture that we have now, to me there's a striking difference between acid and cocaine, one of them took you somewhere, and it was another way of going in, it was another kind of exploration, because of course the images came from the drug but they also came from your psyche, whereas cocaine is strictly a physical drug, a quick kick. It's a rendering of the surface—I think it might be because it's such a visual culture now, with video."

What was important for people in Punk and New Wave was image. For previous subterraneans, image was incidental to a vision of change in society and the self, while for these newer movements image was an end in itself. Insofar as the inner life was concerned, it was important only in order to exorcise it through a kind of ritualized psychodrama, whether in slam dancing or performance art. Image is safe because it's disembodied—you get around better as an image than you can as a self. It allows you flexibility and ironic distance, and it allows you to reject an idea without taking its alternative seriously either. "Like with Blondie," the rock group, says Champagne, "you have the idea of women moving against feminism, for example, back into this aggressively Marilyn Monroe–ish type, only you're quoting it, so you're not serious."

In the perspective of image as self, it's interesting that Marilyn, who sang regularly at the Mudd Club, used no last name. Marilyn when performing looked like a Punk Marilyn Monroe, the latest avatar of an image that fascinated both de Kooning and Warhol. She always dressed the same, often even when she was just going out. "Black tights, black Converse sneakers, then I had this little miniskirt with short sleeves, it was like an A-line, and then over that I would wear a white jacket. And then sometimes I wore little gloves. Because of my Catholic background, I'm very partial to uniforms, I like to sort of wear the same thing and not have to decide. I think having worn a uniform for twelve years has made me really appreciate the simplicity of not having to think and decide what you're going to wear. Also, remember, I was working on my image and becoming known. I was very stylized. My face was very stylized too. I had white makeup, and instead of like red here"—she points to her face —"I had gray. I was like sculpture. I was white-blond, and I would wear green lipstick, and put green on the ends of my hair, green tips, so it was all going out like this and there was green on the end. And then I used to put phosphorescent powder in my hair, and I would have them turn the lights off during the performance and then slowly my hair would begin to glow in the dark."

The Mudd Club was like Berlin in the thirties, according to Marilyn, extremely decadent. As at Max's, they screened people at the door and let in all the regulars, who were mostly sculptors, video artists, writers, musicians, and others in the arts. They got in without cover charge and were given free drink tickets. The drug was cocaine. Unlike previous art bars, the Mudd Club was mainly a disco. "You'd go in, dance, have a drink, talk to someone you know, go upstairs, and then the upstairs was usually private so there were only the groovy people, talk to someone else you know, do some drugs, see who famous was there, look at them, and then just have fun with your friends, sort of dance, drink, walk around. One of the things it was great for, that I really appreciated after seeing the Michael Todd room in the Palladium, is that there was always circulation, it was always possible to circulate. Go to the ladies' room and look at yourself. It only began at midnight. The music was always good. Maybe by two everyone would be relaxed enough."

Talk about drugs made up 25 percent of the conversation, according to Marilyn, maybe 50 percent among artists, writers, and other creative people. Artists Keith Haring and Kenny Scharf were always there—once Scharf pinched Marilyn and she slugged him. He slugged her back. It was the first club to have theme parties, like a two-night Rock 'n' Roll Funeral filmed by Warhol with Viva and Marilyn performing, the Pajama Party, and the New Year's Eve Saturnalia, the whole place done in a Roman motif, with candles and a haremy look. The Mudd Club was a very sexy place but everyone was very asexual, according to Marilyn. Sex was out. "We were somehow just like above it all or something." One of Marilyn's big songs was called "Sex Means Nothing When You're Dead." With the intransigent self deadened for the sake of a manageable, disembodied public image, it follows that sensuality would be minimal. Images may attract, but they don't fuck.

For writer Andrei Codrescu, whose Transylvanian accents are often heard on National Public Radio commenting on the literary scene, "a Punk is somebody who's taken himself hostage and is waiting for somebody to let him out." We're talking in a booth in the Cedar Tavern. The side of Punk that identifies with the image of mannequin or robot seems to have put the self on hold. What is being held off is an underlying despair, which Codrescu thinks affects the generation of which Punk is part. "The values of the middle class, which I've been against as a poet, especially the idea of being totally self-satisfied, with the race for money, the greed that goes along with it, the accumulation of physical objects, the conformity making everything hunky-dory, the mechanical way of behaving, you know, I think those things are bad. I think the enemy is unconsciousness in a sense, the unconscious acceptance of the status quo. I think that the younger people who are now middle class feel a terrible unease. There is a terrible unfulfilled something that they have never satisfactorily explained to themselves, and it eats them up. Which is why they are accepting the arms race and all this shit, you know, because they are ready to die."

Codrescu, part of a generation in transition from the sixties to something that remains to be seen, thinks we are at the culturally deadest point in the last fifteen years. In the face of this situation he believes writers must make greater efforts to reach an audience. "I think a little more stupidity would be in order, you know, less intellectual assumptions, in the sense of thinking you know better about anything, because everything has to be rethought. I'm not satisfied with Allen Ginsberg's definition of the supermarket in that Utopian way [in "A Supermarket in California"] and I don't care for Warhol's that much either, because I've been in there long enough not to get stoned that way. I don't get that high looking at detergent. So there must be somewhere there a new understanding of that particular detergent aisle that is more contemporary and more accurate and really does connect to how people feel about it."

The need to make a connection for underground art that is popular, but not Pop, does not eliminate an even more urgent need for a knowing and critical community of peers against which to test your work. You cannot expect the larger public to be able to judge unfamiliar art. Underground art entrepreneur and writer Richard Kostelanetz uses the image of circles within circles. "Here's an artist who makes a work. He shows it to his immediate peers, and they become the first circle. And if they like it they tell their peers about it and that becomes a second circle, and it goes on outward in that way. At every point along the line the next circle can say no. Now let's say circle fifteen is a commercial publisher, and he's trying to sell to circle sixteen, which is book store manager, who's trying to sell to circle seventeen, which is book buyer. What happens in commercial art is that the work goes from one, the source, to fifteen, who tries to sell to sixteen, who tries to sell to seventeen. Now if sixteen says no, back to fifteen, but then it goes back to one and the artist is where he began. But let's say a more serious artist who gets circles of loyal supporters gets to fifteen, who then tries to sell to sixteen. What happens if it doesn't succeed with sixteen is that he's back to his base, he hasn't gone back to zero." A creative community with its own criteria in resistance to the business establishment is essential to any kind of alternative culture. This quality is the minimal requirement for a culture underground.

Mike Golden, a writer of the generation formed in the seventies, who has worked in commercial publishing but who always has one or two underground publishing ventures going and who claims he communes with the spirit of French poet-crazy Alfred Jarry through the Ouija board, says the underground is a state of mind that cuts across the lines of money, class, success, talent, position, or fame. He cites a commercial musician "who's so far underground he's a mole," who maintains his own noncommercial band, while the Beatles, especially Lennon, tried to be underground but couldn't. "It's a sensibility," he says. "If you like Barbra Streisand they'll take your button away." Subterraneans have to be what he calls mindfuckers, meaning they call reality into question, including their own. Obviously some creative artists call reality into question and some confirm it. But underground artists "are looking for a kind of purity almost antithetical to reality. It is calling reality out and challenging it."

Art critic and activist Lucy Lippard, however, makes an emphatic distinction between two ways that art can challenge status quo reality. We're talking as we walk on a mountain path above Boulder. Critical art, she says, simply offers alternative views of that reality, as Pollock did, while oppositional art is more openly adversarial in a political sense, to the point of activism. "This isn't a value judgment," she is quick to add, though she is much more interested in the second way. She does not deny the value of nonoppositional art for not being specifically political. However, beyond Lippard, such art can include the political dimension by considering the context of its production as part of the work. "There are a lot of activist artists who are doing long-term works which incorporate working with political groups, working with media analysis, teaching, writing, all kinds of things that are all part of what you're doing which is totally aside from making an object. Making an object is the matrix of what you're doing."

A line from a novel by Lippard goes, "Schizophrenics are never convinced that they exist." American culture is schizoid in the sense that it includes many conflicting ideas and tendencies that are insulated from one another so that they never make contact and therefore never get amalgamated into a bigger picture. A view that considers only half the picture is only half real. Considering the process of production part of the reality of any work of art immediately resolves the schizoid conflict between the purity of art and the experience out of which it comes. In this perspective, creative energy traditionally seen as directed to the artifact alone is seen as exercised in and on the world as well. Such a perspective releases the politically committed artist from any guilty compulsion to use the artwork as propaganda, or for other ideological ends. If you want political activism in the art context you can act directly on the world, as Lippard does. But the life of art, apart from its product, itself has social consequences. One of the reasons I'm embarked on this book, which records the experiential history out of which an art-literary movement came, is to make an account of a collective autobiographical experience and justify it as a legitimately creative sphere. For adversarial artists to ignore the political dimensions of that sphere is to help marginalize themselves. There is nothing wrong with that, but there is a choice. Lippard cites Herbert Schiller, the media analyst, to the effect that "aroused consciousness is the greatest tool for institutionalized change that we'll ever get our hands on. And that's really what I work on—arousing people's consciousness, or politically and aesthetically educating them." Most artists, she claims, simply don't understand the political power of culture. "And," she adds, "most political people don't either." Except the cultural conservatives.

When I first started going down to the Village to escape what I considered an antipathetic society a lot of people, including me, really felt that anything connected with the world outside yourself and your own beleaguered enclave was bull shit. It was very American on our part, very innocent, to think you could drop out of the world, and it was an attitude that came to dubious fruition in the commune movement. In the fifties there was such bull shit coming from the outside world that it had its defensive utility. But, as poet Armand Schwerner points out, "There's still bull shit. We protected ourselves against the incursions of the negativity, which seemed to be from the outside, but it was really our projection of our own negativity." After all, most of us were part of the same middle class we were running away from. If the middle class's reflex was to negate part of experience that it was inconvenient to acknowledge, our response was to negate the middle-class world wholesale.

It's 1983. We're in the last of Mickey Ruskin's bars, One University Place, just a few doors up from Washington Square, and it's completely jammed for a Freedom to Write Celebration held by *American Book Review* and also sponsored by the PEN club, in coordination with an *ABR* issue on censorship. I am emceeing and the speakers include Victor Navasky of *The Nation,* Lawrence Ferlinghetti, Allen Ginsberg, Nat Hentoff, and others, and Marilyn is there to sing and dance. One University in some ways resembles Max's, if much reduced in scale. The paintings are on the walls, traded for food and drink, it's well lit, the food is good, the waitresses are pretty and interesting, and it attracts an art crowd including some of the people who used to hang out at Max's. But the ambience is more one of nostalgia for the great days of Max's than that of a fresh scene.

The scene, in fact, had split in two, with the sleazy chic of the Punks moving over to spots in the East Village like the RedBar and the Pyramid Club, and the posh haunts of the new Hipoisie going south of the Village to SoHo and Tribeca. In these bistros you got the sense that the idea of an underground as a style of resistance to the status quo was either no longer hip or little more than style. The Hipoisie had already made it and the Punk entrepreneurs of the East Village bluntly had making it as their aim, and as quickly as possible. Though there were nights when the house was full, they were not screening anyone out at the door of One Uni. They needed the customers. Maybe that's the reason the bartenders called the place Chinese Chance when they answered the phone. One University used to be a Szechuan restaurant, but "Chinese Chance" comes from a poker term that has to do with drawing for a risky inside straight.

A night or two before, I had been up till near four o'clock closing time in the office with Mickey and one of his partners. They were in a state of coke paranoia because of all the publicity the Freedom to Write affair had been getting. They were afraid of a mob scene and were insisting that I hire armed guards to keep order. I pointed out that, luckily, *The Village Voice* had refused to give us any publicity, and that seemed to calm them down some. There was always plenty of coke available in the office and a loaded shotgun leaning in the corner. A lot of heavy drinking, snorting, and mainlining went on among the inner circle. A tone of burn-out and opportunism, a feeling that the party was over, prevailed. They seemed to be afflicted with Sixties Shock Syndrome—the inability of those formed in the Age of Aquarius to readjust to the collapse of the counterculture in the seventies. Though new trends were underway, they vaguely realized they were out of sync, and sought consolation in drink, drugs, or religion, watching one underground veteran after another self-destruct and get his barroom wake. The last words of one victim, spoken in exasperation, were "Fuck you." During one rather short period there were three wakes held at One Uni. The last one was Mickey's. He had been brought home by two friends after a long night doing drugs and left on the floor of his apartment. In the morning his wife found him dead.

At the Freedom to Write Celebration we're listening to Ginsberg talk before reading a poem. He is, in effect, calling the roll of the underground. "What we have here is actually an interesting situation, 'cause I was looking around at the faces. We have a rock band, we have Romanians, civil libertarians, art café patrons and proprietors, it's a Village bar, we have San Francisco alternative-media publishers, we have populist poets, editors of social magazines, high school and college New Wave students, we have world poets, wire service editors, Bohemian columnists, gay art purveyors, old Bohemians from Greenwich Village, underground press editors, American Civil Liberties Union officials, PEN club scholars, angry poets and Buddhist authors and poets, we have pie-throwing parents, civic-minded restaurateurs, old and young Greenwich Village denizens of the 1980's of this century, waiters, waitresses, professors of literature, critics of twentieth-century letters, manuscript dealers, editors and celebrated memoirists, photographers, union activists, a very wide cross section of sensitives and cultural avant-garde as well as radio broadcasters recording and international travelers of the pen ... altogether for civic-minded literary people a very august, dignified, and important occasion."

You had the impression from the media in the eighties that the underground had disappeared. In fact, underground activity was still going on as usual except, since it wasn't coming to market with anything like the coherent thrust and commercial boost it had been getting in the days of the youth culture, most people didn't know what was happening there. The underground had gone underground again. But we have had too many examples, from Poe and Melville through the Abstract Expressionists, to doubt that obscurity, and even poverty, can be weapons against an assiduously cultivated and domineering mediocrity. And who could say when the underground might resurface? When it did, those who had managed to survive the sixties and seventies would know better, perhaps, how to come to grips with the insistent nonconsciousness of the Screw You Decade than they had known how to attack that of the Vietnam era. Perhaps the post-Viet generation would have grown up in a more sophisticated tradition of resistance. Perhaps a renewed underground would have the courage of its contradictions, knowing how to manage the impulse to succeed in terms of the commercial culture without betraying its deepest political and artistic convictions.

The truth is that in this country the myth of the genius in the garret, flaunting an impoverished purity, was always a middle-class soap opera. The guilty need for this fairy tale of virtuous deprivation is itself telling. Its unrecognized message is that genuine art deserves rejection—as if it were not bad enough that it is often in fact rejected. Of course when the alienated artist is accepted in the happy end, the masterpiece that has issued from his isolation will help validate the society that formerly rejected it. But impoverished genius is never a validation of society, it is an indictment. "I would love to be rich and famous," young fiction writer Mark Leyner tells me, "but I think it's impossible through the way I write. But I'll try to become rich and famous some other way. My writing is probably financially futile, but that's not so bad—it keeps the work pure." There is nothing wrong with wealth and fame, Leyner seems to be saying, but you don't even think of compromising your creative work to get it. If he harbors an idea of purity, it is purified of defeatism and hypocrisy, envy and contempt. For subterraneans who don't turn out to be closet Yuppies, and of course many do, fame and fortune can be weapons in the fight for the culture, no less than poverty and obscurity. Opposition continues by other means.

If the enemy is unconsciousness, as Codrescu says, the goal is consciousness. An adversary culture is premised on a resistance to the strictly pragmatic concerns of our commercial culture and its stubborn reluctance to broaden the vision of a partial view from which it profits. As Nat Hentoff observes about the political significance of Ginsberg's *Howl,* "it wasn't so much a call to action as a call to consciousness." All real artists recognize at gut level the effort to lift the dead weight of the nonconscious into consciousness, and they measure one another by that criterion. You feel the shrewdness, as well as the comedy, of Bob Dylan's remark to Allen Ginsberg as reported to me by Ginsberg: "The trouble with you, Allen, is you're not a conscious artist like me." Consciousness is a standard that may look like failure by pragmatic criteria, which is perhaps why Samuel Beckett once said that "to be an artist is to fail, as no other dare fail, that failure is his world and the shrink from it, desertion, art and craft, good housekeeping, living." Nevertheless it is a standard that Beckett, for one, has successfully imposed, as the underground must be ready, when the time is ripe, to emerge and oppose its standards openly to those of the status quo. The time is often ripe when it seems most rotten.

When I was in Poland shortly after the military takeover there, I asked an editor why certain writers insisted on publishing in the illegal nongovernment magazines under their own names instead of using pseudonyms. "We are not subversives," she answered. "It is not an underground movement. This is our country."

This is our country, and our culture too.

INDEX

INDEX

W

1 WHITE HORSE
2 CARMINE ST. POOL
3 VILLAGE VANGUARD
4 LIMELIGHT
5 VILLAGE VOICE
6 LION'S HEAD
7 CIRCLE IN THE SQUARE
8 LOUIS'
9 JULIUS'
10 NINTH CIRCLE
11 LIVING THEATER
12 JEFFERSON MARKET DINER
13 WALDORF CAFETERIA
14 ORIGINAL 8TH ST. BOOKSHOP
15 GERDE'S
16 ROMERO'S
17 MINETTA'S
18 RIENZI
19 KETTLE OF FISH
20 SAN REMO
21 GASLIGHT
22 FIGARO
23 JUDSON CHURCH
24 OPEN DOOR
25 ORIGINAL CEDAR TAVERN
26 ONE UNIVERSITY PLACE
27 TENTH ST. COFFEE SHOP
28 MAX'S KANSAS CITY
29 TENTH ST. GALLERIES
30 HUDSON'S ARMY - NAVY STORE
31 ST. MARK'S CHURCH
32 LE METRO

33 UKRAINIAN NATIONAL HOME BAR
34 ELECTRIC CIRCUS, DOM
35 STEWART'S
36 McSORLEY'S
37 RATNER'S
38 FILLMORE EAST
39 ORIGINAL FIVE SPOT
40 RAPOPORT'S
41 GEM SPA
42 DEUX MÉGOTS, PARADOX
43 UKRAINIAN RESTAURANTS
44 STANLEY'S
45 OLD STANLEY
46 PSYCHEDELICATESSEN
47 EMGAGE COFFEE HOUSE
48 VAZAC BAR
49 CHARLES THEATER
50 ANNEX
51 ORIGINAL PEACE EYE BOOK STORE
52 OLD RELIABLE
53 SLUG'S
54 MUDD CLUB
55 O'ROURKE'S